UNITY OUT OF DIVERSITY

Unity out of Diversity

The Origins and Development of
The University of Humberside

DAVID FOSTER

THE ATHLONE PRESS
London & Atlantic Highlands, NJ

First published 1997 by
THE ATHLONE PRESS LTD
1 Park Drive, London NW11 7SG
and 165 First Avenue,
Atlantic Highlands, NJ 07716

© University of Lincolnshire & Humberside 1997

British Library Cataloguing in Publication Data
A catalogue record for this book is available
from the British Library

ISBN 0 485 11513 1

Library of Congress Cataloging-in-Publication Data
Foster, David, 1938 June 6–
    Unity out of diversity : the origins and development of the
University of Humberside / David Foster.
        p.   cm.
    Includes bibliographical references (p.) and index.
    ISBN 0-485-11513-1 (hc)
    1. University of Lincolnshire and Humberside--History.
    I. Title.
LF332.F67   1997
378.42′53--dc21   97-461
                                                          CIP

Typeset by Bibloset in 10pt Plantin

Printed and bound in Great Britain by
Cambridge University Press

Contents

Foreword
by the Vice Chancellor

The University of Humberside, now the University of Lincolnshire and Humberside, has gone through some dramatic and historic developments in recent years. Indeed, the whole history of the University is one of responsiveness to change and to the needs of the community.

The University can trace its origins back over 130 years. Our foundations were in 1861 as a vocational art college established to train local people in applied art and industrial design for the manufacturing industry of the region – that region then being north of the Humber.

Over the years, a number of other commercial and training colleges were established to meet a local need, first in Hull and then in Grimsby. These colleges were combined to form first in 1976 a College of Higher Education, then a Polytechnic (1990) and, following the 1992 Education Act, a University. Throughout the development, commitment to the needs of local people, the local economy and the region, has remained unchanged. Universities like ours provide important motors of economic development, and we continue to play our part for our new extended region.

Our association with Lincolnshire began in the northern parts of the county, in Grimsby and Scunthorpe, where we established franchise operations with the local further education colleges. The opportunity to become involved in the establishment of a wider university for Lincolnshire arose in the summer of 1995, and it was the type of historic challenge that we could not resist.

There had been several attempts over the centuries to establish a university in Lincoln, but it was not until the 1990s when, following a recommendation from the Confederation of British Industry that the county of Lincolnshire would benefit from having its own university, that momentum was really established.

A Project Company was founded to rally support for the concept of a university and to raise the capital to make it happen. The Lincoln development takes the University into a new era. It is the first completely new city based university campus in the United Kingdom for twenty five years, and the first in recent times to be financed from predominantly local sources. Not only does the county of Lincolnshire now have its own university campus in the heart of the county town, but by working with other local providers we aim to establish a network of further study locations throughout the county.

Approximately 30% of our full time students come from within the region, but increasingly our student population is national and international with overseas developments making an increasing impact not only on our revenue but also on our portfolio of programmes. The mission of this wider University is 'to provide our students world-wide, with the best employment prospects and to equip them to become lifelong learners'. The essentially vocational nature of many of our programmes and the care with which we ensure that they are right for the employers of today is still strongly in line with the thinking of our founding fathers.

'Unity out of Diversity' in Hull, Humberside, Lincolnshire and internationally remains the watchword of this University's development.

Professor Roger King

Acknowledgements

The chance to review the history and development of an institution in which one has been a member of staff for approximately half of one's working life is an infrequent occurrence, and I am grateful to the Vice-Chancellor, Professor R.P.King, for providing the opportunity. Given that the University has emerged from a number of separate institutions in the city, tracing its origins has been an interesting, if occasionally frustrating task in view of the propensity of our predecessors to leave little trace of their existence. Prior to the formation of the College of Higher Education in 1976, records on local authority and voluntary further and higher education are sparse and scattered, and I am greatly indebted to the staff of the Hull City and Humberside Record Offices and of the Hull Local History Library, all of whom have been tireless in their attempts to track down relevant materials. Staff in the University of Humberside Library have been most helpful, first in providing me with unrestricted access to the archives in their care, and second in tracking down secondary sources, no matter how obscure. I am also grateful to staff in the library of the University of Hull, particularly in the Education Library, for their interest and support.

Inevitably, there are numerous people in the city who have memories of work in one or other of the institutions with which this study is concerned, and the opportunities for oral history were legion. However, the emphasis of the work on the emergence and development of the University in the context of public policy and local authority frameworks enabled me to limit discussions to those who were able to contribute directly to the themes under consideration. A number of people have been generous with their time, and have provided possible lines of inquiry, valuable detail, confirmation of interpretations and necessary corrections. Amongst these are staff of the former colleges in Hull who have worked in the later unitary institution after 1976 - particularly T.Berry

(College of Commerce), L.Cross (Kingston-upon-Hull College of Education), A.Powell (Nautical College), I.Wilson (College of Commerce), and M.Wolverson (Regional College of Art). In addition, Mr.E.Jones, Principal of Hull College of Technology 1952-70, and Sister Imelda formerly of Endsleigh Convent have provided valuable material and ideas.

All the chapters have been discussed with Professor King, and my colleagues Professor P.Arnold and Mr.D.Lippiatt have read the entire manuscript. I am grateful to all of them for their comments and criticisms. Any remaining errors or weaknesses are entirely my own.

D.Foster

Chapter 1

Introduction

Founded as Wyke-on-Hull by the monks of nearby Meaux Abbey in the twelfth century, the town changed its name to Kingston-upon-Hull when it was purchased by Edward I in 1293, though it has always been known as Hull. Since that time, Hull developed from a medieval river port serving its local region into one of the major ports of the kingdom. Evidence for population in British towns is scanty prior to the first census of 1801. Reliable estimates suggest that Hull was around 7,500 at the end of the seventeenth century, but that the eighteenth century witnessed substantial growth to 25,613 in 1801, with much of the increase being attributable to inward migration in response to the growth of the port. In common with many towns in the north of England, Hull underwent major transformation in the nineteenth century when the population increased some eightfold to 200,044, with a particularly rapid growth in the 1860s and 1870s, perhaps in response to the expansion of the fishing industry and developments in railway transport. Twentieth century growth has been noticeably slower with a peak of 334,759 being reached in 1951 followed by a slow decline to 254,117 in 1992 as population moved outside the parliamentary borough into the suburbs of the city which are in the East Riding of Yorkshire.

Since medieval times, Hull has been the major port after London on the east coast of England and this fact has dominated the economic development of the city to the virtual exclusion of heavy industry. Its location on the east coast inhibited major developments in international trade beyond Europe, and its major interest has always been in the northern trade, first with the Hanseatic merchants of the north European coast and later with the principal Scandinavian and northern European ports. Initially, the port's influence was limited by its relative isolation from its hinterland of northern England, but the creation of reliable transport links

1

with the West Riding of Yorkshire and Lancashire, first with the construction of canals in the eighteenth century and later during the railway age of the mid-nineteenth century, improved the port's position dramatically,. Both of these developments enhanced the maritime importance of the city, and gave it third rank amongst British ports. However, in the heyday of the British Empire in the late nineteenth and early twentieth centuries, Hull was singularly ill-located for further major developments, and much of the new trade remained in the capital and the west coast ports, leaving Hull with its traditional concentration on northern Europe which it still retains.

The dependence of the city on the maritime trades for its livelihood inhibited the development of any major manufacturing industry. In the medieval period, Hull was predominantly a port serving Yorkshire and other neighbouring counties, with little in the way of manufacturing. Its major exports were wool and later cloth and its import of wine, but by the seventeenth century the range of goods handled was much wider. This pattern continued until the end of the seventeenth century with manufacturing being confined to the metal, leather and textile trades. There was a small shipbuilding industry in the seventeenth century and this developed during the next two hundred years, but it was never on a scale to compete with the rival centres in the north-east and in Scotland. Inevitably, the importance of the sea to the local economy led to the establishment of a range of port-associated industries, but these began to flourish after 1700 when Hull was gradually transformed from a small medieval river port to a modern port with a succession of man-made docks. In the eighteenth century, shipbuilding was the single most important industry, followed by those concerned with the processing of raw materials which entered the port, such as oil-seed extraction, sugar refining, and the manufactures of paint and soap. The fortunes of these industries ebbed and flowed during the subsequent two centuries, but remained the backbone of the local economy whose diversity shielded it from the more severe economic swings which plagued single-industry towns in the north of England. Other major, albeit relatively temporary, contributions to the town's economy were made by two maritime industries. The whaling fishery was established in the port in the 1760s, was particularly important in the early nineteenth century, spawning a number of on-shore industries, but went into decline after 1835. Almost coincident with this decline was the successful establishment of the fishing industry after 1845 when the first trawlers migrated to Hull from the south coast fisheries of Ramsgate and Brixham, heralding a century of prosperity in that area. However, some attempts to plant manufacturing industry in the town failed, as with the short-lived textile industry in the mid nineteenth century, but this was unable to compete with the cotton and woollen areas in Lancashire and the West Riding respectively. Since the Second World War, the fishing industry has gone into dramatic decline, but the city's importance as a port for Northern Europe in particular has continued and been enhanced with the development of good road connections with its hinterland and with the development of the European Union. Consequently, Hull's economic structure is now far more diversified than its popular image as an east coast fishing port would allow.

The consequence of this economic and industrial profile is that the occupational structure of the nineteenth and twentieth centuries has been dominated by semi-skilled and unskilled work, with a good deal of casual labour which varied according to the demands of the port. The implications of this position for the development of technical education, has been substantial, particularly in the period prior to 1950 when educational provision tended to be made in response to local and regional need. When cities of similar size were developing advanced technical education to meet the requirements of local manufacturing industry, such as textiles in Leeds and engineering in Newcastle and Sunderland, Hull's requirements were for a labour force with basic educational skills at best, many of which could be learned on the job. Thus, Hull's apparent lethargy in providing advanced further education during the first sixty years of the twentieth century can be seen, at least in part, as a response to the needs of the local economy.

THE ORIGINS OF THE UNIVERSITY OF HUMBERSIDE

Most of the universities created in 1992 from the former local authority higher education colleges trace their origins, often through one or more amalgamations, to a variety of institutions, some of which were founded in the nineteenth century and all of which were concerned initially with the broad field of further education. The modern University of Humberside has emerged from six separate colleges, the first originating in 1861 and the remaining five founded in the twenty years prior to the outbreak of World War I. Two began life as teacher training colleges and four of the colleges were responsible for further education. All were monotechnics, the latter being concerned respectively with Art and Design (1861), Technical Education (1894), Nautical Education (1895), and Commerce (1911).

However, the education offered in these forerunners of the University was not what we would recognise as further or higher education today; indeed, much of it was little more than secondary education and some of it was concerned with remedying the deficiencies of elementary schooling. The Department of Science and Arts, under whose auspices the Hull School of Art was established in 1861, was a government department founded in 1853 to stimulate interest in technical education; but because provision was dependent on local, voluntary effort and government support confined to grants, development was very limited. Several other factors militated against the development of a strong system of technical education in Britain. Perhaps the major deterrent was the low status which practical and technical education was accorded in the country. At root was a debate about the relationship between theory and practice, with the traditional view advocating the primacy of liberal education which automatically excluded anything practical and a modern view suggesting that pupils needed to be instructed in the practical application of their knowledge. Therefore, mid-nineteenth-century schools offered their pupils a classical and liberal education which prepared some of them for the traditional education of the ancient universities and others for the professions, and within this context practical and technical education had no place. The universities themselves were firmly against the inclusion of technical education in their curricula since they also prepared students for different positions in the occupational and therefore the class structure. However, the problem was one of supply as well as demand. The British tradition of learning on the job, together with the fear of losing trade secrets, encouraged a suspicion of education amongst employers and contributed to the general climate of opinion which undervalued technical education and, in particular, education which integrated theory and practice. A second important factor was the limited availability of elementary

4

education. Until 1870, all efforts at that level were voluntary, and the Education Act of that year, which allowed the establishment of Board Schools, augmented rather than replaced that approach totally. Given that state-provided elementary education only became compulsory and free in 1880 and 1891 respectively, it is little wonder that most institutions in Hull and other towns offered an education which was quite basic, and when the various technical institutions were established the poverty of their recruits was one of their most consistent complaints. Even with the introduction of secondary education after the 1902 Education Act, the majority of children attended all-age schools and left school at age twelve, still academically ill-equipped to pursue further study in a technical institute. A final important characteristic which militated against good quality, high-level provision was the fact that almost all work was undertaken in the evening after young people had undergone a lengthy working day. In the late nineteenth century, a ten hour day was common for young teenagers, shift work was common, and, in a community such as Hull, casual labour was endemic, and it is little wonder that there was little enthusiasm for further education amongst the potential clientele. Thus, it is fair to note that, at the beginning of the twentieth century, post-elementary education in Hull was extremely limited, and the provision from which the University of Humberside was to emerge bore little resemblance to the late twentieth century institution.

The growth of advanced level education in what became known as the public sector has been largely associated in the popular image with technical and technological education, though there has been a noticeable confusion between the two, particularly in the early part of the twentieth century. Commenting on the nineteenth century, one authority noted the problem of defining technical education with any degree of clarity, particularly since it was often confused with secondary education which was often far removed from anything technical (Balfour, p.163-4). With characteristic ambivalence, the 1889 Technical Instruction Act, which enabled local councils to support existing and establish new technical institutions, intended education to combine theoretical principles with manual instruction, but ruled out the teaching of trade in the new schools. The difficulty of distinguishing between further and secondary education, at least initially, could be seen in the position adopted by Sir Robert Morant, Permanent Secretary at the Board of Education, who wished to introduce some theory into the new technical schools but not so much as to create competitors for the new secondary schools. In consequence of this confusion, there emerged a generally accepted view that technical education was generally of a less-advanced and more practical kind than that described as technological, which explains in part the search for increased status which has accompanied the various structural reforms in further education in the twentieth century.

INSTITUTIONAL HISTORY

Although people have been interested in the history of their area for many decades, local history as an academic enterprise was still seeking acceptance and respectability as recently as the 1960s and 1970s. In danger of descending into antiquarianism, it was allegedly concerned with amassing fine detail for its own sake which had little meaning because it was seldom placed in a wider temporal and geographical context. In order to defend itself against such criticism, exponents argued that local history offered a valuable perspective and sometimes a corrective to national interpretations and recorded that which was not merely a local manifestation of a Westminster-led view. Institutional history can easily fall into the same trap of recording developments which are often of interest only to people who have worked and studied in a particular place. One way in which this can be avoided, the approach adopted here, is to consider the development of an institution in the context of the emergence of national policy in its field and against the social and economic background of the times. Details of staff and students have their interest, particularly to those who have worked and studied in a particular place, but it is only in the context of developing public policy during the twentieth century and a response to the socio-economic needs of its region that the origins and growth of a University can be understood. Even so, the experience of one institution's growth against the background of public policy may, of itself, be a complete exception to the norm, and it is only through the use of comparative material that this issue can be explored. However, with one or two notable exceptions, there are few detailed studies of the emergence and development of institutions which provided advanced level further

6

education in the post-Second World War period and which became universities in 1992.[2] However, it has been possible to introduce some comparative material from a range of sources in more general works to put the Hull experience into context.

Perhaps the most striking feature of the national context within which advanced further education developed in Hull has been the massive growth of higher education, particularly since the Second World War. At the beginning of the twentieth century, the number of students in higher education was puny by modern standards. Universities and university colleges had 31,079 students in 1922/23, and this figure had only increased by 20.4% to 37,433 in 1938/39 (Argles 1964, pp.74-75). The picture in further education was even bleaker with only 4,000 on advanced courses (AFE) in 1938/39 (Robbins, Appendix 2B, p.90). The introduction of Ordinary and Higher National Certificates for technical college students after the First World War provided nationally recognised qualifications which combined theory and practice, and they enjoyed steady if unspectacular growth. However, in 1923 only 168 Higher Awards were made, though these had increased more than eightfold to 1,405 in 1944 (Argles 1964, p.67). In contrast, after the Second World War there began a period of growth which, despite occasional financial crises, has continued ever since. The *Robbins Report* of 1963 noted the spectacular ninefold increase in advanced further education from 4,000 in 1938/39 to 38,300 in 1962/63 with the greater part of the growth being concentrated in AFE work since 1954/55 when numbers increased from 9,700 to 38,300); in contrast, university numbers had risen far more steadily from 81,700 in 1954/55 to 118,400 in 1962/63 (Robbins, Vol. II, Appendix A p. 163; Appendix B, p.90). However, this experience was to pale into insignificance with the overall expansion of higher education which occurred subsequent to 1960 which far outstripped the projections made by Robbins who advocated that the 216,000 students in higher education in 1962/63 should be increased to 390,000 by 1973/74 and to 560,000 by 1980/81 (See Table 1.1).

In the thirty years after 1960, students following full-time and part-time higher education increased by almost fourfold, and the growth was spread evenly between the two sectors with 304.9% in the university sector against 299.3% in the public sector; however, the rate of expansion in the public sector was far more

Table 1.1   The Growth of Higher Education in the United Kingdom 1960-1990 (000s)

	Universities			Advanced	Further	Education	Total
	Full-Time	*Part-Time*	*Total*	*Full-Time*	*Part-Time*	*Total*	
1960	111	18.4	129.4	73.8	89.5	163.3	292.7
1965	173	13	186	133	110	243	429
1970	235	43	278	221	121	342	620
1975	269	82	351	246	137	383	734
1980	307	101	408	228	191	419	827
1985	310	120	430	289	216	507	937
1990	370	154	524	377	274	652	1,176
1995							

Source: Educational Statistics 1967, p.43 and 1993, p.8

rapid in the last quarter of the century, with the emergence and development of polytechnics and colleges where the rate of growth was 70.2% compared to 49.3% in the university sector. One important contrast between the sectors has been the much greater importance of part-time advanced education in further education than in the universities. Since 1960, part-time education in the further education sector has never fallen below 35% and in five of the years it was well over 40%; in contrast, part-time education in the universities never rose above 30%, though there was a steady increase of part-time students in universities in the 1980s. A second major contrast between the two sectors has been the importance of sub-degree work in the further education sector and its almost complete absence in the university sector. This point is particularly evident from the number of diplomas and certificates awarded to full-time and part-time students respectively as indicated in Table 1.2. The rate of growth slowed significantly overall after 1970 as polytechnics moved to offer degree courses and as the Art Diplomas were replaced by degrees, but the continuous growth of full-time Higher National Diplomas and maintenance of part-time Higher National Certificates remain significant.

Accompanying the dramatic rate of growth of higher education in the second half of the twentieth century has been the striking continuity of policy, despite the numerous changes in the political complexion of government during the last fifty years, giving rise to the possibility of substantial civil service influence on the development of policy. Indeed, given the short term of office which many ministers normally achieve, particularly in Education which can be a staging post on the way up or down the greasy pole, it is

Table 1.2 Number of Diploma and Certificate Passes Awarded in Advanced Further Education 1960-1979

	Higher National Diploma	Higher National Certificate	Diplomas in Art	Total
1960	952	10,976	1,347	13,275
1963	1,193	12,130	1,361	14,684
1966	2,703	14,293	1,426	18,422
1969	4,386	13,291	1,835	19,512
1970	5,341	12,532	1,900	19,773
1973	6,235	11,294	2,144	19,673
1976	5,568	12,915		18,483
1979	6,843	13,054		19,897

Source: Education Statistics 1969 and 1979

most likely that the more permanent civil servants will have some influence on policy. Ministers have the final decision, but it is clear that, in the British system of government, the opportunities for civil servants to create or influence policy are substantial (Kogan 1971, p.41). It is unlikely that one architect, politician or civil servant, established the policies of concentrating AFE in a few institutions from the 1950s and devised mechanisms to nationalise provision which his or her successors carried out. What is more likely is that reform acquired a logic and momentum of its own, though this ensured that civil servants in the Ministry and Department of Education played a significant role in the formulation and implementation of higher education policy. History often has the effect of producing order from apparent chaos and imposing patterns on events which were unclear at the time, even to the participants. In this case, the pattern seems clear and the developments almost inevitable, but they did not occur without resistance. Local Education Authorities, without exception, opposed the decision to remove polytechnics and colleges from their orbit in 1987-88; individual local education authorities objected to central government decisions, as Hull did when it failed to achieve polytechnic designation in 1967; and individuals opposed central objectives with determination, as did the opponents of the unitary college plan for Hull in 1974/75. Significantly, opposition was consistently unsuccessful.

Equally interesting have been the mechanisms by which innovation and change in higher education have been brought about. Traditionally, major social issues in the United Kingdom have been the subject of a major inquiry, normally by expert committees and occasionally a Royal Commission, whose findings provide an air of legitimacy to any subsequent reforms. The committees' report has offered a basis for subsequent legislation, always providing that a report's recommendations were in harmony with the views of the government of the day and that the party in government at the time of the inquiry had not been replaced by its opponents. However, in the latter part of the twentieth century, this approach has been superseded by a more government-centred technique which may be described as a consultative method. This has allowed government to float ideas and reforms, often in the form of a Green, though more often a White Paper to stimulate public debate, and at some fairly immediate future date publish legislation or issue a Circular which, sometimes under the guise of administrative change, has introduced major policy departures. An example of the first approach is to be seen in the 1987 White Paper which was followed by the 1988 Education Reform Act to incorporate the polytechnics and colleges; the second can be seen in *Circular 7/73* which, following the *James Report* on the future of teacher education, required local education authorities to make proposals for the reform of advanced further education in their areas, and which led to the formation of the unified College of Higher Education in Hull in 1976.

The major transformation which has occurred during this period of rapid change is well-known. The initial voluntary, later local authority provision of higher education has been swept away by the emergence of a national, unified system which is intended to create diversity but which has created conditions which encourage convergence. However, there are also two important themes at the local level which emerge from this study. First is the role of the two Local Education Authorities which have been centrally concerned with the provision of advanced further education in the region prior to 1989, and second is the presence and impact of the University of Hull on the development of local authority provision in the city and the region.

THE EMERGENCE OF A NATIONAL SYSTEM OF HIGHER EDUCATION

The broad sweep of education provision in England over the last century and a half has been characterised by a movement from voluntary to state provision. Historians have long debated the extent of government intervention in society during the mid- and late nineteenth-century, an age which was once thought to have been dominated by the principles of *laissez-faire* on the basis of which government intervention in society was kept to a minimum. However, it is clear that the concept of minimal government was ignored increasingly as the nineteenth century progressed, and there are numerous examples of increasing state intervention, particularly in social fields, albeit often to remedy the ineffectiveness of voluntary provision.[3] Nonetheless, the initiative in the provision of education in mid-century at all levels was taken voluntarily, by individual or groups of philanthropists and by the churches, and the most that could be expected from the mid-Victorian state was some financial encouragement by way of grants, often based on success in examinations.

However, economic competition in the second half of the nineteenth century suggested that the educational systems of some European countries were superior to that of the United Kingdom. Therefore, hesitant moves were made in the late nineteenth century in the form of state-encouraged and state-sponsored education, particularly at the primary level with the advent of School Boards in 1870 empowered to levy local rates for primary provision, and in an historical perspective, this proved to be the commencement of serious state provision which eventually embraced all levels of education. But, even in the late nineteenth century, all secondary and further education provision was in the hands of the voluntary movement, and it was not until the 1880s that a few enthusiasts were finally heard, and legislation reached the statute book in 1889 and 1902 respectively, enabling technical education and requiring secondary education to be provided. The Technical Instruction Act 1889 remained faithful to the Victorian model of dealing with social issues and problems. First a Royal Commission was established to consider the issue; then a piece of permissive legislation was produced which required others than central government to take the initiative in resolving the particular dilemma; and finally, local agencies were established to remedy the problem, though they had to be encouraged to accept their responsibilities and cajoled by central government. In this case, the Technical Instruction Act permitted but did not compel local corporations to levy a rate to support technical education in their domains, and the voluntary principle continued to exist in that councils were empowered to support existing providers as well as establish provision themselves. Nonetheless, the advent of the state into the field of technical education, albeit permissively and locally,. sounded the death-knell of the voluntary movement and by the early twentieth century, much of the provision came directly from local authorities. During the twentieth-century the incipient collectivism of the Victorians burgeoned into full-blown state provision, and the story has been one of progressive involvement of government in education at all levels. The 1902 Education Act established local education authorities, placing upon them the duty of providing primary and secondary education and enabling them to offer further education if they so wished.

From the beginning of the twentieth century, state provision of education at all levels other than university was in the hands of local education authorities, but towards the end of the century there has been a gradual and irreversible movement from local to national control of advanced further education. The strength of a national system locally administered, the classic description of twentieth century provison in England and Wales, is that it can provide a system which is responsive to local and regional needs, but its weakness lies in the fact that such an approach will not necessarily produce the national system required by a modern industrial state without strong central guidance or control. The gradual realisation of this difficulty has led to the decline of local influence and control and the emergence of national domination in all sectors of education, though the development has been confined to the last two decades of the century. In the sphere of further education, in which the origins of the University of Humberside are to be found, this trend can be traced back to 1956 at least, though initially only slow progress was made towards the emergence of a national system of advanced further education.

The twin instruments which enabled successive governments to nationalise advanced further education, and eventually the whole of higher education, were those of concentration of provision and control of funding. It was only after the 1945 *Percy Report* that government began to take a serious interest in the development of further and advanced further education, but it is possible to identify a steady, even remorseless movement towards the modern world in which advanced further education was first concentrated in Colleges of Advanced Technology and to a lesser extent in Regional Colleges of Technology in 1956, then in Polytechnics a decade later, and finally in a few large colleges of higher education such as Hull in 1974-76. The finance available for higher education has always bedevilled progress, and so long as a major burden fell on the local rates, it was perhaps inevitable that provision would be patchy and would depend on the vision of individual civic leaders. Colleges had traditionally been allocated a grant of 60% of the costs of approved courses in advanced technical education, and this was increased to 75% in July 1952, though success would only come to those colleges which met a range of stringent criteria concerning staffing levels and qualifications, research opportunities, and the quality of the educational environment. This support was replaced by the AFE Pool in 1959, a system whereby all local authorities contributed to the cost of advanced further education whether or not they actually provided any. This system remained in place until the advent of the National Advisory Body in 1983 which sought to plan as well as to fund AFE on a national basis, and the national approach was completed for the public sector with incorporation in 1989 under the auspices of the Polytechnics and Colleges Funding Council (PCFC). A similar body was established for the Universities (UFC), and it was only a matter of time before a truly system-wide approach to planning and funding emerged, and this occurred in the 1992 Education Act which offered polytechnics and some colleges the opportunity to obtain university status, thereby producing a unified system of higher education under a single agency, the Higher Education Funding Council for England (HEFCE).

THE ROLE OF LOCAL EDUCATION AUTHORITIES

In the early part of the twentieth century, when central government intervention in education was confined to financial assistance, cajolery and approval or rejection of local schemes, local education authorities were in far more influential positions than they have been in the last decades of the century. Much of what occurred in their area depended on local civic initiative. Unfortunately, that opportunity occurred when the Victorian ideas of minimal government were still present sufficiently to deter local education authorities from taking more than an administrative view of their role. Despite the fact that some local education authorities supported the development of university colleges in their cities, the early twentieth century was not a time for civic educational vision; indeed, it is arguable that the main function of local authorities was administrative rather than policy formation. However, with the emergence of a more collectivist view of political economy and the consequent acceptance by the state of a major role in social policy, local authorities emerged as the principal mechanism for the provision of various elements of national programmes, particularly in education. The introduction of free, compulsory elementary education during the last thirty years of the nineteenth century, the establishment of local education authorities in 1902 with an obligation to provide secondary (1902) and later further (1944) education cemented their role at the centre of a major public service in the United Kingdom. However, in the field of AFE, the history of the latter part of the century has been one in which local government has sought to maintain a role for itself in the face of encroaching national policy towards further education colleges, a contest which ended in defeat with the removal of polytechnics and colleges from local authority control in 1989.

In the field of AFE, the fundamental role of local education authorities was always rather ambivalent because they operated within the context set by national government. Whilst obvious difficulties might emerge where a given local education authority was politically unsympathetic to central government, the principal function was administrative rather than policy-making. Major issues which affected the work of local education authorities, such as the policy of concentration of AFE work in a limited number of institutions between 1956 and 1966 or the removal of the Colleges of Advanced Technology from local control, were taken by central government and implemented locally. Similarly, the increasing controls which central government placed on approval for new AFE courses in colleges and polytechnics, particularly in the 1980s, severely affected the service which a particular authority was able to offer to its constituency. Nonetheless, local authorities were not merely convenient administrative vehicles for national policy. Many centrally-inspired developments offered the opportunity for local initiative which a lively Local Education Authority or a visionary Director of education could exploit. In the case of

Hull, the contrast between the two Local Educational Authorities responsible for the colleges which formed the University is marked. Hull Local Education Authority, responsible for developments from 1891 to 1974, took a narrow view of its responsibilities. Although by no means exceptional amongst its fellow authorities, it appears to have taken a strongly parochial view of its responsibilities, seeking to ensure minimal provision for its immediate constituency rather than seizing the opportunities presented in the 1950s and 1960s to be proactive in developing AFE in the city and the region, and retaining an almost daily interest in the minutiae of college activity rather than developing a strategy for its colleges. In contrast, Humberside Local Education Authority, which assumed responsibility for education in the newly-created county in 1974, adopted a much more positive and creative approach to AFE, with the result that a large unified College of Higher Education was established in the city within two years of the new Authority assuming power. Furthermore, under its aegis, the new College was given the freedom to grow into the largest and perhaps the most prestigious College of Higher Education in England and to be on the verge of polytechnic designation throughout the 1980s.

THE UNIVERSITY OF HULL

It is an interesting thought that, had the aims of the city fathers been fulfilled in the foundation of the University College of Hull in 1928, there may not have been a University of Humberside. The original motivation for a university college was in the context of replacement of the existing Municipal Technical College and enhancement of the level of its work, and it was largely through the influence of the first Principal of the University College, who wished to establish a liberal arts institution, that the original dreams were unfulfilled. Perhaps spurred on by an inability to come to terms with this disappointment, successive civic administrations adopted an ambivalent attitude towards their relationship with the University College, which became a University in 1954, until the city ceased to be responsible for higher education in the city in 1974. The initial attempt and subsequent failure to establish the kind of institution which Hull envisaged appears to have cast a cloud over the development of advanced work in the city during the inter-war years. Equally, a number of attempts were made to reinvent the dream, first by course collaboration in aeronautics, and secondly by several efforts to transfer the Architecture course from the College of Art to the University over a period of forty years. The stimulus for these moves appears to have come from the Guildhall rather than the University, and it is difficult to avoid the impression that the city was prepared to see its own provision diminished if it could be transferred to its neighbour. Significantly, even central government appears to have adopted a similarly ambivalent attitude towards the issue of relationships between town and gown. Whilst the Board of Education and the Ministry blocked moves in Architecture in 1935 and again in 1958, the DES actually proposed an abortive initial teacher education link in 1986.

Chapter 2

The Origins of
Higher Education in Hull

VOLUNTARY PROVISION

Despite the success of the Great Exhibition, which proclaimed Britain's leadership in the industrial world, observers of the wider social and economic scene were highly critical of the country's neglect of technical education and training. Amongst the leading critics of Britain's position and untiring advocates of technical education was Lyon Playfair, an Exhibition Commissioner in 1850, then one of the joint secretaries of the new Science and Art Department in 1853, and five years later professor of Chemistry at Edinburgh. Later, in government, he served as Postmaster General in 1873 and Vice-President of the Council, in charge of education, in 1886. Playfair's tour of Europe in 1851 led to his scathing attack on the U.K.'s paucity of technical education. In his inaugural lecture as Professor of Chemistry at the University of Edinburgh in 1858, he stressed the importance of relating teaching to examining, not then the case in most universities, and in another lecture at St. Andrews in 1873 he bemoaned the universities' willingness to allow the professions, such as teaching, to slip away from their influence, thus losing the opportunity to liberalise the professions. Appointed to the new chair of Engineering at Edinburgh University in 1868, Professor Jenkin contrasted the continental training of engineers in universities with the apprenticeship system in England, arguing that the U.K. should also combine theory with practice and that the theory ought to be taught in universities rather than in newly-founded polytechnics. His successor made the same argument in his inaugural lecture *The Progress of Higher Technical Instruction* in 1885, and T.Hudson Beare, in his 1901 inaugural lecture, *The Education of an Engineer*, noted that Britain had lost its lead in industries such as brewing and dyeing to the Germans who, unlike the British, educated their technical experts in institutions where research was prevalent (Phillipson 1983, p.167-85). However, despite these specific warnings, the large scale demand for university-trained scientists and technologists did not appear in the United Kingdom until the twentieth century.

Much of the early interest in education in Britain was a product of the peculiar national obsession with social class and status. In the late eighteenth century, the main interest in education outside the ancient universities found expression in various types of learned societies for the middle-classes, some of which were eventually succeeded by civic colleges which became the late Victorian universities of industrial and commercial England. As the nineteenth century progressed, there was a growing interest in education of and for the working classes, both amongst private suppliers and by the state. Amongst the social factors which promoted such interest were a desire by some to reduce some of the harsher manifestations of early nineteenth century industrialisation, and the emerging realisation that secondary and higher education might be the very salve which a fractured society required. Furthermore, the general environment, including slightly shorter working weeks and less child labour, gave increasing leisure which made education feasible for both children and adults, particularly through evening class attendance. Economically, too, the benefits of education were beginning to be recognised, at least in terms of assisting particular local developments, and the growth of local transport facilities assisted those who were interested. However, in this area, perhaps the most important stimulus was the growing fear of European economic competition, and the Paris Exhibition of 1867 demonstrated that little serious progress had been made by the later part of the nineteenth century in technical and technological education in Britain.

The principal development in the provision of technical education in Britain was the emergence of the Mechanics Institutes, and others with different names but similar objectives, such as the Preston Institution for the Diffusion of Useful Knowledge; they held firm to the middle-class belief in the value of knowledge as a means of self-improvement and social amelioration. Formed chiefly during the second quarter of the nineteenth century, they catered essentially for craftsmen, foremen and mechanics rather than the sons of managers in industry, and the majority were as important for their lending-library function as for their teaching since much of the target group had little enough leisure during which to attend classes. After founding Anderson's Institution in Glasgow in 1796, Professor John Anderson moved to London to establish the London Mechanics Institute (1804), later Birkbeck College, and by 1851 there were over six hundred institutes which might have provided the germ of a national system of vocational education, but it was not to be, even though some modern universities and technical colleges can trace their origins directly to a local Mechanics Institute. The Colleges of Art grew out of the Schools of Design started in 1836 to train designers for industry, and the Colleges of Commerce from evening classes to train book-keepers and secretaries, then accountants and managers. The major characteristics of these disparate institutions were to remain with British higher education until the later part of the twentieth century. Originally part-time, and therefore essentially local and normally evening centres, they were working-class institutions providing a practical education which normally placed very little emphasis on theoretical principles with little aspiration to offer degree-level work.

Most educational provision in Britain during the nineteenth century was based on the voluntary principal and this remained the position in technical education almost until the end of the century. However, it would be as wrong to conclude that governments were uninterested in improving provision as it would be inappropriate to criticise their lack of direct intervention. The political economy of the period was based upon the concept of minimal government, and where governments did intervene in social and economic matters it was more likely to take the form of investigation of a problem which might lead to enabling legislation encouraging voluntary and local initiative. As early as 1835 the *Report of Select Committee on Arts and Manufactures* had persuaded the government to sponsor Schools of Design to promote the importance of industrial and design education, and the Great Exhibition of 1851 led to the establishment of a Department of Science and Art, within the Privy Council two years later, to improve the provision of technical and industrial education. In true Victorian fashion, the Department sought to fulfil its mission by the introduction of a scheme whereby local initiative could be supplemented by grants payable to institutions on the successful completion of the Department's examinations by their pupils, and this practice continued until the end of the century.

In the last third of the century, one of the most vociferous champions of technical education in Britain was Sir Bernhard Samuelson, a Teesside iron manufacturer and M.P. for Banbury, Oxfordshire. After a tour of major industrial sites in Europe in 1867, the year of the Paris Exhibition which had demonstrated Britain's comparative weakness in industry and design, he chaired a Select Committee on Scientific Instruction (1868) and was a member of the Royal Commission on Scientific Instruction (1870). Both committees deplored the poverty and limited geographical concentration of technical education and the general shortage of science teachers, and made a number of recommendations which would have led to an increased role for central government. However, the philosophy of non-intervention prevailed and little was achieved other than raising the level of the debate. Samuelson's final contribution was to chair the 1881-84 Royal Commission on Technical Instruction whose report he edited. The now familiar comparisons with Europe were rehearsed to Britain's increasing disadvantage; the paucity of good secondary schools and the poor showing of science in elementary schools curricula were noted; and it was proposed that local authorities should be enabled to establish and maintain secondary and technical schools. The legislative result of the work of the Royal Commission was the enabling 1889 Technical Instruction Act which permitted local councils to establish Technical schools and to levy a rate of up to 1d in the £ to support them. Despite the increasingly voluminous evidence of the inadequacy of technical education in Britain, contemporary political philosophy dictated that government might cajole and encourage but not insist on remedying the deficiency, though many towns and cities took advantage of the legislation to establish technical institutes. The strength of feeling against an interventionist approach can be seen in the extent to which Samuelson was involved in major voluntary developments as well as arguing the case for some state-sponsored technical education. At the same time as championing the case in the councils of state, he was lending his support to the bid for government support from Owen's College, Manchester, which became the Victoria University of Manchester, and was involved in fund-raising activities for

the Yorkshire College of Science (1874) which led to the creation
of the University of Leeds (Leonard 1981, p.19-32).

In Hull, the origins of adult, including technical, education,
followed this pattern.[1] Amongst the middle-class organisations
were the Hull Subscription Library founded in 1775, the 1792
Society for Literary Information, and in 1822 Hull Literary &
Philosophical Society was established with Dr. Alderson, a leading
physician in the town, as its first president. Eventually, the Literary
& Philosophical Society merged with the Subscription Library to
form the Royal Institution in Albion Street, but in the 1870s, under
the presidency of Dr. Kelburne King, a local surgeon interested
in science and education, the Literary and Philosophical Society
'assumed a new role as a focus for higher education.' (Allison
1969, p.356). After 1873, led by King and A.K. Rollitt, a local
solicitor and alderman, and other professional men, the Royal
Institution became an active centre for adult education in Hull,
and it was from this group that the first attempt was made to form
a university college in Hull in September 1876. The University
Extension Movement provided university education through a
system of itinerant lecturers from Oxford, Cambridge or London.
Affiliated to Cambridge, the Hull Society provided the sole basis
of higher education in the town in the later nineteenth century.
However, its eventual failure to generate a university college in
the city was attributed partly to its inability to attract other than
the middle classes who alone could afford the time and money to
attend, and partly to the existence of rival voluntary organisations
which also tapped into the limited supply of funds.

For working men, the Mechanics Institute was founded in 1825
under middle-class patronage, but, although it had an important
educational influence in Hull for two decades, its contribution to
Technical education should not be overrated. Mechanics Institutes existed to offer rational recreation, a place for discussion
and the delivery of instructive lectures which seldom displayed
any logical pattern, and the provision of Technical education
was neither the only nor even the primary purpose of such
institutions. Therefore, its long-term influence was comparatively
small, particularly after the 1860s when its social rather than its
educational character dominated its work in Hull, as elsewhere.
After that time, workingmen's needs were met by a number of
voluntary organisations of which the most important was the Young

Peoples' Christian and Literary Institute (1860) which replaced the Mechanics Institute as the focus of popular adult education and after 1869 offered science classes under the auspices of the Science and Arts Department. In addition, there was a range of voluntary bodies which offered both general and specific training in a number of fields, though none were to form the basis of twentieth-century higher education in the city. Amongst the general societies were a Social Institute founded in 1839 on Owenite co-operative principles; the Church Institute (1845) which promoted the study of literature and science in subordination to religion; the YMCA (1847) which was a national, non-denominational body with a strong belief in mutual improvement through the Christian religion; a mutual improvement society in Bowlalley Lane (1853); and the Friends' Adult School which also offered some educational opportunities. Specialist courses were offered in maritime work by two religious bodies concerned chiefly with mariners' welfare; from 1872 Trinity House, which received Science and Art Department grants from 1854, began to provide instruction in a senior department for the certificate examinations of the Board of Trade. The other specialist provision was offered by the Hull and East Riding School of Anatomy and Medicine (1831) which was maintained by local practitioners for their pupils to provide supplementary training to that given in the Hull General Infirmary and in the Hull & Sculcoates Dispensary (Allison 1969, p.356)

In this environment, it is not surprising that technical education failed to gain a substantial foothold in nineteenth-century Hull, though one foundation did survive into the twentieth century, became part of the city's further education provision and was eventually absorbed into the college which became the University of Humberside. In 1860 the Science and Art Department of the Privy Council on Education issued a circular to heads of educational establishments and to large employers in towns where no such school existed, drawing attention to the value of schools of design and the availability of central government grants for such enterprises. Some towns had established such Schools much earlier, such as Coventry (1838), where the stimulus had come from French competition in the ribbon trade, and Macclesfield (1852), but Hull was ahead of many other towns such as Oxford (1865), Sheffield (1867), Leicester (1870), Stafford (1873), and Newcastle (1876) (Stephens 1969, p. 304; Harris, p. 216-9;

Henry, p.3; Hawson (n.d.), p. 71; Hoskins & McKinley 1955, p. 252-68; Greenslade & Johnson 1979, p. 264-5; Richardson & Tomlinson 1916, p.154-5). Local initiative encouraged by modest central government support was typical of later nineteenth-century provison in Britain, and the response in Hull came from a group of individuals led by G.H.Lovell, master of St. James's Boys School, who became Secretary of a committee formed at a public meeting in January 1861 attended by two hundred artisans. Lovell, who hailed from Surrey, had been active in education circles for some time in the town as headmaster of St. James's National School until 1863, was Secretary of the Hull and East Riding Floral and Horticultural Society, and enjoyed local fame as a poet and song-writer. By the mid-sixties, he was the proprietor of a large and flourishing Middle-Class School whose curriculum prepared boys for the civil service, business and commerce. Also instrumental in the development were two members of the local Jewish community, Alderman W.H.Moss, a solicitor who was Secretary to the Hull Dock Company and mayor in 1856 and 1862, and Bethel Jacob, a local jeweller and silversmith, who was president of the Hull Jewish congregation and who became chairman and treasurer of the local committee for the founding of a school. The Mayor was the president, and its honorary committee included Lords Londesborough and Hotham, the town's Members of Parliament, the Recorder, the Sheriff and other notables. (Sheahan 1866, pp. 568, 585, 649-50). From this initiative the School of Art was founded in 1861 as an applied art and industrial design institution to support local industry. Work commenced in the Public Rooms, Jarratt Street, formerly used by the Literary & Philosophical Society, with William Pozzi as its first master, and the School held its first public exhibition in Spring 1862. However, in the view of the local historian of nineteenth-century education in the city, it was its second head, Edwin Chandler, who saw it securely established on the grants earned by both day and evening students at the Science and Art Departments annual examinations. John Menses became master in 1875 and the school was affiliated to the Royal Institution which transferred it to Albion Street (Allison 1969, p.356).

With the notable exception of the School of Art, all efforts made to introduce university and/or vocational education in the town in the later nineteenth century failed to put down roots, and the responsibility must lie with the city as a whole which failed to

Unity out of Diversity

Table 2.1   Colleges in Industrial Cities in the Late Nineteenth Century

City	Population 1891	College	Foundation
Birmingham	401,000	Mason College	1880
Bristol	207,000	University College	1876
Leeds	309,000	Yorkshire College of Science	1875
Liverpool	630,000	University College	1881
Manchester	341,000	Owens College	1850
Newcastle	145,000	Rutherford College	1876
Nottingham	187,000	University College	1881
Sheffield	285,000	Firth College	1879
Southampton	60,000	Hartley College	1862

Source: Green V.H.H. (1969), *British Universities* Harmondsworth
Mitchell B.R. & Deane P. (1962), *British Historical Statistics* Cambridge

recognise that improved educational opportunities would bring economic benefits to society. However, founding a college on a purely voluntary basis in the second half of the nineteenth century required substantial funding, and it was chiefly in the major cities that there was sufficient economic growth and personal wealth to facilitate foundations. Owens College, Manchester was founded through the generosity of one benefactor, as was Hartley College, Southampton, University College, Bristol, Firth College, Sheffield and Mason College, Birmingham. Liverpool College was founded by a group of merchant princes, and the Yorkshire College at Leeds was exceptional in that it did not enjoy the support of any major benefactor and had to rely on the wider community (Table 2.1). All of these early civic colleges became universities, though it is important to note that many offered arts, pure science, and teacher training courses, and prepared students for civil service and professional body examinations. With the exception of Leeds and Birmingham, there was a general indifference to technological education, and there rapidly developed the traditional British approach to higher education, encouraging late adolescent, full-time students (Jones 1968, p.65-6 and 169).

With a population of 154,000, Hull was less populous than most of the towns listed in Table 1.1, though the smaller towns of Newcastle-on-Tyne and Southampton made early provision for their communities on the basis of individual initiative (Richardson & Tomlinson 1916, p.154-5; Green 1969, p.143). However, in contrast to these major centres, there was a lack of substantial private support or major philanthropists who might have provided a lead in late nineteenth century Hull. Nor was Hull able to imitate

24

the occasional collaborative ventures successful in other towns, such as Coventry, where public appeals to the local business community and the general public produced a new building for the School of Design in 1863 and enabled the town to open a new Technical School in 1887 (Stephens 1969, p.304-5). In common with many other medium-sized towns, Hull was content to wait until the legislation of 1889 and 1890 facilitated the introduction of technical education. Perhaps the peculiar structure of the city's economy militated against the establishment of substantial individual fortunes from which donations might have been made. Whilst Hull enjoyed unprecedented economic growth during the latter part of the nineteenth century, it was unable to develop one or more major industries outside the port which might have become the basis for private wealth. Since this was a period when there was neither a tradition nor any desire for municipal corporations to supply the need it was not to be expected that Hull Corporation would fill the gap. Nonetheless, not all reformers were prepared to agree that the Corporation had no role to play. Alderman J.T.Woodhouse, a local solicitor active in the provison of middle-class education, including the foundation of Hymers College as an endowed school, and Mayor in 1891, criticised its lack of endeavour in post-elementary provision and claimed that he 'did not know any town that had been so apathetic on the subject of higher education than Hull' (Hull News 3.10.1891, p.6). However, in that very year, the Corporation finally began to address the problem when it embraced, initially rather tentatively, the 1889 Technical Instruction Act.

MUNICIPAL PROVISION

Apart from the School of Art which was founded in 1861, the various institutions which eventually coalesced to form the present University of Humberside all originated in a twenty-five year period prior to the outbreak of the First World War. Provision was made in a range of institutions in Hull, both private and municipal, and these separate institutions continued, largely under the watchful eye of the city fathers, until the reorganisation of local government made them the responsibility of the new county of Humberside in 1974. It promptly reorganised them to form two separate unitary Colleges of Higher Education and of Further Education in the city.[2]

THE FOUNDATION OF COLLEGES

Unlike some towns and cities, especially in Lancashire and Yorkshire, which can trace their municipal technical institutions back to a Mechanics Institute, Hull had to wait until the end of the century when the combined impact of the 1889 Technical Instruction Act and the 1890 Local Taxation (Customs and Excise) Act enabled local councils to levy a rate and obtain a subsidy to provide technical education. Inherent in this approach towards a national system locally administered, which was to be the basis of further and higher education provision until the end of the twentieth century, there was a contradiction which was never satisfactorily resolved. On the one hand, the Board of Education, particularly after the 1902 Education Act, believed that the national interest was best served by a form of liberal education which was anti-practical in ethos; on the other, the system being established at the turn of the century was meant to be responsive to local needs which, in the case of a city such as Hull, would not be met by a classically-based liberal education. The classical view was reflected in the 1889 Act which prohibited any direct industrial training in the new technical institutes, but for the first half of the twentieth century, local needs prevailed in the absence of any national policy for further education, and provision tended to concentrate on basic rather than advanced education.

Taking advantage of the legislation, Hull Council established a Technical Instruction Committee which met for the first time on 1 June 1891 and which remained responsible for developments until the 1902 Education Act required the Corporation to adopt the role of a Local Education Authority with a duty to provide primary and secondary education and the opportunity to offer further additional education. In response to the 1902 Act, the Corporation established an Education Committee; the bulk of the work was undertaken by Elementary and Higher Education Sub-Committees, with the latter absorbing the functions of the original Technical Education Committee. Thus began an eighty-year period in which the Corporation was responsible for two aspects of work which led to the University of Humberside. Initially, the Corporation concentrated on the establishment of technical education which included art, commerce and nautical training as well as the more traditional scientific and engineering subjects. However, it soon expanded its interests by becoming involved in the provision of teacher training, an enabling function under the 1902 Education Act, and municipal interest in this work was complemented by voluntary endeavour with the foundation of the Endsleigh College in the city by the Roman Catholic Church in 1905.

THE TECHNICAL SCHOOL
The initial foray of the Technical Instruction Committee into the field did not demonstrate a firm local commitment to municipal involvement in the provision of technical education. In addition to members of the Corporation, the committee contained representatives of all the voluntary bodies offering any form of technical education in the town such as the Literary and Philosophical Society, the Young People's Christian and Literary Institute, the Technical Education Council, the Hull School of Art, the University Extension Society, Trinity House School, and the Hull and District Institution of Engineers and Naval Architects. Not surprisingly, the committee chose to support existing rather than establish new provision through the voluntary organisations which were represented on the committee, though this was hard on the children of artisans who could not afford the fees for the voluntary institutes. Grants totalling £1,400, amounting to 25% of the money which the council anticipated that it would receive under the scheme, were made to some of the voluntary bodies for a two year period; one half of the grant was to be spent on apparatus and fixtures, and the Committee was to obtain representation on the governing councils in proportion to the amount of money received from the corporation. The voluntary institutions which benefited were the YPCLI £450; the University Extension Society £225; the Literary and Philosophical Society £225; the Church Institute £200; Hull Grammar School £150; and the School of Art £150 (TIC, 6.10.1891).

The Council's approach of subsidising private at the expense of public bodies, underlined by its initial refusal to make a grant to the Hull School Board, was based on the belief that the voluntary bodies were more deserving because of their greater longevity, that they tended to incur expenditure for general running and maintenance costs which were not levied on the School Board, and, in the case of the Hull School Board, had sufficient resources of their own to provide technical education. Protests from the Hull Trades and Labour Council and the Hull Building Trade Council were made to the Science and Art Department who advised the Corporation that it should support the School Board's attempts to provide technical education, and a grant of £300 was made in 1892. (TIC, 3.11.1891; 25.6.1892; 12.12.1892). Perhaps mindful of local criticism, the Technical Instruction Committee quickly resolved to provide rather than to assist in the provision of technical education in the city, but the relationship between the Council and the voluntary providers remained uncertain until the end of the decade. Some of the voluntary organisations continued to provide education for fee-paying students in the city, and it was only with the intervention of central government that the work of all came under the supervision of the Technical Instruction Committee. Even so, the Young Peoples' Christian and Literary Institute continued to receive support from the Board of Education (TIC, 15.5.1899 & 13.9.1901).

During this early period, when the education provided was little more than post-primary in standard, the Corporation's major interest was in the establishment of its Municipal Technical Institute which was envisaged as an institution directly related to Hull's industry and commerce, and committed to the provision of practical training for the students who were to make up subsequent workforces. The initial plans of the Technical Instruction Committee were ambitious, but neither it nor its successor were able to translate the dream into a vibrant reality. The commitment to local needs was reflected in the membership of the Governing Body of the new College which was to consist of twenty-four corporate and twenty-three non-corporate members drawn principally from local industry and commerce; wider professional support would be sought from the local branch of the Institution of Engineers and Naval Architects and from the Chamber of Commerce. The Institute would consist of five departments reflecting the city's economy, each of which would have a sub-committee consisting of councillors and professionals to oversee its work. Engineering and Cognate Industries would be designed to meet the needs of Hull's most important industries, and the Mercantile and Commercial Department would include foreign languages and commercial geography, thereby recognising Hull's emphasis on distributive rather than manufacturing activity. There would be a Department of Technical Instruction of Women, though women would be welcome on all courses and not just those concentrating on domestic economy, and a Technological Department would concentrate on local industries, though the provision that recourse to the Department of Science and Art would be needed suggested that this would be direct industrial training work currently prohibited by the Act. Significantly, there was also to be a Higher Instruction in Science Department, including Chemistry and Physical Science, which would seek to counter the lamentable provision of advanced work inhibited by the high costs of staff and equipment. In order to attract students from the working classes, fees would be low and could be remitted in meritorious cases, and there would be a system of scholarships, exhibitions and prizes (TIC, 29.3.1893).

Crucial to the creation of a successful College rather than the provision of a number of disparate classes was the engagement of an ambitious and energetic Principal, to which position Dr. J.T.Riley was appointed in 1893. At that time second master at Bradford Technical College and previously of Mason College, Birmingham, Riley had wide experience in organising, developing and teaching classes to degree level, and in establishing laboratories and new buildings (TIC, 28.8.1893). He was to become the central figure in the development of technical education in the city for the first quarter of the twentieth century, firstly in his position as Principal, a post which he occupied for nine years, and then as the city's first Director of Education after the 1902 Education Act created the LEA until his retirement in 1926. Riley's initial scheme for the College was more cautious than that of his employer, but followed the outline established by the Committee in seeking to serve the central elements of Hulls' economy. There were to be two departments in Engineering and in Mercantile and Commercial Education. In Engineering, there was to be a two-year preparatory course since most students were ignorant in mathematics, science and drawing, and this would be followed by a two-year course in the Higher Technical Department where there would be full-time courses in Marine and Mechanical Engineering, Civil Engineering and Naval Architecture, and possibly day release courses in marine engineering design and mathematics applied to design. In addition, he hoped to provide courses of training for sea-going engineers. Courses in other areas would follow, and the Art School would become a department of the Institute. Full-time fees in the Higher Technical Department would be five guineas per term with scholarships for best students. In Commercial Education there would be a three-year course. The estimated building and equipment demands associated with the plans would amount to £25,780 (FGP, 6.4.1894).

The provision of suitable premises for the new Technical Institute was as vital to its success as was the appointment of a dynamic Principal, but it is here that the contrast between ambition and reality is greatest. Initially, perhaps naively in view of generally unco-operative relations, the Council hoped to use buildings of the School Board in the evenings for some of its work, and it was anticipated that the provision of Engineering and Higher Science courses, which required specialised equipment in permanent locations, could take place in the voluntary societies' buildings, especially in the Literary and Philosophical Society's laboratory (TIC, 27.5.1892). It was inevitable that the new institution would begin life in temporary premises, but more grandiose plans for a comprehensive approach to the problem of providing for the education of its citizens soon emerged in the form of collaboration with the Public Libraries and the Property Committees for a building housing public hall, public library and technical school. Unfortunately, this was quickly abandoned on the grounds of expense, a problem which was to recur with depressing frequency during subsequent decades (TIC/FGP, 19.6.1893). Eventually, a temporary engineering school was established in premises leased in Observer Street for three years, and the College began life in seven different buildings scattered across the city (PAR 1895/96). The issue of a permanent home for the College was finally resolved with the purchase and adaptation of Park Street Orphans' Home. Significantly, the lowest of nine tenders, £8193, was accepted for the conversion work, and the work was only completed two years after the College first occupied its new premises in 1898 (TIC 14.2.1898; PAR 1899/1900).

During the first fifteen years of the College's life, technical education was offered in a somewhat haphazard way in a number of centres across the city, albeit all under the supervision of the Higher Education Sub-Committee. In an attempt to deal with the uncoordinated provison identified by the Board of Education's

Table 2.2   Full-Time Student Numbers Per Annum in Hull Technical Institute
1894-1929

	1894-1903	*1906-1920*	*1920-1929*
Engineering	32.8	22.9	26.8
Chemistry	14.4	17.8	25.4

Source: Principals' *Annual Reports*

inspectors in 1909, the Committee rationalised provision by hiving off lower level work to four branch colleges, thus enabling the Technical College to concentrate on higher level work, but the general problems discussed above continued, and the work of the senior school, as it was often described, suffered accordingly. Further and major reorganisation occurred within a year. Evening classes in the College were so full that the Director of Education, Dr. Riley, proposed hiving-off some work to a new organisation to be known as the Hull Evening School of Commerce, though the old approach continued with its location in the premises occupied in the daytime by the central secondary School. The new college was also to have a range of branch feeder colleges (HESC 16.11.1909; 13.12.1910) However, reorganisation did not result in any improvements in the existing premises, and the second Principal of the Technical Institute, T.H. Luxton, was campaigning for completely new ones within a year in order to provide largely low-level secretarial and languages training for local students; in fact, even in its first year a couple of students passed the Intermediate examination for B.Sc. (Econ.) of London University.

Table 2.2 indicates the small-scale character of full-time education in the Technical Institute through to 1930, a situation which ensured that the Colleges in Hull were essentially evening institutes with only small numbers of students attending in the day. Furthermore, work was very largely at a non-advanced level, a feature which was common to many similar institutions; the Board of Education, for example, was critical of the dominance of elementary work at the Harris Institute, Preston in 1907/8 (Timmins et al. 1979, p.20). In the early years of the Hull Technical Institute, many students were involved in the external examinations offered by the Board of Education, the City and Guild London Institute, the Lancashire and Cheshire Institute and the Royal Society of Arts, but, in contrast, only a handful of students matriculated and went on to take the intermediate and final examinations for the

London external degrees in science, engineering and economics. Nonetheless, sufficient progress had been made by 1910/11 for the Principal to note its ability to provide courses to pass degree standard, though the shortage of students and lethargy of employers could lead to the closure of the College unless improvements were forthcoming. In a city the size of Hull, four Intermediate passes in 1912/13 and six Finals a year later and one Intermediate and four Final successes in 1914 were disappointing (PAR 1911/12; 1912/13; 1913/14).

THE SCHOOL OF ART
In common with many Technical Instruction Committees, in 1893 the Corporation agreed to take over the control and management of the School of Art, thus making it the first institution to be provided under municipal support (TIC/F&GP, 21.6.1893). The first few years were spent establishing it on a firm footing, including the construction of new premises, and attempts were made to expand and reorganise the provison of art education in the School. During the early years of municipal control, the School sought to provide a bridge between art and crafts on the one hand and the needs of local industry on the other. In the view of Mr. Exley, Principal 1911 to 1920, too much of art education was concerned with the 'premature manufacture of works for exhibition' instead of the support of local industries which was its real concern (PAR, 1913/14). Thus, in order to provide a good general education in art and to train competent teachers, the School was re-organised in 1913 into six major areas – drawing, painting, modelling, pictorial design, industrial design and Architecture. Behind the attempt to link art education with industry was the belief that the task was less the training of craftsmen and more the production of educated students who would realise the importance of art and design which was at the heart of everyday life. This was a laudable aim to set before the city, but initially at least, local employers were less enthusiastic about the opportunities than the staff of the School. This link with the real world remained at the centre of the School's purpose as indicated by the Principal E.A.S. Bonney who noted in his first report in 1929/30 that its aims were first to train young people for work in manufacturing and handicraft industries, artists and teachers, and second to offer courses in art appreciation which would contribute to a liberal education. Thus,

the departments of Design, Painting and Decorating, Architecture, Embroidery, Dressmaking and Dress Design were augmented by a professional art circle and a bookbinding department, and this role was underlined by renaming the School to the City of Hull College of Arts and Crafts which was felt to reflect its importance in the sixth largest city in the kingdom and which would enable it to extend its influence in the region.

The School of Art was located in its nineteenth-century premises in Albion Street and, despite the energy of the staff and in particular the Principal, the premises were thought to be so inadequate by 1899 that its official recognition by the Science and Art Department of the Privy Council was endangered (TIC/AC 12.11.1896; 7.4.1899). Therefore, in 1900, moves began to find better premises for the School with a notice in the local press for a suitable site. On the strength of a number of visits to art schools in various parts of the country, which revealed the poverty of the Hull environment compared even to smaller centres, it was recommended that a new school should be built in Hull. The proposals were nothing if not ambitious. It was hoped that the new School would be on a site near to the Art Gallery and Free Library and thus central enough to avoid the development of annexes in different parts of the city, that it should contain an Art Museum and Cast gallery, and should be responsible for all art education in the district. A further indication of the ambitions of its promoters was the recommendation that the new School should be able to accommodate at least two hundred day and two hundred and fifty evening students, more than double the numbers then attending, and that it should consist of a basement and two floors lit from the north or north-east. It was anticipated that the cost would be £15,000 to £17,000 or a 0.254p rate (AC 12.1.1900). The Council received twelve offers of land, including the Literary and Philosophical Society premises in Albion Street and the Mechanics Institute building nearby, but eventually a site on Anlaby Road was approved and purchased, and a competition for the design of the School was established (AC 10.10. 1900, 8.11.1900, & 2.8.1901). The committee approved c. £10,000 for the building, excluding furniture and fittings, which was to be in Renaissance style, but this was increased to an absolute maximum of £12,000 after its adequacy was questioned by Jenkins & Harbour, a firm of London architects who wished to compete (AC 21.11.1901). The winning architects were Messrs Lanchester,

Stewart & Rickards, and the building contract was awarded to
Messrs. Hockney & Liggins whose estimate of £12,058 was the
cheapest. The Council borrowed £5,380 for the purchase of the
land and sought a further £14,000 for building and fittings, and
the new School was opened on 6 October 1905 (AC 7.5.1902
and 30.5.1902). Naturally, the Higher Education Sub-Committee
of the Council's Education Committee, which had taken over
responsibility for the area in 1902, was very pleased with its first
new building, but His Majesty's inspectors were less impressed with
the fact that the library was well below the standard of a school of
its size and importance.

Initially, the School of Art catered primarily for Hull boys who
attended principally in the evening though, by 1896, pupils from
the East Riding were attending the day classes. Growing from an
annual attendance of eighty-six students in 1895/96 to around three
hundred and sixty in the years from 1908 to 1912, the small staff of
three full-time and five part-time teachers, in addition to the Head,
found that they had to concentrate on remedying the basic defects
in the education of their recruits whose previous educational attainment had been poor. It is clear that the academic achievements of
the School were very limited, and examination results were at best
modest, with HMI urging that systematic improvements be made
to bring the School up to the standard of others in the region.

THE NAUTICAL SCHOOLS
In the sphere of nautical education, the haphazard provision of
training in the period prior to the First World War was the
result of a combination of voluntary and local authority effort.
Although classes in navigation appear to have been given from the
mid-1890s, the first mention of an institution is the Hull Nautical
School of Cookery, founded in 1899 under the management of
a small number of shipowners. It soon became apparent that
this organisation was unable or unwilling to bear the burdens of
training for the whole industry, and in 1899 it asked the Technical
Instruction Committee to take it over and maintain it from its funds
(TIC 31.12.1901). A school of cookery was approved by the Board
of Education (HESC 15.12.1905). The inspectors urged the Local
Authority to devise 'a more adequate – though not too ambitious
or costly – scheme, with a view to providing a more commodious
and better equipped school' (HMI Report 1907). In 1906, the

Local Authority noted that there were plans for a new School for Fishermen by the instructor at the Fishermen's school (HESC 16.11.1906), and in 1908 moves were made by the Hull Fishing Vessel Owners' Association and joined by the Joint Amalgamated Arbitration and Navigation Committee and the Port of Hull Trawl Fishermen's Protective Society. (HESC 12.1.1909). Subsequently, the Local Authority agreed to purchase a thousand square yards of land adjacent to that which the society had bought. The school was built on the west side of the Boulevard adjoining a Catholic church at 8/6d per sq. yd. (HESC, 11.5.1909 and 13.7.1909), and almost immediately received a glowing report from the Board of Education (PAR, 1910).

The Nautical Training School appears to have suffered most severely from the problems which faced the other technical education schools in the city. The initial premises were very poor, consisting of 'three small rooms in the upper portion of a building erected to serve as a shop and dwelling-house, situated not far from the fish dock,' with the result that floor and bench space were inadequate, storage facilities very poor, and the more ordinary conveniences of a school absent. Particularly problematic was the consequence which required men of all ranks and ages to work at the same table which resulted in skippers and older persons avoiding classes. Instruction was given by one teacher only, albeit with great commitment and enthusiasm, to enable students who might wish to take the Board of Trade Certificate examinations, but the nature of the industry militated against regular attendance (HMI Report, 1907).

However, the structure of the industry served by the College influenced the character and quality of the education offered. Characterised as it was by casual employment with periods at sea, regular attendance in College was impossible for the majority of the boys. Therefore, although annual enrolments in the first few years of the twentieth century reached four hundred, it represented only 10% of those who worked on Hull trawlers, and these students attended only while on shore for a few days, or for a few weeks when out of employment (PAR 1906/7-1918/19). Consequently, it could only operate as a Junior Technical School for boys between the ages of 13.25 to 15.25, after which they would begin a four-year apprenticeship on sea-going trawlers, during which time they would attend for advanced courses when on shore. These problems remained with nautical education and training throughout the twentieth century, and although the Nautical College was one of those which merged to form Hull College of Higher Education in 1976, the vast majority of its work was and always has been at a non-advanced level.

TEACHER TRAINING

Apart from a number of teacher training colleges which were founded by the churches, late nineteenth-century training was basically through the pupil-teacher method which was recognised as a totally inadequate way of training elementary school teachers by the 1898 Departmental Committee of Inquiry. According to Prime Minister A.J. Balfour, speaking during the debates on the 1902 Education Bill, 36% of students did not pass the certificate examination and 55% of existing teachers had never been to training college (Hencke, p.23). Therefore, recognising that existing training in independent colleges and through the pupil-teacher system would be even more inadequate for the educational system to be introduced by the 1902 Bill than it was, the government gave local authorities the right to establish teacher training colleges, thereby adding a final group of colleges to the system. By 1907, the desirable method of training was school until 17 or 18 followed by two years at teacher training college.

The stimulus for the foundation of a Municipal Training College in Hull was shortage of certified teachers in the city's schools. However, the inability of the Technical College to expand into a higher education establishment because of the cramped nature of its existing site and its unattractive environment provided the opportunity to float the idea of a comprehensive provision of advanced education in the city which was to recur at various intervals during the first half of the twentieth century. The Local Authority accepted the proposal of W.H.Owen, a local barrister on the Higher Education Sub-Committee, for the development of a new site for higher education in Hull which would include a Training College, a new Technical College and a University College, though the Board of Education, whose approval for the scheme was necessary, received the idea with a distinct lack of enthusiasm. Whilst accepting the need for a training college in the city, the Board noted that such a college would have to be completely separate from any other institution in order to qualify for the Board's building grant of 75%, and suggested that a joint college encompassing a range of levels of work would find it impossible to attract the right kind of staff at salaries paid to training college employees. The council accepted the view, but sought to obtain land for the training college, which would allow expansion as necessary and possibly in the future, thereby reserving the right to revive its conception of a comprehensive higher education establishment in the city (HESC, 18.11.1907), which it did after the First World War. The architects, Messrs. Crouch, Butler & Savage of Birmingham, won the competition for the design of the buildings and the Local Authority received from the Board of Education 75% towards the £3,170 purchase price of the land on Cottingham Road (HESC, 26.10.1909). The College opened in September 1913 with 49 women and 64 men students. Its first Principal was Mr. I.B.John, formerly principal of Dudley College, and the Higher Education Sub-Committee was to be its Governing Body (21.1 & 13.5.1913).

The origins of teacher training in England had been found in the voluntary movement in which the churches were prominent, dominated by the Anglicans. The development of the voluntary Endsleigh Training College in 1905 by the Sisters of Mercy in their Beverley Road Convent occurred against a background of denominational strife in Hull, and Endsleigh's origins were set against the background of a vicious late nineteenth-century campaign in the city in to prevent the development of a Catholic school system.[3] On 30 June, 1905 the diocese of Middlesborough sought permission for the Sisters of Mercy to establish a college in Hull primarily for girls who had served as pupil teachers in the Roman Catholic diocese, though this intent was soon widened to all girls especially those from the neighbouring Leeds diocese and to embrace those who wished to teach without becoming pupil teachers. The Board of Education sought a range of guarantees in the face of great determination from the church which sought to move ahead without the requisite number of qualified staff, and somewhat grudgingly gave approval in July 1905 after an HMI visit the previous January. Modelled on the college at Mount Pleasant, Liverpool, the College sought to produce good Catholic girls and good Catholic mothers, the hidden curriculum of the college. The College began with sixteen students, bought adjacent land and began a building programme. By 1907/8 approval for an intake

Table 2.3   Recruitment of Students to Endsleigh by Roman Catholic Diocese 1907-18

Liverpool	20	Ireland	6
Middlesborough	19	Westminster	3
Hexham & Newcastle	16	Southwark	3
Salford	12.5	Other Dioceses	8
Leeds	12		

Source: McClelland, p.237

of ninety-two increased to ninety-three, where it remained until approval was given to grow to 180 in 1928.

The new College was successful in attracting students from around the country, but its early years were fraught with severe problems resulting from the low quality and subsequent achievements of students, poor teaching methods and inadequate staffing. Even HMI Dale, himself a member of the Roman Catholic church, who appears to have succumbed to Sister Dawson's blandishments rather too readily, could not ignore the fact that the poor quality of work was attributable to the principal's practice of admitting students who had not passed the scholarship examination. Therefore, he advocated that the students take shorter academic courses since they were not expected to shine, and spend time in the open air since they were not physically strong ! Not only was academic performance weak, particularly in the basic subjects of English and Mathematics, but the standard of teaching left much to be desired, partly on account of the lack of competent lay teachers and their very rapid turnover. Had there been a ready supply of trained and capable teachers from the Order, the weaknesses may have been remedied, but this was not the case. However, HMI also recognised the determination of the governors to create a high standard college, and urged the Board to give it its chance, though the historian of the College's early years suggests that the sympathy of the College's first HMI had 'hindered (the principal) from coming to grips with the reality of running a training college' (McClelland 1993, p.313).

The situation improved with the appointment of a new HMI Dickson, a lady who was not taken in by Sister Dawson's subterfuges to disguise the reality of the situation in the College. In addition to highlighting the faults in teaching, such as the tendency to memorise facts and details rather than encourage original thought, the new inspector was instrumental in obtaining the removal of a particularly ineffective instructor and persuading the authorities to introduce the idea of regular training of two nuns each year. Clearly, some improvements followed, although the poor quality of staffing, particularly under the influence of the war and the 1918 'flu epidemic, was instrumental in the Board of Education's refusal to allow numbers to rise to one hundred for the 1918/19 intake (p.265)

The first Principal, Sister Dawson, though not an educationist, has been credited with great leadership in the face of successive attacks by HMI on the poor quality of the College. On her retirement in 1918, the Board of Education sought an assurance through the Catholic Education Council that staffing would be largely from members of the religious order in charge of the college to reduce turn-over. The new Principal was Sr. O'Hara, a very successful mistress of method since 1912, and one of the first nuns to attend Cambridge for training under the scheme introduced in 1911. With the appointment of an academic in place of an administrator, the situation began to improve, though the Board was unwilling to approve Sr. Martin as Vice-Principal because she did not have university qualifications. However, by 1938 the academic problems associated with its early work had been resolved and there were one hundred and eighteen students at the College. At the beginning of the Second World War, the College was evacuated to a country house in east Yorkshire, returning to Hull in 1943 before the end of the war where it occupied some premises in the Municipal Training College since its own buildings were being used by St. Mary's Grammar School who had been bombed out of their own premises.

ANALYSIS

Further Education in Hull did not make a particularly auspicious start, and even the Chair of the Higher Education Sub-Committee, reviewing its performance in 1918, confessed that the LEA's attitude had been at best opportunistic and generally reactive. A partial explanation for the LEA's torpor may be found in the concurrent need to consolidate the Board School system of elementary education and to provide a system of secondary education under the 1902 Education Act, both of which took priority over other considerations, but the national record was mixed but

Table 2.4   Population of Hull and Six Comparable Cities (000s)

	1881	*1891*	*1901*	*1911*
Coventry	42	53	70	106
Hull	154	200	240	278
Leicester	122	175	212	227
Newcastle	145	186	215	267
Oxford	46	49	53	57
Preston	97	108	113	117

Source: Mitchell & Deane, *British Historical Statistics*, 1.7 1962

undistinguished in this period. Nationally, there were only some 4,000 full-time and 4,000 part-time day students, and at the end of the first decade of the new century technical education suffered principally from neglect. In Hull, as in Liverpool (Argles, p.62-3) technical education was available, though chiefly in part-time, evening-only classes, delivered in scattered, second-hand premises to relatively apathetic students in support of a local economy whose enthusiasm for training was limited, in part by the occupational structure of the town. both in itself and in comparison with other towns of similar size. However, some towns were able to make significant progress, many of which were smaller than Hull. Municipal Technical Instruction Committees in Leicester, Newcastle, and Stafford produced new, purpose-built technical Schools in 1892, 1894, and 1896 respectively. After 1890, Leicester appears to have been fortunate in the continuing voluntary contribution to municipal provision. There, employer interest was maintained through the donation of modern equipment and the establishment of prizes and scholarships, and the same Authority had undertaken a rationalisation of its provision by 1914 with advanced work being done in the Technical College and non-advanced carried out in the Evening Schools (Hoskins & McKinley 1955, p.304-5). However, whilst the Council's performance in comparison to other towns is unimpressive, its success has to be evaluated in the context of the environment in which it operated, and there is little doubt that the structure of the local economy and, in particular, its employment opportunities and requirements generated an attitude amongst employers, parents and potential students which was not conducive to the successful development of further education.

The success of civic colleges in the late nineteenth and early twentieth centuries depended on there being a sufficient population to supply students from a community which recognised the social and economic benefits of education, and superficially at least, Hull appeared to be in a strong position.[4] In terms of population, Hull had experienced significant growth in the second half of the nineteenth century, with the municipal borough increasing by 183.7% to 240,259 in 1901, a rate of growth which was aided by substantial migration into the town. In addition, the economy of the town was generally expanding. At the beginning of the twentieth century, Hull's economy was based firmly on the port, with trade concentrated on northern Europe, and the last few years prior to 1914 saw a level of prosperity in the city which was not to be reached again for many decades. Economic growth was based on the emergence of one main shipping company, Wilson's, on the development of port-related industries such as seed-crushing, grain-milling and fishing, and on the growth of transport services. However, this prosperity was founded on industries which demanded much casual and relatively unskilled labour, and the absence of any large consumer population in the area militated against occupational diversification. Although there was a shipbuilding industry in Hull, established since the seventeenth century, the city was not an important national centre, and its requirements hardly provided the springboard for the development of engineering education. As a result, the limited employment opportunities in specialist engineering persuaded pupils to go elsewhere (PAR 1907/8). Thus, the peculiar demands and the natural volatility of the local labour market, aggravated by depressions, such as occurred in 1904, and strikes such as the engineering strike in 1906, created a very modest demand for education, particularly amongst evening-only students (PAR 1904/5; 1906/7).

Against this background, it is not surprising to find the college Principals lamenting the attitude of employers towards technical education. In many cases anything more than basic education was an irrelevance, but, even where it might have been effective, industry was less than helpful in encouraging the colleges. The major problem was that industry was unwilling to support training for their employees, whilst their willingness to employ equally boys who were trained and boys who were not, undermined the thrust of the colleges' work. In nautical education, the absence of a really effective apprenticeship scheme in the industry discouraged some from attending when they could obtain equally good employment without training; even the occasional firm which did have a scheme seldom bothered to ensure that their apprentices were attending as required. Experience suggested that this would lead to declining enrolments; boys from the School appeared to have no better prospects and the lure of employment and money was considerable (Advisory Committee Report 12.4.1921). Further setbacks came within a couple of years when the Fishing Vessels Owners' Association withdrew their apprenticeship scheme which meant that their ships were staffed entirely by casual labour. This left no role for School other than providing initial training for men and boys in the mercantile marine, and providing in-service courses for fishermen when they were on shore (10.4.1923).

Even where there was an interest in additional technical education, the quality of schools in Hull left much to be desired and appears to have hindered the development of the colleges. During the School Board era 1870-1902, there was a major expansion of voluntary schools seeking to safeguard the denominational position, but it was in the new rate-aided sector that the major developments took place. Unfortunately, successive School Boards took a parsimonious approach to the provision of elementary education, with standards being notoriously low compared to the national position. Amongst the principal characteristics of the Board School system in Hull were a lower education rate than any comparably-sized city, a curriculum restricted to grant-earning subjects, and excessive employment of untrained teachers and poor salaries, though three higher-grade schools were opened providing practical and scientific education. Despite this latter innovation, the students recruited by the Colleges had a very poor basic knowledge for scientific and engineering studies, and those recruited were often only willing to stay for a couple of years. Describing the reformed system after 1902, the local historian of the city's educational provision noted that 'to some extent the early (Education) committee inherited the outlook as well as the institutions of the School Board: in higher education especially, it was slow to rise to its new responsibilities and opportunities, and sometimes did so only after remonstrance from the Board of Education ' (Allison 1969, p.357).

In the early part of the century, the Board of Education introduced specific regulations designed to improve the quality of secondary and technical education in the country as a whole, and the severity of their impact in Hull further underlined the poverty of education provision and the attitudes towards its value. This was the case in 1907/8 when the Board required future students sitting its examinations to undertake four years in secondary education before entering technical colleges. Given the structure of employment in the city, this acted as a deterrent to technical education since they would remain at College until 18+ at which age it was very difficult to obtain initial employment in a market where the demand was for younger employees. (PAR 1897/98; 1904/5; 1906/7; 1907/8). A second attempt to raise standards, this time in Art, was made in 1911/12 when similarly stringent demands were placed on candidates for examination. Those who wished to obtain an Art Teacher's Certificate had to attend secondary education until the age of 16+ and then undertake a continuous course at an Art School for five or six years; students requiring certification in industrial design would have to follow evening only or part-time course of at least four years after the age of sixteen. Throughout the second decade of the century, the Head of the School of Art, Mr. Exley, continually drew attention in his annual reports to the contrast between the desirably high standards being set by the Board and the ability of his students to reach them. High attainment was further discouraged by the prevailing tendency of the majority of the pupils to attend four or even five evenings per week, a regime which was extremely difficult to sustain for four or more years. Similarly, the Board of Education's view that the minimum age on enrolment should be fourteen after two years at secondary school exacerbated the recruitment problems of the Nautical School (PAR, 15.6.1920)

The prospect of undertaking a technical education course was not particularly attractive even before the Board reformed its examinations. Higher education, and secondary education also until 1944, was firmly opposed to the inclusion of technical education within its orbit on the grounds of status and class, because it was preparing students for particular roles within the class structure. Consequently, technical education, concerned with the practical aspects of life and thus preparing its students for working-class occupations. had its low status confirmed. As a result, the most able boys, and their parents, preferred to enter the professions rather than science and engineering training, thus ensuring that technical education was at best a poor relation and at worst seen as a sector for those who had failed to achieve anything better, a point made with great consistency by Hull college principals. Even when students could be found, they must have been of an heroic mould not to have been inhibited by the combined conditions of work and study. Some boys were working a normal week, attending College on two evenings per week, and, on occasions, following an evening class with a 6 a.m. start the next day! Even under normal conditions, the imposition and acceptance of overtime working prevented students from undertaking home-work (PAR 1897/98;1901/2; 1906/7).

Chapter 3

Inter-War Provision in Hull

Immediately after the conclusion of the First World War, the abortive pre-war scheme for a university college in the city, initiated by W.H.Owen in 1905, was revived, and the protracted negotiations over the establishment of the University College of Hull, which occupied much of the 1920s until its opening in 1928, were to cast a shadow over Local Authority provision of post-secondary education in the city for the whole of the inter-war period. Because Hull's makeshift and scattered buildings compared unfavourably with technical education premises in other large towns, post-war reconstruction presented an opportunity to improve the modest pre-war provision, perhaps by providing comprehensive higher education in the city, though none could have thought that it would take the best part of a century to realise. Luxton, Principal of the Technical College, encapsulated the educationists' vision, though it is worth noting that even he did not aspire to the full-time education offered in the civic universities of the North and Midlands. He believed that:

> the ideal condition for Hull would appear to be a great central institution providing for all advanced evening class work of every description for the whole city, whether scientific, technological, literary, commercial or domestic – a university in character, fed by a well-arranged system of preparatory technical, commercial and domestic science schools, and working in the closest co-ordination with the Secondary Schools and the Elementary Schools under the LEA.
> (PAR 1910/11)

Such an approach would enable Hull to overcome its very poor educational knowledge and achievements in economics, engineering and shipbuilding and to seize the potential to become a world scientific centre for chemically-based industries of oil, grease, soap, paint and varnish. This vision required a substantial building programme equipped with first-class scientific, technical and commercial libraries, high-quality workshops and laboratories, and staffed liberally to encourage extensive reading and research. Only then would 'the local Technical Colleges . . . become the Mecca of the manufacturer, their staffs the honoured confidantes of their managers, and their students . . . given every opportunity of deserved promotion and every encouragement to advanced work.' (PAR 1913/14)

A UNIVERSITY COLLEGE FOR HULL?[1]

In 1918, a sub-committee set up by the Education Committee to consider the needs of post-war education in the city aimed 'to stimulate and equip the City for taking full advantage of the opportunities for industry and commerce in a new era of the world.' Reviewing the previous performance of the LEA, the committee recognised that the City Fathers had failed to grasp the opportunities before it, and its purely reactive role had led to an opportunistic approach to educational and commercial policy. Therefore, seizing the new opportunity and recognising that a new system must offer to students 'the means of acquiring the scientific knowledge, the technical and technological theory and practice of the varied principles and organisation which make up the vast sum of modern industry and commerce,' the committee proposed an ambitious, if thoroughly local plan of action. The existing Technical Institution was to be greatly expanded to provide advanced science, technology, commerce and general subjects to university degree standard, to undertake consultancy and experimental work in close co-operation with local employers and industry, and to offer advanced evening classes in any department according to demand. The courses to be offered would reflect directly the needs of local industry and commerce. Degree level subjects included applied chemistry, shipbuilding, building, agriculture, modern languages and literature, and students would take London external degrees in engineering, pure science and commerce; applied chemistry was to be studied with special reference to those products imported through or refined in the town, such as oils, fats, soaps, and tar.

In addition to this concentration and enhancement of work taught in the Technical and Commercial Colleges, appropriate elements of work, such as Architecture, would be transferred from other municipal colleges to the new University College. Use would be made of the existing facilities in education based on the Municipal Training College already on an adjacent site on Cottingham Road, and it was accepted that it would probably be necessary to include some arts courses to obtain wider public support. Perhaps mindful of the weaknesses of pre-war secondary education in the city, the new institutions would be supplied by a feeder, but totally separate junior sector, and by the secondary schools in Hull. However, the strictly local and even limited character of the venture was indicated by its wish to provide an opportunity for degree-level education for all who had failed to provide a place at a university. Clearly, the vision of the educational leadership in the city did not encompass the recruitment of students from a wider area. Nonetheless, in the light of existing provision, it was a bold scheme which could not be accomplished by expansion on the present constricted site of the Technical College, and its dispersed character, together with that of the Evening College of Commerce, suggested that a new, large and unified site was required for the scheme, including a social wing housing the library and other public facilities, and perhaps even an industrial and commercial museum (Report of the Sub-Committee on the Required Provision for Technical Instruction in the City of Hull 1918).

Thus, the scene was set for the realisation of the dreams of Owen, Riley, Luxton and others that Hull should have a university-level institution with a strong scientific and technological bias towards the needs of local and regional industry and commerce. This concept was not without its opponents, and the voluntary university extension movement staggered into life again with a proposal that the university college should be an amalgam of all bodies interested in higher education, voluntary and corporate, but that the bias should be towards the former. Seen for what it was, an attempt to revive the flagging fortunes of the old elitist, middle-class and generalist idea of a university, it failed to gain support. However, some of the concepts implicit in the idea were to seem strangely prophetic when viewed from the perspective of 1930. In January 1919, the council set aside £150,000 for the purchase of land next to the Training College for the development of a Technical College, after which the two might be combined into a university. However, the Council's initiative came at a difficult time economically which caused the Board of Education to refuse permission for the transfer of land for higher education purposes since 'it was premature now to conclude that a large development of post-secondary full-time education in Hull will be necessary to meet either a local or a general demand from Commerce and Industry.' (HESC 27.10.1921). The economic constraints of the Board's position were heavily underlined by its immediate acceptance of T.H.Ferens's (2) offer in 1922 to buy the land and donate it to the Council for its original purpose, an approval which had the advantage of reserving the land for higher education, unless the necessary government approval was forthcoming for a change of use.

The Board's refusal of support appears to have produced a slight hiatus in developments locally, with little immediate progress being made towards the development of any kind of major institution on the land which Ferens had provided. The stimulus for further action appears to have been the LEA's proposal to erect a junior Technical College on Cottingham Road to resolve the problems of overcrowding in Park Street, a move which would pre-empt all attempts to found a university college. This turn of events led to Ferens' pre-emptive gift of £250,000 to establish a university college on the site, somewhat perversely welcomed by the Higher Education Sub-Committee as providing for the development of the technical, scientific and humanities education of the city, despite the fact that it prevented the construction of a junior Technical College (HESC, 12.10.1925). In 1925, Riley's proposed academic structure included four faculties – Arts, Economics, Pure Science and Applied Science – though there was criticism from leading academics whose advice was sought by Ferens. The eventual proposal of the committee, asked by Ferens to produce a plan, was to confirm the Riley proposal but to separate Education from Arts to create an additional faculty. Advanced work in Engineering and Chemistry would be transferred from other Hull institutions, and Education at the Training College would be incorporated into the University College. Thus, apart from the formal incorporation of the Training College and the recognition that there should be an Arts faculty, the original municipal conception remained intact.

However, not everyone shared Riley's conception of the new

institution, not least the newly-appointed principal A.E.Morgan who came from University College, Exeter in 1926. Since his appointment was actively engineered by the Organising Board of the University College, Morgan was able to stipulate a number of crucial conditions on his appointment, all of which were conceded and were to affect the character and direction of higher education provision in the city for the remainder of the century. In addition to requiring a further £250,000 endowment, he obtained from the LEA the £150,000 earlier dedicated to a technical college, and demanded that Technology be excluded from the curriculum. The University of Hull's historian suggests that this apparent *volte face* by the Appointments Committee, which swept away the original conception of a university college in Hull, was the work of Ferens, even though the decision was contrary to his business philosophy and required acquiescence in the views of a man whose agnosticism contrasted with the benefactor's stern Wesleyanism. However, it is clear that Ferens had consulted a number of eminent academics, including the chairman of the University Grants Committee, and it is possible that they may have given advice which led Ferens to accept a different vision for the new university college. The immediate upshot was the resignation of Riley as Secretary to the Organising Board whose vision of a technological University College serving the interests of the city was destroyed by the conditions attaching to Morgan's appointment.

Riley's disillusion reminded Morgan of the need to retain the goodwill of the Education Authority, and his initial building plans contained considerable provision for Technology, albeit in temporary buildings. However, by January 1927 it was clear that this was merely a smokescreen and that Technology would not be included; in Morgan's view 'the only possible foundation of a true university institution is to be found in the faculties of Arts and Pure Science' (Morgan to Moore, 18 January 1927, Bamford 1976, p.32). His first scheme, therefore, excluded Engineering and Education, though the hope was expressed that the Training Colleges, both municipal and voluntary, might become affiliated to the University College, with students who wished to obtain degrees attending the latter for their academic subjects and the former for their teacher training. Clearly, the complete reversal of policy was the work of Morgan, with the aid of outside advisors, and his vision of a university prevailed, as an intellectual organism unsullied by formal connection with vocationally-oriented colleges and free from external control, though willing to accepted undedicated finance,. Although Lord Eustace Percy, President of the Board of Education, regretted the change of policy locally, the Board agreed to the Council's capital expenditure of £150,000 in April 1927, but did not accede to the £2,500 LEA maintenance grant, offering instead the sum of £1,000 for two years under further education regulations. This was refused, as it would have meant that University College would have to be open to government Inspection. The ambivalence of the Local Authority remained, however, as shown by its inclusion of a similar sum in its rates estimate for donation to the University College (HESC 30.11.1927), and also by its joint venture to establish a course in aeronautical training with the Technical College from 1930-1945, though this eventually foundered. The initial conception was odd in the light of Morgan's initial decision to exclude engineering from the curriculum, but the University Grants Committee's failure to support the initiative in 1945 was, at least in part, a reflection of the University College's failure to build up this area, and of the national picture since Hull's initiative had mainly local impact.

FURTHER EDUCATION IN THE INTER-WAR YEARS

Much of the Local Authority's energy had gone into its promotion of, and collaboration with, the University College plan, and, with its failure from the LEA's perspective, there were no alternative plans for the development of advanced further education in the city. Nonetheless, the Local Authority's relationship with the new University College continued to be somewhat ambivalent. Although the new institution was quite different from that which the city's educational leadership had envisaged, this did not prevent it from continuing to flirt with the University College during subsequent decades, sometimes to the apparent detriment of its own development of advanced further education provision. The Authority's apparent acquiescence in its second-class position vis-à-vis the University College can be seen by its agreement that it should restrict itself to students already working in industry and commerce mainly through part-time evening only classes and leave the full-time degree-level work to the latter. There was some limited co-operation between the two institutions, with full-time students from the Blackburn Aircraft Company following a two-year diploma, though this transferred to the Technical College after the war (Mitchell 1975, p.6).

Architecture was another area in which the Local Authority appeared content to allow its responsibilities to be taken over. Two attempts were made to transfer Architecture courses from the College of Arts and Crafts to the University College, thus enabling the latter to offer a degree, only for the moves to be blocked by central government. The first was in 1934, but this was abandoned in the light of strong discouragement from the Board of Education (Bamford 1975, p.92). A second attempt was made during the war years 1941-44 when both parties seemed willing to collaborate, but the University College wished to establish a department of Architecture, based on the transfer of courses from the College of Arts and Crafts, approval for which was not forthcoming from the Board of Education. In the view of the University's historian, 'it is difficult to avoid the feeling that the courage, faith, and the spirit of adventure were missing, ' (Bamford 1975, p.98). Another view might be to marvel at the municipality's willingness, even enthusiasm, for the transfer which would have had the effect of removing Architecture from its natural links with art and industrial design.

In the area of teacher education there was a national feeling that colleges should develop closer relationships with universities, with college courses being recognised for degrees or diplomas. Consideration by the 1925 Departmental Committee on the Training of Teachers failed to grasp the opportunity to establish area committees to oversee the training and certification of teachers, as proposed by Hull, preferring instead to set up regional Joint Examinations Boards for the certificate examination, though the Board of Education retained the right to examine practical teaching. Locally, the College would have liked to develop links with the new University College of Hull in this respect, but the Board of Education felt that the latter was too young to become an examining body for teacher training. Thus, the Municipal Teacher Training College and Endsleigh College were associated with Leeds University for examination purposes until the post-war reforms established the Area Training Organisations. Yet the Local Authority persisted in its desire to forge greater links with the University College. During the Second World War, proposals were made to transfer its Training College to the University in 1940 and the architectural courses of the College of Arts and Crafts in 1942, but the near closure of the university and its parlous financial situation prevented this from happening.

The ambivalent attitude of the LEA towards the University College and its own provision of advanced further education is rather puzzling. It may be that the various manoeuvres discussed above represented attempts to achieve the thwarted ambitions of the 1920s by transferring to the University College a range of vocational subjects, thus securing something of its original vision. However, even had success attended these moves, it would have only been partial. The subjects in which efforts were made were the relatively prestigious areas of Architecture and teacher education, thus continuing to exclude those areas of Technology which were most in need of enhancement in the city's provision. On the other hand, successful transfer of some courses to the University College would have reduced the obligations and therefore the financial commitment of the Local Authority and such an explanation, whilst unable to be confirmed from the evidence available, is consonant with the reputation for parsimony which seems to have attended the city's educational provision in the first half of the century.

It is not surprising then that there was a reversion to the pre-war policy of drift in the face of the continuation of problems which were only too evident before 1914. Perusal of the Principals' reports, which exist in the Local Authority papers only until 1930, indicate continuing poor quality students, lack of support from industry and commerce, and outdated and obsolescent equipment in depressing and crowded premises. Comparative evidence is difficult to obtain, but it appears that Hull's experience was unexceptional. The 1930s in Constantine College, Middlesborough was also a period in which resources were limited, accommodation inadequate, and library improvements needed. (Leonard, p.55-67). On the other hand, the take-over of the Harris Institute by the Preston Corporation in 1928 led to a more positive approach by the local authority, aided also by considerable assistance from local industrialists (Timmins et al. 1979, p.32).

However, since technical education was seen as being directly for the benefit of specific localities, it was inevitable that general social and economic conditions would have a major impact on developments. In Hull, the depressed economy of the inter-war period, particularly the 'thirties, ensured that few students came forward to undertake advanced and degree level work. After the First World War, Hull's economy was characterised by a reduced rate of population growth, a stable, but above-average unemployment rate, the failure of an expanding labour force to find industrial employment, and the decline of port and port-related work leading to an over-dependence on domestic industries and services. Population grew much more slowly, showing only a 12.8% increase 1911-1931 to 313,544, while the unemployment position in the city was greater in Hull than in the rest of England. The lack of heavy industry in the town ensured that it avoided the worst excesses of the national depression 1929-31, but the consistently above-average unemployment for the inter-war years resulted from the great expansion of the port's unskilled labour force which was particularly susceptible to changing trading conditions, and the comparative shortage of employment for women. The real problem for the development of technical education in Hull in the inter-war years was the fact that the growth in its occupational structure tended to be concentrated in those areas which did not require high-level training. Of the increase in employment of 16, 840 between 1923 and 1937, 82.5% were in non-industrial employment, associated chiefly with transport, public utilities, hotels and distribution. Conversely, employment in shipbuilding and ship-repairing declined by a half, and there were reductions in dock, labour and canal services, chemicals and oils, cocoa and chocolate. The fact that, in 1947, 51% of employed men worked either in the port or in occupations related to the port, suggests that Hull's economic difficulties resulted largely from the port's inability to continue expanding at its earlier rapid rate rather than its failure to diversify (Allison K.J. (1969), p.215-286).

THE TECHNICAL COLLEGE

The work of the Technical College continued independently, though with no greater success, and in the company of all the problems which were noted earlier. The failure either to achieve a University College of the type which the city had anticipated, and the consequent inability to relocate existing work to the new Cottingham Road site merely exacerbated the problems of further education in the city. As a result, the Local Authority was compelled to requisition further annexes across the city with the result that work was being offered in sub-standard accommodation. The annual reports of the Principals in this period repeat the arguments advanced before the First World War, suggesting that the failure of the Local Authority to achieve its University objective had not only absorbed much of its energies in the years after 1918, but had produced a sense of disillusionment personified by Riley's resignation in 1926.

Overall student numbers on full-time day courses remained relatively low with some improvement on pre-war standards. Advanced work, principally part-time evening-only, continued as 'a small but stable tip to the iceberg throughout the thirties' (Mitchell, 7), and although the numbers entering for examinations for London degrees showed an improvement on the pre-war picture, they remained a disappointment for a city the size of Hull. However, Hull's experience was not dissimilar from other further education colleges. At Constantine College, Middlesborough, which had only been founded in 1929 there were less than thirty full-time students per annum between 1930/31 and 1936/37 in a town less than half the size of Hull (Leonard 1981, p.174).

THE COLLEGE OF COMMERCE

Developments in the College of Commerce continued to be hindered by the poor quality of students coming from Hull's secondary schools and by the general lack of interest amongst the commercial and professional employers in the city (PAR, 1912/13). There was a growing demand for this type of education, especially amongst female students, but it is clear that the tendency for a large minority of students to study individual subjects rather than coherent courses inhibited the development of the School's work and encouraged it to concentrate on low level work associated with Junior Technical Schools. (PAR 1921/22). Within this framework, overall numbers grew from 1050 in 1912/13 to 1598 in 1931/32 (PAR 1912/13 and 1931/32), and it was claimed that, by the mid-twenties, it was one of the largest schools of its kind in the country (PAR 1923/24). Partly to answer the increasing student demand for places, but more importantly to increase the status of the school and the level of its work, the Local Authority agreed to establish a College of Commerce, separate from the Technical

Table 3.1   Full-Time Students at Hull Technical Institute 1920-32

	1920-1	1921-2	1922-3	1923-4	1924-5	1925-6	1926-7	1927-8	1928-9
Eng.	42	27	32	32	22	29	21	17	19
Chem.	32	29	32	32	16	24	20	20	24
Marine				11	22	26	32	59	54

Source: Principals' Annual Reports 1920-30

Table 3.2   Degree Students at Hull Municipal Technical College 1924-28

	Total Successes	Intermediate Level	Final Degree Level
1923-24	21		
1924-25	12		
1925-26	10	8	2
1926-27	6	3	3
1927-28	8	5	3

Source: Principals' Annual Reports 1920-30

Table 3.3   Degree Students at Hull Municipal Technical College 1930-39

	Total Students	Intermediate Level	Final Degree Level
1930	70	54	16
1933	93	63	30
1936	110	89	21
1939	134	115	19

Source: Mitchell 1975, p.65

College, for all day and evening work in premises in Brunswick Avenue in 1930.

THE SCHOOL OF ART

After the First World War, the School of Art continued to grow even though, according to J.J.Brownsword, the new Head of the School appointed in 1920, 'Hull is credited with not being an Art loving City' (PAR, 1920/21 Report). Furthermore, there was both an increase in enrolments and an improvement in relations with industry, though the latter fact did not prevent regular pleas for greater co-operation from industry. It is clear that successive Heads saw themselves as having a missionary role within the city. In addition to urging employers to take a more active role in the work of the School which was encouraged by student success at national exhibitions, Brownsword was critical of the city council which did 'little or nothing to convince the student of the actuality and desirability of his studies.' (1922/23). What he had in mind was the employment of students, if only temporarily, by the city council which would provide them with positive encouragement.

An important element of the School's work was the development of courses in Architecture with design as a dominant feature, and this led to the eventual recognition of its courses by the Royal Institute of British Architects (RIBA), though it was 1935 before the Higher Education Sub-Committee gave approval for arrangements for an Architecture degree, and three years later before the RIBA recognised the three-year, full-time day course for exemption from its Intermediate level examinations.

TEACHER TRAINING BETWEEN THE WARS
The impact of the First World War led to a serious diminution in the number of men at the Municipal Training College so that by 1916/17 only five of the one hundred and twenty-two students were men, and the Principal himself was released at the end of 1915 to undertake munitions work as part of the war effort (HESC, 14.12.1915). After the war, the college became a women's only college after the first two years of the peace, with men being trained in universities or in colleges allied to universities, a situation which pertained until 1959. In 1923, the College's existence was threatened by the national economic climate; LEAs were encouraged to reduce their expenditure, and the local Geddes committee proposed closure of the college as an economy measure. The proposal must have been attractive to the Local Authority which contributed c.£7,250 of the £17,460, but, to its credit the Hull LEA decided to keep the college open, and an additional grant was obtained from the Board (Bibby 1963, p.29). Behind this simple argument was the perennial problem which resulted from the concept of a national system locally administered which was to dog public higher education until the 1980s. Institutions pointed to the educational desirability of recruiting students to colleges from outside of a given authority, whilst LEAs noted that they were effectively subsidising the education of students from elsewhere. Much of this was mitigated by the Board of Education grant, and eventually resolved by the pooling system, but it was some years before that was applied to teacher training.

The war years were notable only for two initiatives, the one redolent of the past, the other very much a consequence of prevailing conditions. In 1940, on the resignation of Miss Cumberbirch

Table 3.4   Origin of Teacher Training Students at the Municipal College 1919-29

Year	Total Students	New Students	Hull & Riding	Year	Total Students	New Students	Hull & E. Riding
1919-20	153	79	19	1924-25	148	77	22
1920-21				1925-26	150	73	30
1921-22	152	79	22	1926-27	150	80	20
1922-23	153	74	28	1927-28	150	71	48
1923-24	146	76	26	1928-29	150	79	49

Source: Principals Annual Reports 1919/20 to 1928/29

as Principal, the Higher Education Sub-Committee revived its dream of comprehensive provison in the city and sought a possible, though undefined relationship with the University College, but this was temporarily thwarted by the evacuation of the latter's Day Training College from Hull to Cambridge (HESC, 7.5 & 25.9.1940). Inevitably, the Second World War impinged severely on the work of the College, particularly in a city such as Hull which was in the front line of German bombing raids. The result was that the college moved students to Bingley and Ripon, and in September 1942, the whole college moved to Halifax, a year later to Ripon, and in July 1943, temporarily closed.

Chapter 4

Later Twentieth Century Provision 1944–1970

THE 1948 REORGANISATION PLAN

The country began to plan for post-war reconstruction prior to the end of the Second World War and, in education, this took the form of a White Paper *Educational Reconstruction* (1943) which paved the way for the famous 1944 Education Act. It placed on Local Education Authorities 'the duty of securing the means of preparation for work and leisure.' Although this was the first time that central government had placed such a requirement on local authorities, some indication of the relative priorities within the education budget could be gleaned from the White Paper's plan to spend £12 millions on Technical, commercial and art education but only £2.49 millions on technical and adult work. The Act also required local authorities to produce plans for the development of all sectors of their education service, and in January 1948 Hull prepared an ambitious scheme for further and adult education. The proposals revived elements of the 1918 scheme with its vision of comprehensive further education provision centralised on the Queens' Gardens site in the centre of the city, close to the seat of local government. The ultimate goal was to bring the disparate colleges together, into a 'unified whole along the lines of a polytechnic, improving standards and developing into a responsible institution (which) will be in a position to acquire a status comparable to that of a university' (1947 Plan p.27). Closely associated with the new education centre were four independently-controlled junior technical colleges, located in the city suburbs and acting as feeder institutions to the Queen's Gardens complex, thus underlining the essentially local provision of further education common across the country at that time. The plan for further and adult educational development was completed by a proposal for an adult education college which would be devoted to liberal studies, and hope was expressed that it might be possible to purchase a country house in East Yorkshire to serve as an adult residential centre. Excluded from the plan was the Nautical College which was left to expand its work in improved premises in the Boulevard where it remained for some twenty years before plans were made for a new building adjacent to the city centre complex. Teacher training did not figure in the overall plan for the city, and the Municipal College returned to its original site after wartime evacuation to become an affiliate of the new University of Hull Institute of Education in 1948. Endsleigh College, for which the city had no responsibility, also joined the new Institute of Education and reverted to its Beverley Road site after temporary accommodation in Cottingham Road had been found during the war.

As with the 1918 plan, the reality was far from the vision. The capital costs of the plan were unclear and it was unlikely that it would be realised in the immediate aftermath of a war which had crippled the nation economically. Perhaps realising that it would take some time before any building programme came to fruition even if its plans were approved by the Ministry of Education, the LEA purchased land to extend the existing premises of the College of Commerce in Brunswick Avenue and erected temporary accommodation in Queen's Gardens for both the Technical College and the College of Arts and Crafts. Furthermore, the plan for the governance of the new provision fell far short of the ideas in the government's desire for strong governing bodies representing local independent interests with all reasonable freedom to develop the work of a major college. In contrast, Hull continued to use its appropriate sub-committee, now the Colleges and Schools Sub-Committee of the Education Committee, as the governing body for all its colleges, and that sub-committee maintained a very detailed supervision of the minutiae of college organisation and management, but failed to provide any overall strategy for the development of further education in the city. The spirit of the Circular was accepted by an in-principle decision to give all further education colleges their own governing body (CSSC 23.9.1949), but the sub-committee constituted itself as the governing body of each institution, thus enabling the Local Authority to continue its detailed control of its institutions. It was not until the late fifties that this proposal was realised in the exact form in which central government intended in 1946.

The Ministry did not approve Hull's overall plan until 1953 and, even then, deferred a decision on the concept of junior feeder colleges which were quite crucial to the success of the integrated scheme. Nonetheless, the use of Queen's Gardens was given the go-ahead in 1949 and, after some hiccups, in 1952/53 work began on the first phase, consisting of workshop blocks which were occupied in 1956. Phase two, the construction of the main building for the Technical College, was also subject to approval and planning delays, but was eventually included in the 1956/57 building programme, and was opened in 1962. However, this nine-storey structure and its associated workshops only accommodated the Technical College, and the other providers of art and crafts, commercial, and nautical education remained in their scattered and inadequate premises.

Attempts to obtain buildings for the Colleges of Commerce and Regional College of Art in 1962/63, to which the College of Arts and Crafts had been converted in 1947 (CSSC 17.9.1947), failed to obtain Ministry approval, but the former was allowed to go ahead soon after and its new premises next to the College of Technology in Queen's Gardens were opened in 1968. Somewhat mysteriously, unsolicited approval was given for extensions to the Nautical College for inclusion in the 1964/65 programme, but this became a proposal for a new college in 1965 which was opened on the edge of the Queen's Gardens site in 1974. At the same time, a new building for the Regional College of Art was approved in 1968 and opened on the central site in 1974. Thereby, the physical vision of 1948 was finally completed, although all of the component colleges were still making extensive use of annexes in different parts of the city. The complementary educational vision of a single comprehensive institution for further education was still not realised when the Hull Education Authority transferred its responsibilities to the new Humberside Education Authority in 1974. Then, the four further education colleges in the city remained separate entities, and the emergence of a unitary college with a single vigorous governing body had to wait until 1976. By that time, the national educational environment had changed considerably, and that development also encompassed the Colleges of Education.

FURTHER EDUCATION PROVISION 1945-1956

In the decades after the war, central government began to take a greater interest in further education, and there began the long fifty-year period during which a locally-organised and administered system of further and advanced further education was replaced by a truly national system of further and higher education. There was widespread agreement, reflected in the report of the 1945 Percy Committee, that the inferior status of technical education in the United Kingdom resulted in a lack of focus and direction for colleges and in high failure rates amongst students doing advanced work in the colleges. Thus, the first twenty-years of the post-war period were characterised by a debate on the expansion and location of such work. All parties to the debate agreed with the Percy Committee that the United Kingdom needed to improve significantly its provision of further education, in both quantity and quality, and since the need would not be met by the universities, other arrangements would have to be made. However, at that point, unanimity disappeared. One important question concerned definitions encapsulating the issue of status and class. Technical education had often been conceived of as narrowly vocational and directly associated with the world of industry, despite central government attempts to ensure that courses emphasised practice combined with theory; the result was that such colleges had become mainly working-class institutions. This view tended to receive employer support whose reluctance to become involved in further education may well have reflected a wider antipathy to theoretical education and a sympathy for on-the-job training personified by widespread apprenticeship schemes. Technological education, on the other hand, was of a higher order and required recognition of this through the qualifications offered. Unfortunately, the blurring of this distinction meant that universities, with their emphasis on theoretical education, tended to avoid strong technological emphasis, and resisted the granting of degree status to such courses and awards. Thus, one facet of the debate after 1945 was the nature, title and status of technological awards which everyone agreed to be necessary for economic development. The Percy Committee proposed that there should be a new and prestigious award outside the universities, but this ran up against the universities' monopoly of degree-awarding powers. The 1951

White Paper *Higher Technological Education* proposed a new College
of Technologists to approve courses and awards, but this fell with
the change of government in 1951. The Ministry of Education
resolved the issue by announcing in 1955 the formation of the
National Council for Technological Awards to oversee the introduction and guarantee the standards of a new award to be known
as the Diploma in Technology.

A parallel issue concerned the location of technical and particularly Technological education. The former would inevitably
remain in the many local technical colleges spread throughout the
country, but the latter revolved around the issue of concentration
or dispersal. The *Percy Report* recommended the development of a
few specialised degree-level technological institutions, co-ordinated
by Regional Advisory Councils under a National Council for Technology, but initial government policy appeared to favour dispersal
of courses as evidenced by the introduction in 1951 of a 75% grant
for all courses at advanced level, thus recognising their regional
and national character. Under this approach, the award would be
centralised and given national credibility whereas the provision
would be dispersed throughout the country. Paradoxically, the
1956 White Paper, *Technical Education*, moved in the opposite
direction, recommending that there should be a 'vigorous increase'
in advanced further education work in twenty-four colleges of
further education, though this was not intended to inhibit the
development of such work, especially of a part-time mode, in other
institutions. The subsequent government circular which converted
this proposal into policy rationalised provision into four categories
of institution appearing to favour a policy of concentration for
full-time and sandwich advanced further education, whilst allowing
for the dispersed provision of part-time courses. The neatness of the
distinction ignored the economic problems which would arise in
area colleges offering primarily advanced level work in a part-time
mode only without the necessary full-time base to provide adequate
resources and staffing, but the potential diminution of part-time
provision which such a policy implied appears to have been
sacrificed on the altar of concentration. The policy envisaged a
hierarchy of institutions which would be ranked according to the
level and mode of courses offered. At the apex were to be eight
to ten Colleges of Advanced Technology providing a full range
and substantial volume of work, exclusively at advanced level, on

a full-time and sandwich basis; part-time work could remain but lower level work would disappear. At the second level were to be twenty-four Regional Colleges, each at that time in receipt of the 75% grant for advanced work, which would have a substantial volume of advanced work, largely full-time and sandwich, but retaining part-time and lower-level work; these colleges were to be designated on the basis of the distribution of industry and population. Below this would be area colleges which would offer some advanced work, though it would be largely part-time, which meant proliferation. Finally, local colleges would offer the bare minimum of advanced courses. Whilst in retrospect, one can detect the continuity of policy from 1956 through to the establishment of the polytechnic sector, no specific binary policy evolved in 1956, nor was it anticipated that the new Colleges of Advanced Technology would leave the local authority sector.

Further education in Hull developed against this background, and the local experience during the third quarter of the century was one of disappointment and frustration, particularly in the failure to achieve regional college status under the 1956 reorganisation and to obtain polytechnic designation ten years later. The delays in obtaining approval and then implementing the 1948 reorganisation plan meant that further educational provision in the city continued in its inter-war mode, and all the problems of that period remained. The LEA continued to exercise detailed control, rather than provide educational leadership for its colleges, and had great difficulty, despite its plans, of providing adequate premises for their work. A partial response to central government desire for strong and active governing bodies was made with reluctance in Hull ten years after the publication of the Circular which raised the issue, showing the jealousy with which the City Council guarded its powers. The Governing Body of each College existed as a sub-committee of the Education Committee of the Council. Councillors dominated each Governing Body, with almost identical membership on each, and the monthly meetings of each Board occurred on the same day each month. Whilst each included representatives of industrial, commercial, professional and University of Hull interests as appropriate, the independent governors had no voting powers on any financial matters (HEC 23.4.1956).

Whilst the LEA developed an impressive scheme for the location of further education in the centre of the city, there was little central

direction of educational development. It is true that the College
of Arts and Crafts became the Regional College of Art in 1947,
and the College of Commerce made an apparently promising
start with immediate moves to hive off the junior work so as
to enable the College to focus on advanced work in two main
departments of Professional Studies and General Commercial
Subjects. (CSSC 27.10.1947). But symptomatic of the lack of
decisiveness within the LEA was the handling of a vacancy in the
College of Commerce. The resignation of the Principal, Mr. A.F.
George, in 1951 inaugurated a period of four years in which the
Chief Inspector of Education in the city, Mr. P. Barber, acted as
Principal of the College, and was only confirmed in that position
after an HMI report of 1954 had commended him for giving central
direction to the College for the first time (CSSC 12.6.195, and
18.3.1955).

One of the major disappointments in the city was the failure
to develop a substantial base of advanced level work in the
post-war period, and this contributed to the failure to obtain
wider recognition in the fifties and sixties. There was some support
for advanced developments in all the colleges, though it was on
a relatively small scale. The College of Commerce was one of
only forty institutions to offer the new Diploma in Management
Studies from 1961, and initially this course recruited quite well
in comparison to the other major centres in Yorkshire (*Yorkshire
Council for Further Education Annual Report 1962/63*, (YCFE), p.5).
The College of Art was allowed to offer the new National Diploma
in Design from 1951/52, and the Technical College began its own
HND in Aeronautics in 1957/58. Similarly, external bodies were
supportive of the quality of work done, with the Royal Institute
of Chemistry offering particularly glowing commentary in 1962
(CTBGP 4.12.1962). However, whilst there was a significant
increase in student numbers studying in the city's colleges, the most
popular courses were those at non-advanced level, and there was
a noticeable dearth of students working towards London external
degrees. For example, there was a 50% increase to over 2,000
students in the College of Commerce from 1947 to 1954, but
it was mainly attributable to the growth in part-time day classes
and the recruitment of more mature students. Its Department of
General Commercial Subjects had 1,047 students, with shorthand
and typing the single most popular subject and almost 10% of

Table 4.1   Hull College of Commerce: Students by Mode of Attendance 1950/51 and 1958/59

	Full-Time	PTD & PTDE	Evening Only	Total
1950/51	65	369	1,332	1,766
1958/59	234	644	2,142	3,020

Source: *General Report on Commerce 1952-59* Report Files 1959/60 No.

its students undertaking GCE courses, whilst the Department of Professional Studies had 500 students and a further 719 in languages classes in seven European languages. In contrast, by the end of the 'fifties, only 3% of students were studying at university level, some of whom were University of Hull accountancy students attending on a part-time day basis, though 55% were following other advanced courses, principally the Higher National Certificate in Commerce which was expected to replace local commercial courses associated with shipping. In fact, there were only eighteen full-time and three part-time evening-only students on the preliminary and ten full-time day, five evening-only on the finals B.Sc.(Econ) London courses. This problem continued to plague the College throughout the post-war period and may well have been instrumental in determining the unsuccessful outcome of the Local Authority' s bid for polytechnic designation in 1966.

In the Technical College advanced level work grew, with two hundred and forty-two students following degree courses, of whom eighty-nine were attending full-time, twenty-one on HND, two hundred and seventy-six on HNC courses and a further seventy-seven on advanced professional examinations in 1946/47 (Mitchell, p.11 and 14n). However, its work at this level was plagued with similar problems associated with the size of classes, particularly in the full-time mode. One of the problems inherent in piece-meal provision of advanced courses was the inefficiency of the small classes undertaking degree work, and this was so serious that the Local Authority was advised by HMI to review their continuation. In 1958, the Board of Governors resolved to ignore Ministry warnings about the small classes in its B.Sc. Engineering course, though it claimed that these problems were rectified by the time that the course had commenced (CTBG 8.7.1958 & 14.10.1958).

Further education continued to be offered in poor quality premises in the post-war period. The Regional College of Art suffered serious accommodation problems and the LEA felt obliged to erect temporary huts on the Queen's Gardens site and to rent additional premises in Regent Street for Architecture (CSSC 8.11.1948). An HMI report in 1949 produced the familiar litany of problems confronting the Nautical College, particularly the totally inadequate premises which offered no library, common room, or canteen facilities, and even failed to provide a private room for the Principal. A similar report on the College of Commerce five years later drew attention to the poor services offered to students in terms of library facilities, kitchen/dining accommodation, and toilets, but more important was the overall problems facing anyone trying to develop an institution concentrating on advanced level work. Although the junior and senior work had been separated from 1947, junior classes still used the Brunswick Avenue premises during the day so that the College had exclusive use only during the evenings. Even more important was the fact that the premises were themselves outdated and, as the College expanded, it was compelled to make use of annexes in other educational premises in the city, all equally unsuitable for its work and designed to make its task even more difficult. By 1966, the College operated in no less than eleven annexes (*HMI Report* October 1954 and Principal's General Report on Commercial Education in Hull, both in Hull City Archives, TCE/4/927; 'Focus on Hull- its schools, colleges and industry' and 'Hull Polytechnic,' both in *Technical Education and Industrial Training*, 9,7, July 1967)

Morale must have been further undermined by the LEA's ambivalent attitude towards relationships between its Colleges and the University of Hull which came to the fore again with yet another proposal to transfer the Architecture courses from the Regional College of Art to the University of Hull, granted its charter in 1954. On this occasion, the idea seems to have originated with the York and East Yorkshire Architectural Society which wished to transfer the course to the University since a University degree was obtained in a broader social and educational environment than that available in a college. Additional benefits claimed for the proposal included the fact that a degree rather than a diploma was the passport to scholarships for further study and for many posts in government service; degree standards tended to be higher than diploma standards since competition for entry was both keener and based on national rather than regional recruitment; and the combination of teaching and research in a University would provide a better course than in the College which was oriented purely to the former. However, the University of Hull was only prepared to consider the establishment of a department with the full co-operation of the city fathers, and the LEA decided 'to continue, for the present, to provide architectural training at the Regional College of Art and Crafts (CSSC 1956/57, Reports No.3 and Minutes 15.1.1957). Perhaps more important was the unwillingness of the University Grants Commission to sanction such a development.

However, as in the inter-war period, the relative failure of the city to provide for the development of a vigorous system of advanced further education was, at least in part, a response to the environment in which the Council operated. The wider economic environment in the city certainly did not encourage the development of the Colleges. Hull suffered severe damage during the Second World War and the set-back to the local economy was prolonged. In the post-war period, it lost its position as the principal port for seeds and nuts to Liverpool, and suffered a recession in the grain trade during the 1950s, largely due to lower milling capacity resulting from war damage. Between 1951 and 1963, unemployment in the city was consistently above the national average, and the chemicals and building industries failed to expand. Also, the continuing domination of the occupational structure by relatively unskilled labour, with school-leavers requiring less than one year's training for employment, meant that further education, particularly at an advanced level was undervalued (Allison 1969, 283-4). The war also affected Hull schools quite badly. 11,000 school places were lost during the bombing, and this, together with the raising of the school-leaving age to 14 in 1947 added up to a heavy demand for new school buildings (Allison 1969, 360-1).

In this context, the development of further education was a lesser priority locally, and local industrial, commercial and professional support remained lukewarm. The College of Commerce made some progress in improving its relationships with industry and commerce through the establishment of active Advisory Committees for banking, general commercial subjects, sales management and shipbroking, though not in the crucial areas of management studies and transport. However, this collaboration did not lead to the desired enhancement of day-release students. In contrast to other cities, Hull was very poorly provided with part-time day

courses, largely because employers, particularly banks, accountancy and insurance companies, were unwilling to release students
from work. There were no part-time day or sandwich courses in
the crucial area of management studies, and the overall increase
in part-time day students during the 'fifties was only 300 to 600,
a relatively small number for a city the size of Hull. Part of the
point of a strong governing body, with adequate industrial and
professional interest, was to increase the symbiosis between the two,
thus enabling the college facilities to become better known amongst
its potential clientele. The LEA's wish to retain tight control,
especially in economic matters, hindered colleges' development
and contributed to the lack of industrial support. (*HMI Report
on Nautical Education*, in CSSC 18.2.1949). The progress made
in this area remained disappointing into the fifties, indicated by the
Yorkshire Council for Further Education's refusal to recommend
the purchase of a sea-going training vessel for the Humber on the
grounds of cost and 'the absence of any enthusiasm from local
industry.' (*26th Annual Report of YCFE 1953/54* in CSSC Report
1954/55, no.6)

THE SEARCH FOR HIGHER STATUS I: REGIONAL COL-
LEGE DESIGNATION

One of the major purposes of the 1956 *White Paper* and subsequent
reforms was to create a limited number of important centres of
excellence through the concentration of resources in a more limited
number of institutions. From the vantage point of forty years on,
Hull's hope for inclusion in this group of colleges was rather opti-
mistic. Nevertheless, in spite of its problems, the Local Authority
was hopeful that it would be recognised as a major national centre,
though its failure to achieve the 75% central government grant
towards its AFE provison ensured that Hull would not become
a College of Advanced Technology (CAT). However, with the
publication of the 1956 *Circular 305* it hoped that it might become
a Regional College with a substantial amount of advanced work,
'including in particular full-time and sandwich courses, but in
which the volume and character of advanced work(including
part-time work) are not such as to make it realistic for the college
to concentrate entirely on such work.' (WP 1956, #11).

In 1957 attempts were made to obtain the 75% grant, hoping to benefit from the likelihood that colleges in receipt of the grant but not designated as CATS would become regional colleges, but without success. Within two years, the system of grants was discontinued nationally to be replaced by the Advanced Further Education (AFE) Pool system which sought to share more equitably between providers and consumers the cost of advanced further education, and this necessitated new criteria for the consideration of any further designations. *Circular 3/61* declared its willingness to consider new applications, but the criteria listed only strengthened the policy of concentration and ensured that Hull would remain outside the charmed circle. Under the *Circular*, new proposals for full-time and sandwich courses in applied science and Technology would only be entertained if the college concerned had a range of well-subscribed full-time and sandwich courses, was appropriately staffed, engaged in supportive research, and housed in adequate premises. Equally important was that colleges be suitably governed which meant a degree of freedom to which Hull colleges were unaccustomed, and the involvement of neighbouring Local Authorities from which students were drawn. In such circumstances, there was little likelihood of Hull being awarded Regional College status.

One of the inevitable consequences for those institutions which failed to achieve CAT or Regional College status, like Hull, was that they would be encouraged to focus on lower level work, thus finding it more difficult to meet the demands for advanced-level part-time work in their areas. Reflecting the new situation, the 1961 White Paper *Better Opportunities in Technical Education* showed a new interest in lower level work, announcing special courses for operatives, remodelling craft courses, and emphasising the importance of technical-level courses. These initiatives coincided with new buildings in Hull, led to significant growth in numbers, though at advanced level single figure year groups were the norm and full-time and sandwich students still limited. In the College of Technology in 1962/63, there were only 691 advanced level students, of whom 452 were full-time and 24 on sandwich courses. Of these, only 60 were following degree courses. By comparison, Constantine College, Middlesborough and Oxford College of Technology, both in smaller towns, had 648 and 850 full-time advanced level students respectively in the same year, and the latter was offering a full range of degree programmes from 1960. (Leonard 1981, p.176; Henry p.29; Crossley 1979, p.460-1). There was some encouragement for advanced level work in 1962 when the College was approved to offer Part II courses leading to the Graduate Certificate of the Royal Institute of Chemistry, but the real problems facing the College were clear three years later when the Regional Advisory Council rejected six of its seven proposals for courses leading to CNAA degrees (Mitchell 1975, p.32).

THE SEARCH FOR STATUS II: POLYTECHNIC DESIG-
NATION

The progressive concentration of full-time and sandwich advanced further education into a limited number of institutions was com-
pleted by the designation of polytechnics in the late 1960s which gave official recognition to the so-called binary policy in English and Welsh higher education. In its White Paper *A Plan for Poly-
technics and Colleges* (1965) the Ministry announced its intention to establish thirty polytechnics in England and Wales based on the existing Colleges of Technology, and reform commenced a year later with *Circular 8/66* which invited local education authorities to prepare plans for the future of advanced further education in general and the establishment of polytechnics in particular. The selection of locations for polytechnics in the late 1960s implies a policy based on criteria, important amongst which was the intention of 'achieving a reasonably balanced provision in different fields of study over the country as a whole.' In fact, the locations approved showed a marked concentration on urban and industrial areas along a central corridor from London through to the industrial north. The eastern half of the country was particularly poorly served, and in the case of Hull, the nearest polytechnic was at Leeds, some fifty miles to the west. In Yorkshire and Humberside, the major cities of Leeds and Sheffield were obvious candidates, but other possibilities existed in Middlesborough, Huddersfield and Hull. In the event, Hull was the only one which was not designated, though the Yorkshire and Humberside Council for Further Education expressed its regret to the Ministry and offered its services to the Authority in preparing a resubmission (*YCFE Annual Report*

1965/6). The historians of the process of establishment of the polytechnics note that some unsuccessful proposals created 'a certain amount of bitterness and scandal,' and report that many people felt that the DES had encouraged the Hull LEA to think that its application would be successful, so that 'the rejection led to more disillusionment than might otherwise have been expected and to invidious comparisons with some of the proposals which did get accepted.' (Burgess & Pratt 1974, p.129). The absence of any evidence directly accounting for the decision mean that the observer is left to speculate why Hull failed to achieve polytechnic designation, though it seems likely that the Ministry's refusal was the logical end to some twenty years of lost opportunities in the city.

Whilst the requirements of local and regional industry were central to the development of any national policy, a major criteria which colleges had to satisfy to achieve designation revolved around the scale and level of their educational provision in 1966 and the likelihood of significant development. In terms of sheer volume, Hull compared favourably with a number of other colleges seeking designation. With a total in excess of 13,000 students, the combined colleges provided one of the largest single concentrations in the country. One of Hull's strengths was its part-time work, totalling at least 9,000 in Commerce (3,000), and Technology (6,000), giving a total student number in excess of all but twelve of the centres which received polytechnic designation. With a College of Technology in a new £1.75m. building in Queen's Gardens, and both a College of Commerce and a College of Art soon to join it on a central campus, there appeared to be a strong case for designation. National policy was concerned specifically with concentrating and strengthening the base of full-time and sandwich courses, and in this respect that Hull was found wanting. The full-time work in the city's colleges totalled 1174 students – Art (274), Commerce (300) and Technology (600) – and this was more than the 1965-66 numbers in at least nine of the successful candidates for polytechnic designation, all of whom had 1,000 or less (Pratt & Burgess, p.68), but the vast majority in Commerce and Technology was part-time. Perhaps more problematic for Hull was the importance attached by the Ministry to the capacity for growth to perhaps 2,000 full-time and sandwich students, though it is difficult to understand the magical properties attributed to that figure as opposed to, say, 1,500 or 2,500. Although Hull's industrial base included a number of the newer technological industries such as aeronautics which could probably have flourished within a polytechnic culture, recent history pointed to a highly diversified economy based upon a strong demand for relatively unskilled labour which might have suggested that the colleges were meeting known and even anticipated needs.

The policy of concentration of courses placed perhaps even greater emphasis on efficiency of operation, following the argument of the 1966 *Pilkington Report for NACEIC* that class sizes of less than twenty-four students were inefficient. The subsequent DES *Circular 11/66* imposed a regime on course approvals which militated against Hull's case. The minimum enrolment on new full-time course approvals was to be twenty-four, and on part-time day courses fifteen with work study and twenty without; evening-only courses would be approved on an ad hoc basis when full-time courses existed in same academic area. More stringent still was the requirement that a centre that wished to establish a new area of work must have a minimum of fifty students in that field. The only exceptions to these conditions were courses in novel and specialist fields, postgraduate courses, and areas which were deemed necessary but could not accommodate the requisite numbers. New part-time courses could only be approved if there was nothing available in 'reasonable travelling distance' which was defined as up to one hour in day-time depending on age, time-of-day and transport facilities. Even existing courses were to be reviewed under the *Circular*, and inefficient courses would be allowed to continue without full enrolment only 'until the resources, of both staff and accommodation, already committed can be otherwise employed.' Advanced further education courses in Hull had been plagued consistently by the failure to enrol significant numbers, and in 1966, apart from the twenty-four students on the Graduate of the Royal Institute of Chemistry course, no full-time course could muster double figures and the largest sandwich course was 16 (Mitchell 1975, p.47-8). Against a background of concentration of resources in larger centres, resulting partly from a national policy of austerity, Hull found itself in a very weak position and DES planners could not have been encouraged by the failure to establish viable full-time advanced level courses, presumably a major factor in refusal of degree course proposals at regional level a year earlier.

Hull's potential weakness as a centre for the concentration of advanced courses was further indicated by its very wide portfolio of mainly low-level courses offered in its colleges, so that 90% of the students in the combined colleges were on non-advanced courses. Although the College of Technology had a flourishing mechanical engineering department with a London B.Sc. external degree and HND courses in mechanical and aeronautical engineering, and a parallel electrical engineering department, its comprehensive offerings included hairdressing and pre-nursing courses which hardly augured well for an institution which was expected to concentrate on advanced level work. The College of Commerce also offered courses which ranged from the postgraduate Diploma in Management Studies through HND down to GCE O level, and included the full-time diploma course of the Central Training Council for Teachers of the Mentally Subnormal, a mainly mature student course. The College of Art, in contrast, was almost exclusively advanced level, with its students treated as adults, and a 90% pass-rate expected. Completing the quartet was the Nautical College which was a combination of secondary school, soon to be amalgamated with Trinity House nautical school in the city, a range of non-advanced further education courses in mercantile and fishing studies, and a small amount of advanced work for masters' tickets. Its students ranged from sixteen to fifty years of age. Therefore, apart from the College of Art, the proposed institution represented 'the city's curious concept of what a polytechnic should be,' leading one anonymous contemporary to conclude that 'what, sadly, could never be contemplated is the formation of a polytechnic on present showing' (*Technical Education and Training*, 9,7, July 1967, pp. 300 & 302).

All further education colleges were products of their Local Education Authorities, and it is certainly possible that the record of Hull did not inspire confidence in the Department of Education and Science. Hull's failure to achieve polytechnic designation in 1967 seems more likely to have been the logical response to the feeble development of advanced further education in the city during the previous decade rather than any Machiavellian desire to deny the city and its region its just deserts. In fact, one contemporary commentator felt that the city's received its just deserts, noting that elected representatives and permanent officials bore a serious responsibility for the fact that there was 'nothing within the administration and standards of the system that could possibly merit polytechnic status . . . . . . Hull against

Lanchester or Enfield makes a very bad joke.' (*Technical Education and Training*, 9,7, July 1967. (p.43-5).

It could be argued that the Authority was particularly dilatory in responding to central government exhortation concerning the government of colleges. A variety of *Circulars* had encouraged Authorities to provide greater freedom for the Governing Bodies of Colleges of Further Education, and draft Instrument and Articles for polytechnics were designed to give such institutions maximum autonomy within certain controls exercised by the LEA. Furthermore, the DES required staff representation on Boards of Governors and established Academic Boards which would give staff a strong advisory role in the government of the institution. These ideas ran counter to the whole tenor of college government in Hull which had been characterised by minute control by local councillors, with minimal input from independent governors who had no voice on matters of expenditure, and no involvement by staff. Even as late as 1970, the Principal of the College of Technology was challenged by councillors on his Governing Body for carrying unnecessary stock amounting to four to six months materials (CTBG, Report Files 1970/71, no.38). Perhaps equally important in influencing the eventual decision was the absence of evidence that the Education Committee and its various sub-committees had ever engaged in policy discussions concerning the development of further education in the city. Despite the ambitious reconstruction plans after both World Wars, and completion of the building aspects of the 1948 plan in the early 1970s, there is no record of discussions concerning the educational strategy which might have been adopted in the city, and the observer is struck by the totally reactive approach to further education provision.

This point was reinforced by the Authority's attitude towards buildings. Whilst it is true that central government approval was required for major building projects, such as the Queen's Gardens complex, the overall picture is one of reaction to external criticism rather than creative approaches to problems. Thus, the Principal of the College of Art anticipated serious problems in gaining recognition for the new Diploma in Art and Design on account of the limited accommodation available and it took the externally-engineered crisis in Architecture to prompt expenditure on apparatus and equipment (Report Files 1961/62, no.24; 1968/69, no.5). Similarly, it took a conditional approval of the

Diploma in Art and Design to produce both building improvements and staff enhancements (CABG 12.6.1966; 20.9.1966;
7.2.1967). The force of this criticism may be tempered by the
fact that one college was in new premises and the other three were
waiting for new homes on adjacent sites, thus completing the higher
education campus which the city fathers had envisaged at the end
of the 1940s. However, it was a future based on promises and a
vision which, when completed in the early 1970s with the opening
of the Nautical College, did not create great confidence in some
observers. Whilst the Hull College of Technology was in a new
building costing £1.75 million and opened in 1962, it was seen as
'the neat tip of an untidy educational ice-berg' (*Technical Education
and Training*, 1967).

In contrast, the other colleges were poorly housed, though all
were waiting for the development of new premises. The College
of Commerce was in 'an early English education style building'
in Brunswick Avenue and in a further eleven annexes or rooms in
other colleges in the city, though it hoped to move to a new site
next to the College of Commerce. Similarly, the College of Art
had a principal home and six annexes. The former, purpose-built
in 1905, housed the School of Architecture, but the remainder of
the School was 'scattered widely in various school premises, the
conditions of which are geared more to small children than to
art students.' Worst of all was the Nautical College whose further
education work took place in 'a converted Catholic church and
a variety of huts in bad repair.' Given the city's history and
economy, this college might have been thought of as the jewel
in the crown; instead, it offered 'conditions worse than any other
in the city' (*Ibid.*, p.302). Further evidence of the LEA's highly
parochial concept of further education can be seen in its failure
to respond to *Circular 320* issued in 1957. To assist its policy of
concentration, which would mean students living away from home,
the Ministry encouraged authorities to build hostels for advanced
level students and urged the need for private study space and social
and recreational facilities, but it was only in 1970, under HMI
persuasion, that it was felt necessary to consider construction if
polytechnic status was ever to be gained. By then, it was too late.

After the disappointment of 1967, the real problem for the city
was to maintain provision which met the needs of the area in the
face of government policy. The major losers from the policy of

concentration were part-time students, from whom there was a substantial demand in Hull. The Colleges would find it difficult to provide advanced work for them, when there was no full-time base for such work. Equally, it was likely that well-qualified staff would move away from Hull to centres which were offering more attractive careers thus further decreasing the prospects of evening-only students most of whom would be unable to travel to Leeds and/or Sheffield. The Principal of the College of Commerce consoled himself with the thought that further education had repeatedly shown itself capable of bursting through the restrictions placed on it by the planners who had sought concentration unsuccessfully ten years previously, with the CATs and Regional Colleges, and he anticipated that the new policy would meet the same fate (T.Berry, *Times Educational Supplement*, 19 May 1967)

The impact of non-designation was potentially quite severe. As well as the possible failure to recruit full-time students and the potential loss of well-qualified staff, observers felt that there was a threat to proposed CNAA recognition of the College of Technology and a threatened loss of RIBA accreditation. (*TES*, 7.5.1967, p.1510). In fact, although the figures are spasmodic, it can be suggested tentatively that the immediate aftermath was less universally bleak than some had predicted (Table 4.2). Total numbers of students studying at advanced level in the city actually increased after the failure to gain designation, though the growth was far from consistent across the colleges. In Commerce, the picture was mixed with a decline in degree level work, which was only offered to Part I level, but an encouraging growth in the HND Business Studies sandwich course and a maintenance of numbers in the part-time HNC courses. In Art, there was small growth, underlining the fact that this area was recruiting nationally despite the failure to achieve polytechnic designation, and its standing was confirmed by CNAA approval for Fine Art and Graphic Design degrees in 1974/75. The major decline occurred in Technology where the worst fears of the educationists in the city were realised. The overall decline in student numbers was catastrophic in full-time and sandwich areas, with the exception of the HND Sandwich courses in Engineering and Aeronautics which recovered in 1970, and discouraging in part-time ones. However, 1969/70 was the last year that the B.Sc. courses were advertised and by 1971/72, the only full-time courses in the College of Technology

Table 4.2   Advanced Level Students taking Examinations in Technology, Commerce and Art 1966-70

	1966	1967	1968	1969
B.Sc. Finals	22	15	16	9
B.Sc. Parts I & II	35	19	18	4
Graduate Royal Institute of Chemistry Part I	15	13	3	31*
GRIC Part II	15	24	30	
HNC Engineering	37	26	7	27
HNC Engineering	340	243	217	222
DMS			62	41
B.Sc. Econ Part I			8	6
HND Business			73	93
HNC Business			42	50
HNC Engineering Administration			24	42
Diploma in Art & Design		11	18	25**
Diploma in Architecture		7	12	18
Total Students	466	358	524	566

* Figure for both Part I and Part II combined
** Includes 10 resits from the previous year

Source: Figures compiled from miscellaneous reports to the various Governing Bodies, found in the Annual Report Files of the Education Committee.

were those leading to the Royal Institute of Chemistry awards and the HND Engineering sandwich course.

The overall impact of the failure to achieve polytechnic designation on the city's advanced further education provision may best be seen by comparison with other institutions which were designated. At Constantine College, Middlesborough eight separate departments, covering engineering, science, business and management, and mathematics, enrolled 792 and 957 full-time and sandwich students on degree and higher diploma courses in 1968/69 and 1969/70 respectively, and by the period 1970/71 to 1974/75, this number had grown to an annual average of 1,194 (Leonard 1981, p.181-2).

A further by-product of the failure was the threatened loss to the University of Hull of the School of Architecture, the third attempt to bring about such a transfer of work. The School of Architecture was obviously a source of considerable concern and the RIBA visitation in May 1963 had drawn attention to a series of problems which were reflected in the persistently low recruitment figures. Both the outlook and the organisation of the School were out-of-date, and students were alleged to suffer from a narrowness of approach which derived from their academic and geographical isolation. Continuing recognition was only granted on the understanding that serious efforts would be made to improve the overall standing of the School which the Local Authority sought to achieve by opening discussions with the University of Hull to whom it offered municipal resources to facilitate the transfer. The situation was exacerbated by the failure to achieve polytechnic designation which the RIBA had seen as one means of removing the isolation of students; on the other hand, the professional body had suggested that failure to achieve designation would lead to the unavoidable withdrawal of recognition. However, whilst the University appear to have been willing to help the Authority, the low priority which the University Grants Committee accorded to Architecture meant that there was little hope of a School being established in the University. Equally, the Ministry of Education's unwillingness to support any other form of affiliation between the School and the university placed the onus back on the LEA which agreed in principle to support the continuation of the School. A development plan was put into operation to increase undergraduate student numbers, introduce a postgraduate course, and appoint two research officers, and the School weathered the storm. (HEC, Report Files 1963/64 no.18; 1967/68 no.8; 1968/69 no.5; 1969/70 no.2; 1970/71 no.5)

Thus, in terms of full-time advanced work, particularly at degree level, the national policy of concentration appeared to be working, albeit negatively in the case of Hull, and the failure to achieve designation was a sad ending to the Local Authority's responsibility for further education. In rejecting the bid for designation, the DES noted that it 'would be prepared to review the question of establishing a polytechnic in the Humberside area in the event of major developments resulting in substantial changes in the present position,' (HEC, 14.4.1967, p.41), but the major developments which might lead to success were unspecified. However, this was the period in which the city had been promised a Humber Bridge during the 1965 bye-election, and it was widely anticipated that this would lead to economic regeneration on both banks of the river. It is at least possible that this may have been in the Minister's mind, though it was at least arguable that a polytechnic might have encouraged economic and industrial growth rather than be a response to it. Despite the lack of clarity on this issue, the LEA refused to be completely downcast, and in 1970 asked the DES to review its earlier rejection, based perhaps on the expansion of work at the College of Commerce, then in its new building and appearing to have a bright future, on the approved building plans for the College of Art and the second phase for the Nautical College, and on the fact that work on the Humber Bridge had commenced. An unfavourable response led the LEA to agree in 1972 to press the new county of Humberside's claim for polytechnic status for the city, and its final act in this area was to participate in a joint, though unsuccessful delegation with Humberside councillors, to persuade the Department of Education and Science to review the position again (HEC F&GP, 13.3.1970; HEC 17.4.1972 & 17.5.1973).

TEACHER TRAINING 1945-75

The post-war years in teacher training witnessed major changes which had a significant impact on the two colleges in the city. Significant changes in the structure of teacher training and the validation of courses, together with a dramatic expansion in numbers in the 1960s transformed the face of teacher training in Hull, and presented a marked contrast to the experience of advanced further education in the city. All aspects of teacher training were much more closely controlled by central government, with Local Education Authorities tending to be little more than conduits for the implementation of policy, and therefore the Municipal Training College did not suffer from the same kind of policy vacuum as affected its sister colleges. Endsleigh College remained in the hands of the Roman Catholic Church during the third quarter of the century and responded accordingly to government policy. Equally, the Training Colleges remained unaffected by the furore surrounding polytechnic designation in 1966-67 since there was no move nationally to include them in the designations. In fact, at that time, Colleges of Education, as they had become after the *Robbins Report* (1963), cherished their links with their local universities, and looked to a strengthening of those links rather than any formal relationships with further education colleges which were seen as somewhat lesser beings.

At the outbreak of the Second World War, the essential characteristic of the national system of teacher training was that it was piecemeal, with the colleges isolated from the mainstream of post-school education. Responsibility for teacher training remained divided. The new Ministry of Education, Local Education Authorities and Governing Bodies controlled administration and finance; academic responsibilities rested with the universities who awarded the qualifications which were below degree standard; and the necessary co-ordination was achieved through interlocking membership of appropriate bodies. The administrative and financial responsibility involved a partnership between the Minister who controlled the overall supply of teachers, and therefore the overall numbers in training and the balance of need between sectors and subjects, and the LEAs who worked within the teacher training Pool. But although the system was national rather than local, there was a good deal of local pride and interest on the part of individual LEAs. Within this system, the voluntary colleges operated independently except where a parent body exercised control over capital finance.

During the war, both Training Colleges in the city had been evacuated from their premises, the Municipal College moving to Bingley and then Ripon in the West Riding and Endsleigh College taking over some of the vacated premises by the former's removal to the west of the county. The Municipal Training College reopened in Hull in 1944 after it evacuation to West Yorkshire, and Endsleigh College returned to its original site. Evacuation provided the LEA with an opportunity to revive its interest in a more comprehensive provision of courses in the city and to renew its flirtation with the University College. In 1944, prior to the reopening of the Municipal College in Hull, and Endsleigh's move back to Beverley Road, the Education Committee considered participating in a plan to create a University College School of Education, including elements of all colleges under the control of the Council. Although this initiative failed, it is interesting to note that it was the minority proposal recommended by the McNair Committee which had been set up to advise the government on the establishment of an integrated system of teacher training, but this also failed.

The McNair Committee was divided between those who wished teacher-training to become part of the university system and those who feared that such a move would lead to an overly-academic approach. However, the Committee's Report, *Teachers and Youth Leaders* (1944), was the basis for the subsequent rejection of plans to integrate teacher training with universities, and led to the establishment of Institutes of Education based in universities and acting as Area Training Organisations (ATO) responsible for academic standards, the co-ordination of teaching practice, and the planning of training and provision in its area. An Institute of Education was established in Hull in 1948 and the University College was directly responsible for the production of teachers and their further professional well-being, an 'experience somewhat alien to the typical university work of educating students from 18 to 21, and granting degrees.' (Bibby 1963, p146). The Institute had a governing body, usually chaired by the Vice Chancellor, which was responsible for the whole work of the institute, aided by academic and professional boards advised by subject boards of studies. The latter consisted entirely of specialists in the University and the Colleges, thus affording the latter a good deal of influence in the development of their subjects within the context of teacher training and providing an opportunity for improving the academic content, coherence and standards of their course. Previously dependent on Leeds for examination work, the two Hull colleges were able to join the newly-established ATO based upon the University College of Hull which acted as their validating body until the late 1970s. Initial discussions, involving both the Colleges of Commerce and of Arts and Crafts as well as the two Training Colleges and the University College department, had begun in a spirit of co-operation, but the eventual Institute was based on the three main teacher training institutions and was only achieved within the concept of institutional autonomy within a co-operative system (Bibby, p.148).

The structure and organisation of teacher training resurfaced in the Robbins Report, *Higher Education* (1963) whose wide-ranging concerns included the possible modification of 'the present arrangements for planning and co-ordinating the development of the various types of institution.' With respect to teacher training, the Report broadly revived those proposals of the 1944 McNair Committee which had not been implemented. In order to improve their status and their work, it was recommended that training colleges should be renamed Colleges of Education, be more closely integrated with universities through Schools of Education from whom they would receive finance, and be given independent governing bodies. At the heart of the proposals, and the only one eventually accepted, was the proposal that the best College of

Education students should undertake a four-year course leading to a Bachelor of Education degree, the first step on the road to creating an all-graduate teaching profession. What the proposal overlooked was the potential for creating small, non-viable classes at degree level, thus repeating the problem already apparent in the advanced further education sector which the 1956 reorganisation had recognised and which the 1966 polytechnic creations were designed to address.

The ATOs fostered much co-operation between university and colleges at subject level where elaborate committee structures were the order of the day, but the latter were still in a position of tutelage and, despite the fact that they were autonomous institutions, were certainly not treated as equals. (Bibby 1963, p.182). This feature was nowhere better illustrated than by the University of Hull's attitude to the award of degrees to College students taught entirely in the colleges. With the extension of teacher training courses to three years in 1960 and the Robbins Report proposal three years later to introduce a four-year B.Ed. degree, Hull introduced a non-honours award. By 1970, it was one of only two or three universities that remained unwilling to upgrade the award to honours, and this reflected poorly on the colleges and their attempt to attract well-qualified students. Relations between the University and its colleges was summed up by the last Principal of Kingston-upon-Hull College of Education as 'a kind of fifty-year courtship, with several lost opportunities for consummation, followed by close working relationships across the autonomous divide for almost thirty years' (Bibby 1963, p.267).

The early 1950s was a period of quiet consolidation for teacher training in Hull before the advent of rapid growth beginning at the end of the decade. At Endsleigh College in 1957, by which time there were one hundred and eighty students all resident, an HMI report noted the relative inadequacy of the premises, and the hindrance to development caused by the continuing presence of St. Mary's pupils. The general conclusion of the report were extremely good – a caring community which was succeeding in spite of the limitations placed on students by shortage of space and materials. Student quality was obviously improved with 38 of 130 (29%) in Year 1 and 32 of 119 (27%) in the second year holding one or more A levels (*HMI Report 1957* in University Archive).

In addition to reforms to enhance the level of work in teacher

Table 4.3   Major growth post-1963 in Teacher Training in Hull

	1949	1954	1963	1970
Kingston	160	170	505	750
Endsleigh	180	180	525	635

Source: Bibby 1963, p.181

training and to increase the status of the teaching profession, the post-war period also saw a major expansion of the system, first in the aftermath of war with the construction of numerous emergency colleges and second in response to demographic and political changes in the fifties and sixties. The impact of emergency training after the war had little impact on the Hull colleges, but, in common with the rest of the country, the sixties was a period of dramatic expansion. In response to the post-war bulge, the introduction of the three-year training course in 1960, and proposals to raise the school leaving age to 16 in 1970, Colleges of Education became a major force in higher education provision as the numbers in teacher training quadrupled during the decade, with some colleges being as large as pre-war universities.

The criteria for the expansion of individual colleges, which included location in or near to a University town, the ease with which teaching practice places could be provided, the ability to recruit new entrants to the profession, an inclination for large and medium-sized colleges, and an increase in number of mixed colleges, was very much to the advantage of the two colleges in the city, both of which underwent considerable expansion. By 1962/63, there were one hundred and forty six colleges nationally of which only one had over 1,000 students. The second largest group of thirteen, including Kingston-upon-Hull College of Education, had 500-749, and the third of fifty-five with 250-499 included Endsleigh College of Education. (*Robbins Report* Appendix 2 (A), Part II). The impact on both colleges was dramatic and necessitated a major building programme. At the Municipal Training College land on campus was available, and at Endsleigh land was purchased from the neighbouring Sailors Children's Society to provide more teaching facilities whilst new halls of residence and a chapel were built on Beverley Road.

Chapter 5

The Reorganisation of Further and Higher Education in Hull 1972–1976

Hull's failure to achieve polytechnic status for its colleges in 1966/67 was an immediate setback for advanced further education in the city, particularly in the area of science and technology, though the longer-term impact was less severe than might at first have been expected. In the early 1970s, a separate and apparently unconnected central government initiative, concerned with initial teacher training, provided another opportunity to reconsider the future of higher education in the city, and despite much internal wrangling, this helped to place advanced further education in the city on a firmer footing.

During the 1960s initial teacher education had undergone major expansion nationally, and the relationships between individual colleges and their providers, principally local education authorities, had been strengthened with the government's rejection of the Robbins Committee's proposal that colleges should forge closer links with their local universities. By the end of the 1960s, two contentious issues were beginning to emerge. First, there was growing concern over the nature and content of teacher training, which had been largely ignored during the heady expansion earlier in the decade, with rival camps arguing the case for a more professional or a more academic training course. Second, there were signs, played down by the Department of Education and Science, that the proposed rate of expansion of teacher education into the 1970s would produce a glut of qualified teachers. Some of the evidence for the new scenario came from two official sources.

In 1969, the Parliamentary Select Committee of Education and Science decided to investigate teacher training during that session, and a year later the Secretary of State for Education, Edward Short, invited Area Training Organisations to examine the curriculum of Colleges of Education. The impact of these two initiatives was such that a major inquiry into the future of teacher education became almost inevitable, and the new Conservative government elected in 1970 immediately established a Committee, chaired by Lord James who later became Vice-Chancellor of the University of York, which began work the following January. At first sight, the committee's function was to report on the content of initial teacher education and make recommendations on the numbers therein, but more significant in the long-term was the invitation to consider these issues in the context of colleges, polytechnics and other further education institutions maintained by local education authorities. In fact, five polytechnics created in the late 1960s had established small departments of education, and they provided a model for ending the isolation of teacher training. Against this background, the James Report and subsequent government Circulars paved the way for a major reorganisation of local authority teacher training and its absorption within advanced further education.

The proposals created a new situation for Hull in that any unified institution arising out of the proposals would include teacher training which, given the numbers elsewhere in the city on advanced level courses, appeared to be in a position to dominate the debate. Consequently, 1973-75 were years of intense discussion and dissension in the city, with strong professional resistance from teacher trainers to the concept of a unitary institution which eventually emerged only as a result of a forceful approach from the new Humberside LEA which became responsible for developments on 1 April 1974, but which, in a shadow role, had been involved in developments rather earlier.

THE NATIONAL FRAMEWORK FOR REFORM

Thus, the 1972 James Report, *Teacher Education and Training,* apparently concerned with the detail of the academic content of and the numbers in initial teacher training, became the platform for a much wider reform of the structure of local authority higher education which reaffirmed and strengthened the binary policy enunciated in the mid-1960s. The 1972 White Paper, *Education: A Framework for Expansion* proposed to continue recent growth in higher education against a background of severe reductions in teacher training. It maintained the Robbins principle of availability of higher education for all qualified students, thus meeting the needs of the economy, the personal ambitions of students and the wider aims of society and, like most White and Green Papers of the next fifteen years, concentrated on the size and structure rather than the purposes of higher education. By 1971/72, overall full-time and sandwich student numbers were estimated at 463,000 which represented 114.1% growth over the previous ten years, and it was anticipated that there would be a further 66% rise to 750,000 by 1981/82. These estimates assumed an increase in the age participation rate from 15% to 22% by 1981, thus implying that the majority of the expansion would be taken up by full-time, standard age rather than mature students, and there was a significant absence of proposals to increase the existing 70,000 part-time day places. By 1981 the university and public sector elements would be broadly equal in size, with 375,000 in each, and this implied a much more significant growth rate in the polytechnics and colleges (204,000 to 375,000 full-time and sandwich students – 83.8%) than in the universities (236,000 to 375,000 – 57.9%). The major part of the expansion in the public sector would take place in the polytechnics which would expand to 180,000, though colleges of further education and colleges of education would provide an additional 155,000 places. Crucial to the achievement of these targets for the public sector was the intended reduction of initial teacher training from 114,000 to 60,000-70,000 over the decade which would facilitate the diversification of a great many of the existing Colleges of Education, whether alone or by joining forces with Further Education Colleges, thus producing new institutions which would be hardly distinguishable from Polytechnics or other Further Education Colleges. An indication of government's emerging concern with the cost to the Treasury of expanding higher education can be seen in the expectation that universities and colleges would encourage students to live at home, and the expectation that the costs of growth, largely staffing, should be achieved by a move of SSRs to 10:1 in both sectors. Government also hoped that new course developments would focus on the new

1. The first men students, Cottingham Road, 1913

2. Hull Municipal Training College, classroom

3. Hull Municipal Training College, assembly hall

4. The library, 1960

5. Hull Municipal Training College, men's hostel dining room

6. Women's commonroom, 1950

7. Students in costume collecting for Rag Day, 1930s

two-year, non-vocational Diploma of Higher Education proposed by the 1972 James Report.

The White Paper and subsequent government statements made it clear that trainee teachers should be educated alongside other higher education students wherever possible, thus signifying the virtual end of the monotechnic approach, and contained some hints as to the nature of new colleges, many of whom would play a major role in meeting the expansion of higher education proposed by government. Some would become major institutions of higher education either singly or in partnership with other neighbouring institutions, though merger with a university was not encouraged, and it was envisaged that the new colleges would 'not be easily distinguishable by function from a polytechnic or other further education college.' (WP 1972, #160) Central to these institutions was a flexible teacher supply which might be achieved by the introduction of consecutive training preferably with unit-based courses, thereby neatly introducing the concept of deferred choice of professional outlet until higher education had been sampled. In short, the government was committed to a major change in the role of Colleges of Education, though it neither anticipated nor sought to establish the creation of a distinctive sector. Nonetheless, the colleges of higher education began to emerge as a force after 1976, personified in the formation of the Standing Conference of Principals of Colleges and Institutes of Higher Education (SCOP) as its pressure group, though its chief unifying characteristic was still its internal diversity, a function of size, location and history.

The subsequent DES Circular 7/73 *The Development of Higher Education in the Non-University Sector*, noting the need for 'major reconstruction of the role of Colleges of Education both inside and outside teacher training,' invited local education authorities, both existing and new, to review need in their areas. The *Circular* suggested that its approach to local authority proposals would have some regard to the need for a regional policy which would seek to redress existing imbalance of provision between regions both by expansion in under-provided areas and control in areas where provision was generous; as a general guide, it was to be assumed that urban centres or regions of at least 250,000 population ought to have an institution of higher education. Local Authorities were also offered advice in terms of the planning process. If new institutions were to be proposed, which might include non-advanced further education (NAFE) work, consideration should be given to the need for economies of scale, though those with predominantly arts and social science courses could be viable at 1-2,000 which was smaller than the polytechnics; proposals should also avoid creating further residence and transport problems by concentrating large numbers of students in one centre, and should also note the desirability of providing for local students, both full-time and part-time. Reflecting the traditional local control of further education, the *Circular* emphasised that the initiative for reform lay with the latter whilst recognising that the planning process was complicated by the concurrent reform of local government. Nonetheless, in its eagerness to press forward with its educational reforms, the government required existing local authorities to make interim responses to its *Circular* by November 1973 with the new authorities submitting final plans as quickly as possible on their assumption of responsibility on 1 April 1974.

THE HUMBERSIDE RESPONSE TO CIRCULAR 7/73

In 1972, non-advanced further education, advanced further education and teacher training in the Humberside region was located in a number of urban centres and was the responsibility of a number of separate local authorities. By far the largest was the city of Hull with its significant municipal and voluntary provision, whilst further courses were also offered at the specialist East Riding College of Agriculture and in five other general colleges, though only at Grimsby was there any advanced level work, closely related to the food and fishing industries which formed the economic base of the town. Therefore, Hull became the focus of debate on *Circular 7/73*, though its appearance in May and its request for a response by November came at a time of major disruption for local authorities grappling with the complexities of local government reorganisation. There is little doubt that local authorities were too preoccupied with wider problems to be able or willing to fight the DES's destructive teacher-training policies, and both the timing and the timetable of the *Circular* were hardly based on coincidence (Lukes 1975, p.79). The Hull Education Authority approached the task of developing interim proposals without enthusiasm in view of the impending transfer of its educational responsibilities to the new

County of Humberside on 1 April, 1974, and its officers appear to have presided over a protracted period of consultation with the governing bodies and academic boards of the five institutions under its wing, and also engaged in consultation with the voluntary College of Education in the city.

The central forum for the production of an interim proposal to the DES was a regular meeting of the Principals of the five LEA colleges, sometimes attended by the Director or Deputy Director of Education for Hull, though with no apparent consultation with the shadow Humberside Authority.[1] In the early discussions, which lasted for most of the remainder of 1973, the majority of the Principals were absorbed, in varying degrees, by a desire to protect the position of their own colleges and either ignored or rejected the opportunity to contribute to a radical reform of advanced further education provision in the city. Most vociferous in his opposition to reform, and initially to any kind of merger, was Dr. C. Bibby, Principal of Kingston-upon-Hull College of Education, who was particularly concerned to protect what he saw as the distinctive, vocational character of teacher education which he believed would be lost in a merged institution, particularly one which also offered further education. Therefore, he favoured the retention of independent status for Kingston-upon-Hull College of Education or, failing that, a merger with Endsleigh College of Education to preserve a monotechnic institution for teacher education in the city, though the issues involved in merging a voluntary and a municipal college were never addressed. However, recognising that the six hundred initial teacher education places allocated to the Humberside Authority by the DES were unlikely to create a viable institution without some diversification, Bibby argued that some minimal diversification into courses of training for the 'para-pedagogic professions' such as careers education, child guidance, health visiting, librarianship, probation and social welfare, which might consist of c.15% of the college's student body, would retain the necessary character for an institution dedicated to professional training. Bibby's commitment to a monotechnic approach was shared by Mr. A. Sugden, Principal of the Regional College of Art who feared particularly for the future of Fine Art education in a comprehensive institution and who was committed to defending and extending advanced level work in his institution. Throughout the local discussions, Bibby continued a vociferous and widespread campaign for his ideals, including seeking the support of the Minister of Education, R. Prentice, the former Minister of Education and M.P. for Grimsby Antony Crosland, and the recently elected Leader of the Opposition Margaret Thatcher, all without success, and he eventually encouraged his Academic Board to make a separate response to the DES to accompany the County Council's submission in January 1975.

The other Principals were either less vocal or more ambivalent about their position. Captain Simpson, Principal of the Nautical College, was concerned to develop a comprehensive provision for nautical education in the city so as to enhance his college's national reputation. This would involve further strengthening of its non-advanced work to provide a suitable base for the development of higher diploma and degree courses which the College lacked and which were vital if it was to develop the national reputation it sought. Mr.T.Berry, Principal of the College of Commerce, recognised the case for the federal proposal which would provide public sector higher education in the city with a much needed boost, and felt that it might strengthen the case for polytechnic designation which would enable the work of the College of Commerce to be enhanced. In contrast Dr.R.Rogers, Principal of the College of Technology embraced the opportunity presented by reorganisation to press for a College of Further and Higher Education. However, by June 1973 all five were supporting the idea of a merged institution as the most academically effective and cost-efficient means of collaboration, though disagreeing on its character. The majority favoured a confederation of colleges with a Principal chosen in rotation from the existing personnel, which would preserve institutional autonomy and retain existing college loyalties, but which would provide for mutual recognition and student transfer within the institute. The minority argued for a federal solution which would have a permanent Director with control over academic development and the allocation of finance and accommodation, though the degree of authority ceded to the centre in this proposal was unclear.

In the early discussions, the Hull LEA appears to have given the principals their head, but, mindful of the *Circular's* request for interim plans in November 1973, held two formal meetings with them to formulate a response. Having discussed the federal/confederal organisation on 5 November which appeared to form the basis of a response to the DES, the Principals were nonplussed to be confronted by a proposal nine days later from Dr. R.D.A. Crafter, the Deputy Director of Education for Hull, for a unitary institution based on a merger of the five colleges with Endsleigh College of Education having federated status within it. The new institution would have a single Governing Body and Academic Board and a permanent Director with overall responsibility for organisation, management, discipline and the appointment of staff, though the possibility of each maintained college needing a Principal for control of his own former college was acknowledged. Clearly, the Principals were taken by surprise, and Crafter's proposal revealed continuing divisions concerning the character of the new institution. Bibby pledged to do all in his power to block the scheme, and was supported by Sugden who felt that it would prevent an enlightened and progressive future for both further and higher education on Humberside, particularly in the field of fine art. Simpson re-iterated his concern with the future development of advanced level work in nautical education and would back the scheme most likely to achieve that. Berry was more inclined than others to accept the case for a unitary institution, though only if it quickly led to the designation of a polytechnic; and Rogers supported the scheme (Bibby to Hobson, 13.12.1973; Bibby to T.Berry 3.12.1973). Given the difficulties and the impending assumption of responsibility by Humberside, Hull Education Authority sought approval to delay a firm response to the DES. At the end of the year, the Director of Education for Hull, Mr.S.Hobson, advised the DES of the Authority's inability to achieve a unified position and listed the two major proposals and noted the 'fundamental divergences of opinion about what the new shape of higher education in the city should be.' (Hobson to R.C.Pulford, 3.1.1974). In view of local government reorganisation, the DES accepted Hobson's letter as Hull's interim response since it did not contain specific proposals. (Pulford to Bibby, 30.4.1974)

Apart from reflecting local differences of view, the Hull Education Authority's ambivalence provided an opportunity for DES interest in reorganisation to manifest itself. The predominant role of the DES in the reorganisation of teacher education was made clear by Mr.H.A.Harding, the Assistant Under Secretary of State in charge of the project, as early as May 1974. In a lecture to a Study

Conference on Colleges of Education and Reorganisation, held at
Coombe Lodge Further Education Staff College in May 1974,
Harding drew attention to the primacy of national reorganisation
as part of the government's plans to achieve a major reduction in
initial, and a great expansion of in-service, teacher education within
existing resources and structures. The government's objectives
would be best met by encouraging mergers between Colleges of
Education, Polytechnics and other Further Education establishments in order to provide the diversity of courses required. In
terms of structures, the DES favoured amalgamations into unitary
institutions, though it recognised that federations could be a satisfactory answer to problems caused by the involvement of voluntary
colleges, and looser types of association may be necessary where
colleges were separated by considerable distances (Harding 1974).
The DES position had been appreciated by Dr. Bibby who was in
little doubt that many local proposals involving the reorganisation
of Colleges of Education were inspired by civil servants in the DES
(Bibby 1975, pp.19-29), and detailed involvement of the DES in
the Hull debate was confirmed by its advice to the principal of
Endsleigh College in May 1974 that 'the Department proposed
to establish a polytechnic in Humberside with its own Faculty
of Education and Social Studies', in which Endsleigh would not
figure, but the College might wish to sell its buildings and land
to Humberside County Council for use in the new institution.
Its later cursory dismissal of the two schemes proposed in the
Hull LEA's interim response, confirmed its desire to see a policy
of concentration of higher education provision within the city
and provided significant support for Humberside's unswerving
commitment to the concept of a unified institution.

The extent to which the DES policy of concentration was pressed
upon or shared by Humberside may never be known conclusively.
The Chair of the Humberside Education Committee, Councillor
W.Martin, advised the consultative meeting on 15 July 1974 that
the DES anticipated that the national reforms would lead to the
emergence of about one hundred higher education institutions of
which Humberside would be one, and there appears to have been
little doubt that, if Humberside wished to develop higher education
within the county, a scheme which sought to maintain the identity
of the existing colleges was doomed to failure. However, as the
Circular noted, the DES had no powers of compulsion. The

initiative lay with the local authority, though the DES power to grant or withhold approval for any proposed reorganisation was highly significant and appears to have been used openly, both to reject local proposals and to impose its own schemes on reluctant authorities to such an extent as to lead College Principals to describe the process of consultation as a 'smokescreen' (Bibby in *THES*, 12.7.1974). However, it is clear that, in exercising clear political leadership in favour of a Polytechnic in Hull to meet the region's social and economic needs by remedying the inadequate provision of advanced further education within the county and the wider Yorkshire and Humberside regional planning area, the new LEA's view was consistent with a long-standing local ambition. Therefore, it seems likely that Crafter's plan, tabled on 14 November, reflected the views of the new Education Authority to whom he had been appointed Deputy Director of Education in October 1973 and the Authority's chief problem was the tactical difficulty of persuading the professionals involved in the debate to accept its policy and agree to the establishment of a unitary College of Higher Education, rather than the strategic one of the nature of reorganisation within the county.

The new authority assumed power on 1 April 1974 and established a special sub-committee of the Education Committee to formulate its response to *Circular 7/73*. Apart from the maintenance of a monotechnic, teacher-training institution which no one outside the Colleges of Education appeared to favour, the options facing the Local Authority were variants of partial or total mergers. One possibility which emerged from the *James Report* was the establishment of a liberal arts college on the American model, but that carried with it the probability of being confined to the new two-year, pre-professional course which James favoured, thus failing to meet the Authority's ambitions for a Polytechnic. A second option was to create a Community College which catered for 16/19 year-olds and provided both in-service education, professional updating, and more general non-vocational education for the community, though there was little evidence that previous U.K. governments had been particularly enthusiastic about professional and non-vocational education, and the concentration on 16/19 for full-time work would similarly miss the opportunity to develop advanced work in the city. A third choice would have been to form a vocational or professional college from Kingston-upon-Hull and

Endsleigh Colleges of Education in which teacher training was the predominant function with some additions of courses for related caring professions, but heavy concentration on teacher training would have left such a college vulnerable to future readjustments and have restricted the possibility of developing advanced further education in the county. The final possibility was to seek comprehensive provision in the city, either through an institution which combined further and higher education, or through two institutions, one emphasising higher education and seeking the status of a Polytechnic and the other concentrating on further education. This approach would guarantee the development of both advanced and non-advanced further education in the city, and provide a flexible, centralised higher education institution which was capable of responding to the social and economic needs of the region and capable of making a major contribution to the expansion of the non-university sector of higher education. In the nine months leading up to its response in January 1975, at least fourteen meetings were held, most between County Council officers and the Principals of the Colleges, but two major consultative sessions with members of college governing bodies presided over by the chair of the Local Education Committee, sought an agreed proposal which could be submitted to the DES. Clearly, the exhaustive process in which the Authority engaged indicated the importance that it attached to producing a scheme which was acceptable to the professionals who would have to implement it, though its determination to create a major unitary institution, perhaps designated a Polytechnic, was never in doubt.

The two major items for resolution were the breadth of the scheme to be proposed and the nature of the unitary institution devised. In the early stages of consultation, the Authority involved the Principals of all Further Education Colleges in Humberside, thus providing an opportunity to consider the establishment of a comprehensive, post-16 system of further and higher education within the county, a position complicated by the existence of well-regarded, advanced level work in food and fisheries studies at Grimsby College of Technology. The decision to focus on Hull was made rather quickly, though Grimsby College and the LEA were anxious to ensure the continued development of advanced courses on the South Bank which were directly related to the town's Economy. However, the early decision on

94

the geographical aspects of the problem did not resolve the issue of the nature of the new unitary institution, and there was still considerable debate about the comprehensiveness of its provision, and its structure, organisation and management remained a bone of contention. The consultations were plagued by the continuing division among the professionals over the most appropriate form of merged institution, and the further fracture between those who felt that a merged comprehensive institution would threaten their work, and those who felt that it would provide them with the new opportunities they were seeking. During the summer, Local Authority politicians and officers had to put pressure on the professionals to make proposals to the round of County Council committees in September 1974 which recognised the wishes of the elected representatives. In the event the governing bodies of four of the five colleges agreed to support the proposal for a unitary institution, with Kingston-upon-Hull College of Education still intent on defending its organisational identity as the only means of preserving the corporate sense of teacher education, and the county's submission was approved by the Education Committee in December 1974 (2).

Humberside's response to *Circular 7/73* proposed the merger of the five local authority colleges in Hull into a unitary institution of higher education, to be established in September 1976, with a single Governing Council and Director, and an Academic Board supported by several Faculty Boards. The longer term aim was to establish an institution which would provide predominantly higher education, with non-advanced work in a newly-created College of Further Education, though the Authority reserved the right to include some non-advanced work in the higher education college, especially where the vertical integration of courses made it desirable. The actual division of work, courses and staff between the two would be a matter for future deliberation. Given the uncertainty surrounding its future, Endsleigh College was to be involved fully in planning the new institution, but within a few months its Governors had decided that the College would have to close at the end of the Summer Term 1976, and its offer to sell its land and buildings to the County Council was gratefully accepted in view of the government ruling that any growth in higher education had to be achieved by using available resources. In contrast, other institutions in the county were excluded from

Table 5.1 Proposed Division of Students and Levels of work between the Colleges of Further and Higher Education

	HCHE	HCFE
To.al Students (FTEs)	5,858 (3,517)	7,989 (2,215)
Total Students on Full-Time and Sandwich Courses (FTEs)	3,218 (2,762)	870 (675)
Total Students on Part-Time Courses	2,640 (755)	7,119 (1,540)
Burnham Gradings I-III (FTEs)	69.1% (76.03%)	3.44%
IV	30.9% (23.97%)	38.09%
V		58.47%

the merger, though it was hoped that close working relationships would develop with Grimsby College of Technology and that the county's College of Agriculture at nearby Bishop Burton might also be a possible centre for the development of higher education in the future, a vision which was realised with the development of University higher diploma and degree work in the early 1990s at both institutions.

The scheme was based on the maintenance of existing provision where appropriate, but also on anticipated growth in areas of increasing importance to students, industry, commerce and the professions, as well as the county itself. The two colleges would have a combined population of c.600 academic staff and c.14,000 (5,800 FTEs) students, though the fact that only 30% (47% FTEs) of students were enrolled on advanced courses, principally in the declining area of teacher education, pointed to the need for considerable expansion in advanced provison if polytechnic ambitions were to be realised. The proposed division of work between the two institutions as shown in Table 5.1.

It was anticipated that the College of Higher Education would favour the development of multi- and inter-disciplinary courses, perhaps giving prominence to a 'single coherent Dip.H.E. scheme with units taken from the various Faculties of the new institution and from other colleges,' and would seek a significant expansion in degree-level work in vocational areas which were important to the county such as business studies, engineering production with management studies, law and accountancy, maritime studies, marine engineering and communications, social work, and Technology.

The Authority established an Interim Planning Committee (IPC) which would have a Joint Academic Committee (JAC) consisting initially of five Principals plus one student per college, chaired by Mr.J. Bower, Humberside's Chief Education Officer, and a Joint

Panel (JP) to consider the Instrument and Articles of the new Colleges. Provison was made for widespread consultation with the Area Training Organisation for teacher education, the Yorkshire and Humberside Regional Advisory Council, the Humberside Teachers Joint Consultative Council, and the professional associations and unions who represented the staff of the merging colleges, but the JAC would make proposals on academic policy and development, resources, organisation, establishment and student unions. Although most firm decisions could only be made when the leadership of the College had been appointed, it was assumed that initially the College of Higher Education would be organised into five faculties 'synonymous with the interest of the present colleges,' each headed by an Assistant Director. All resources of the existing colleges were to be given to the new institution.

The *Circular* required responses to include a first estimate of the capital implications of the scheme and, although the resources of the existing five colleges were available for the reorganisation, the Authority was unable to be precise in its response. One of the major questions facing the planning group related to the building stock of the two new Colleges, and the actual division of facilities between the Colleges of Further and Higher Education. This problem was compounded by the contrast between the quality of the environment in the former Colleges of Education, generously funded by central government for residence and social facilities as well as teaching, and the relative poverty of the former local technical colleges which provided almost entirely for non-resident students and which often had been under-resourced. A major concern was the long-standing inadequacy of facilities for higher education at Queen's Garden, the site of the existing College of Technology, and substantial investment would be required, particularly to provide a library and the necessary social and recreational facilities. More generally, there was a need for accommodation for central administrative services and additional specialist and non-specialist buildings, though some of this could be able to be created by the adaptation of existing premises on the various sites. With this in mind, the Local Authority had reserved 6.5 acres of land around the existing Queen's Gardens buildings for developments, including a hall of residence, and estimated that capital expenditure of the order of £2.3 millions would be necessary. At the time of the response, the position was complicated by the uncertainty surrounding the role of Endsleigh College, but its decision to close in 1976 and the offer of its property to the Authority improved the situation and obviated the necessity for a new hall of residence in the Queen's Gardens area. (HBFE Sub., 7.3.1975, #705).

In approving the Local Authority submission, the DES rejected the arguments put forward by Kingston-upon-Hull College of Education in favour of flexibility and the symbiotic potential for teachers being trained alongside other students. It suggested that the new Hull College of Higher Education should seek co-operation with the University of Hull through the establishment of a High Level Advisory Co-ordinating Board, an idea which sat rather uncomfortably with the Department's general support for the binary divide in higher education, its specific discouragement of university/college relationships, and its expectation that most colleges would seek validation from the Council for National Academic Awards.

Thus, the original vision of a single scientific, technological and vocational institution offering advanced level work in the city, first unveiled in the early decades of the century, was fulfilled. Though there seems little doubt that DES pressure behind the scenes was important in realising the objective, the role of the new Humberside LEA was crucial locally. The understandably dilatory approach of the Hull LEA was replaced in 1973/74 by a vigorous new County Council with an ambition to create a polytechnic in Hull, and the emergence of Hull College of Higher Education was a tribute to the energy with which elected members and senior officers pursued their goal of a unified institution, though they found the DES less co-operative with respect to status and nomenclature.

Chapter 6

The Establishment of Hull College of Higher Education 1976–82[1]

INTRODUCTION

The range of issues facing any new institution are legion, but they are inevitably more complex when that institution results from a merger of existing colleges, not all of which were enthusiastic about the future, and the problems are exacerbated when this work has to be carried out within a context of substantial decline in the major area of the new College's advanced level work. The range of problems needing immediate attention was almost overwhelming, and a systematic approach in which the formulation of a mission is followed by the development of a strategy and an embryonic organisation was impossible. Not only had the legal entity of the new College to be determined, but new courses had to be developed rapidly to give the College an academic identity, requiring resolution of the demarcation line between further and higher education work. In addition, staff had to be organised and adequately located in new departments to reflect the College's work which involved addressing the immediate problem of staff insecurity resulting from planned reductions in teacher education.

The first few years of the new College were characterised by intense developments involving the expenditure of restless energy by some and the experience of considerable discomfort for others. Once a temporary framework for the governance and management of the College had been established by the Local Authority, work began to define the academic character of the institution requiring regional and national support for course proposals and the approval of validating bodies. A vital element of any development was the resolution of staffing issues resulting from major reductions in teacher education which would involve considerable re-training, judicious new appointments and, in some cases, redundancy. Crucial to success was the establishment and development of good working relationships between the College and the LEA and it is a measure of the commitment of both parties that the College was successfully launched on its way by the end of the decade. It proved a watershed for a number of internal and external reasons.

THE GOVERNANCE AND MANAGEMENT OF THE COLLEGE

Since the legal establishment of a new institution takes time, it was necessary to set up temporary systems to enable the LEA and the College to begin to confront the main tasks ahead. The JPC drafted Instrument and Articles of Government for submission to the Secretary of State based on model documents provided by the DES, and these provided the legal framework for the control and management of the two Colleges; the Instrument and Articles of Government for Hull College of Higher Education, remained the legal basis for the government of the College until incorporation in 1989, though some changes were introduced to the membership of the Governing Council with the formation of Humberside College of Higher Education in 1983. The IPC, consisting of forty-four members representing all parties interested in the re-organisation of further and higher education in the county, created the framework for both the College of Higher Education and the College of Further Education. Under the chairmanship of J.Bower, the county's Chief Education Officer, it first met on 3 December, 1975 and continued in being until its final meeting on 20 January, 1977. The IPC was responsible for the initial establishment of Hull College of Higher Education, overseeing both its first Development Plan and the delicate issues concerning staff deployment, development and, in some cases, redundancy (IPC 20.1.1977, #5.1).

The IPC established a Directorate consisting of the Director-Designate, J.M.Stoddart, formerly Assistant Director at North-East London Polytechnic and who took up office on 1 January 1976, and three of the Principals of the former colleges which had merged to form Hull College of Higher Education, Mr.

Berry, Dr. Bibby, and Dr. Rogers, acting as Pro-Rectors with specific responsibilities for academic and resource planning and for staffing in the new institution. The Directorate was supported by a Chief Administrative Officer, appointed from the Humberside Education Authority. Both Sugden and Simpson retired at the time of the merger, and Sister Joan McNamara of Endsleigh College was appointed Senior Tutor, though she also retired in 1979. The task facing the new Director and his senior colleagues was formidable. Not only did they have to create a new College and lead it into the future, but they had to do so within a system of checks and balances which included the Academic Board, which the Director chaired, the Governing Council, of which he was a member, and the LEA with whom good relationships were essential if the new College was to succeed.

After the interim period, which ended with the first meeting of the Governing Council in March 1977, the College was governed under a standard Instrument and Articles of Government common in the public sector. The structure of College government was inherited from the 1960s and earlier, and was based more on the technical college tradition where the LEA had complete control than on the College of Education pattern where the local authority was little more than a conduit for the transfer of central government funding and the application of government policy. However, to this idea of social control and responsiveness exercised by the LEA was added the university-derived concept of academic freedom whereby members of staff of a college were actively involved in the development of its work, thereby providing an important contrast with the former colleges' previous experience under the Hull Education Authority. Under the Instrument and Articles, Humberside County Council, as the maintaining authority, had complete power over finance, employment and staffing, equipment and space, and the nature of the academic programme, though in executing these functions it was advised by the Governing Council of the College. The LEA controlled expenditure through the receipt of financial estimates submitted to it by the Governing Council, and the prior consent of the County Council was required if the College wished to exceed approved estimates or to undertake expenditure which would have a carry-over impact on subsequent financial years. Control of capital expenditure also rested with the Authority, though it was dependent on central government allocations, and the College's needs had to be prioritised within the Education Authority's overall capital requirements. The LEA decided on the tuition fees and rates of payment for part-time staff. The only discretion available to the Governing Council was to spend within approved estimates, to vire between headings up to £10,000, later increased to £15,000, and to authorise repairs, maintenance and minor alterations initially up to £2,500 and increased to £5,000 per job. As a result of this financial control, the LEA was able to control the staffing base of the College and was the employer of all staff who worked there. Therefore, all staff were appointed to the College in the service of the County Council and were subject to its conditions of service; in the case of non-teaching staff, appropriate National Joint Council terms and conditions applied, and the remuneration and grades of such staff had to be agreed with and approved by the Authority. Finally, it was responsible for determining the general educational character of the College and its place in the local education system, though in exercising this function it was advised by the Governing Council of the College. (Articles HCHE, #2).

Within this supervisory framework, the Governing Council was responsible for the 'general direction of the College and for promoting its efficiency and development' with the assistance of whatever sub-committees it may have chosen to establish (Articles HCHE, #3). To assist it in its work, it set up standing committees for Policy and Finance and for Personnel, Establishment & Premises on which the Chair and Vice-Chair sat ex-officio. (GCP 22.3.1977, #29). The membership of the Governing Council reflected both the local character of the College and the version of collegiality by which such institutions were governed. The former character of the College was underlined by the County Council's nomination of twelve of its forty-six members, by the membership of two Governors appointed by the neighbouring University of Hull, formerly the validating body for the College's teacher education courses, and by the requirement for four further representatives of secondary, further and higher education in the region. A form of derived collegiality, in which members of the College were involved in but did not have control over decisions affecting institutional development, was respected by the Director's membership of the Board, and by a further seventeen members elected from amongst staff and students. This core body of local politicians and college members then appointed up to twelve additional members with experience of industry, commerce, trades and the professions, of whom at least three had to have trades union experience, and a further four were co-opted to represent the regional education scene with one from a major establishment of higher education, two from the full-time teaching staff of county further education colleges, and one from a Humberside school identified through consultation with appropriate teachers' organisations. Both the size and the professional and political composition of this body were in marked contrast to that which replaced it at the incorporation of the College in 1989.

The university-derived element in the arrangements for governance extended from staff membership of the Governing Council to the pseudo-collegiality of its Academic Board which consisted of a rather unwieldy fifty-nine members, including twenty-three ex-officio members from the Directorate, Heads of School and Heads of Services, thirty-two elected and four co-opted. The Board was responsible to Governing Council for all aspects of the academic work of the College, including new developments, the admission, selection, suspension and expulsion of students, staff development, advice to the Director on staffing establishments and the allocation of funds. It exercised these responsibilities through a wide-range of sub-committees where the real work was done.

Within this formal structure, the health of a College depended heavily on the context set by the LEA and on the personality of the Director. Certainly, the omens were good, with a new Authority seeking to make its mark and quickly developing a degree of civic pride in its new creation. Within the constraints placed upon it by central government policy and encroaching central control during the 1980s, Humberside generally shared the College's ambitions and supported its development. Given the dissension which had accompanied the emergence of the College and the pressing need to expunge the past and establish new loyalties to a new institution, it was almost inevitable that the post of Director should go to an external candidate. Fortunately, good relationships were formed between the LEA and the Director whose visionary and aggressive approach was exactly what the new College required. In keeping with the further education tradition, the Director, assisted by permanent deputies, had a reasonable measure of Executive authority, though the existence of Academic Board and its committee structure required a political approach to ensure that the leadership's ideas prevailed. The devices employed to ensure that this occurred were already familiar in many polytechnics. Policy was formulated in the weekly Directorate meeting, progressed through the range of committees, all of which were chaired by Directorate members, and finally agreed by Academic Board for transmission onto Governing Council and the LEA. Thus, the system provided an opportunity for academic staff to make a positive contribution to the strategic development of the institution, though it is doubtful if Academic Boards were capable of seriously frustrating the policy objectives of the Directorate. Nonetheless, the latter required a degree of political acumen if the system was to operate smoothly, and Hull possessed a Director with both the vision to see where the College was going and the decisiveness to ensure that it reached its destination.

THE ACADEMIC CHARACTER OF THE COLLEGE

Outline planning began before its official designation in September 1976 and the fundamental question was what would be the nature of the new College, resolution of which would enable many others to be addressed. In establishing previous reforms of the system of higher education, governments had given a very clear indication of the nature of new institutions, first, in the case of the Colleges of Advanced Technology in 1956 and second, in the Polytechnics a decade later. However, the reforms of 1974-76 were more concerned with the expansion of the national system of higher education and the development of a larger and more flexible public sector, based largely on the diversification of the former Colleges of Education, than with the creation of particular types of institutions. The DES appears to have envisaged the concentration of higher education into larger urban units on the one had, thus implying mergers between Polytechnics and some Colleges of Education, and on the other the downgrading of Colleges of Education to further education, concentrating perhaps on the new two-year Diploma of Higher Education proposed by the *James Report* of 1972. Occasional glimpses of ministerial views could be discerned, as in the case of the Minister of State for Higher Education, Gordon Oakes, who, when officially opening the College in 1978, underlined its comprehensive nature, its local significance and its partnership with industry as means of preventing academic drift (G.Oakes, speech at Opening of HCHE, 19.3.1978). However, these often amounted to little more than post-hoc rationalisations, and most colleges were left to determine their own future within the parameters set by national controls of courses and finance.

As a new sector emerged, sometimes described as a third force in higher education, its chief characteristic was its diversity as every institution seized the opportunity to negotiate its own future with its maintaining authority, municipal or voluntary, and with the Department of Education and Science. The LEA took the initiative in determining the character of Hull College of Higher Education by providing a brief to develop advanced education at undergraduate and higher technical level in the locality and the region, thus requiring a development plan which would convert the brief into reality and would set the tone and establish the character of the new College. Setting itself firmly in the tradition of the polytechnics, a status to which both Authority and College aspired, Hull College of Higher Education saw itself as the major public sector institution in the region, comprehensive in character with courses at all levels from craft to postgraduate but with an emphasis on advanced courses to meet the needs of industry, commerce, and the professions in the county and beyond. At its inception, Hull was one of the largest and most comprehensive of the sixteen new, polytechnic-type colleges of higher education, with some 4,000 full-time equivalent students studying a wide range of academic areas, at a variety of levels, including 65% on advanced further education courses, and, despite the inherited reduction of teacher training places from 1,200 in 1972 to 480 by 1979, the College made an immediate and major commitment to growth which it hoped to achieve in two phases. The first phase consisted of limited growth to meet the expected national, regional and local student demand, including adult and part-time. Realistically, it focused on a range of courses which built upon existing strengths, utilised spare accommodation and provided a means by which the serious staffing difficulties resulting from the reduction in teacher education could be addressed, (IPC Sub-Committee, HCHC Development Plan, 5.7.1976). In approving the plan, Humberside Education Authority granted a supplementary estimate for validation and development amounting to £149,000 in 1976/77 and £341,000 in a full year, and an agreement to prioritise the necessary building conversions for both Further and Higher Education in the County's plans. (HBEC 8.7.1976, #1481-1483).

The development of an academic programme in the public sector was not merely a matter for College intention, but subject to a range of controls outside of its institutions. A vital tool in the DES armoury for controlling developments in the public sector was the procedure for course approvals which required every college to seek the support of the Regional Advisory Council (RAC) before the Regional Staff Inspector (RSI) advised the Secretary of State on the desirability of approving a particular proposal. A highly significant element of the reform of higher education from 1974 to 1976 was the tightening of the course approvals mechanism through the issue of *Circular 6/74* which encouraged colleges to apply for approval to develop a Diploma in Higher Education. However, proposals needed to be linked to degrees in the same academic areas, and, more importantly, they were to be in areas which were in common with existing or proposed Bachelor of Education courses and capable of being offered without additional staffing. RACs were creatures of the local authorities whom they existed to advise and their deliberations could be affected as much by the competition between local authorities and other Regional Colleges as by educational considerations, but the Yorkshire and Humberside RAC gave firm support to the College's strategy. Immediate approval was obtained for new degree courses in Business Studies, Combined Studies, Environmental Studies, Law, and Social Studies, and a Diploma of Higher Education, and these were augmented within a year by further support for a full-time degree in Architecture, a part-time degree in Education for serving teachers, Certificates in Social Service and Social Work, and a postgraduate Diploma in Schools Counselling (IPC 3.12.1975). National confidence in the College's potential was confirmed by RSI and DES approval which would enable it to move towards its target population of 5,100 by 1982/83, a figure which represented 27.6% growth on 1976.

The immediate results of this strategy can be seen in the commencement of new courses in areas where resources were adequate for first phase development, namely Business Studies, Humanities, Social Studies, Teacher Education and Architecture. Initial approvals were gained and courses started in 1977 for a BA in Business Studies, the new Diploma in Higher Education (DHE) and the Certificate of Qualification in Social Work; approval in principle was also given for a two-year year, post-DHE B.Ed degree. The new courses were located in buildings vacated by the reduction in initial teacher training, and staff similarly displaced were also absorbed as far as possible, but the success was achieved on a slender resource base. The second phase was more ambitious in that it anticipated work in Design Studies and new advanced work in Maritime & Engineering Studies. All would require staff, accommodation and equipment, and key staff would be in Maritime and Engineering Studies, also vital if the potential for growth in phase one Administration and Management Studies was to be realised. Despite these anticipated limitations on future growth, by the time of the official opening in March 1978, the Director was able to claim, with some justification, that the initial response to the Local Authority's brief had been successful, with the introduction of full-time and part-time degrees, the establishment of short course and conference work, and a commitment to community education (J.M.Stoddart, speech at Official Opening of HCHE 19.3.1978).

During the reorganisation of further and higher education in the city, the LEA had been anxious to make provision for both sectors with some favouring their location in one institution. However, the eventual decision to establish both Further and Higher Education Colleges required an appropriate division of work between the two. At first sight, this might appear a relatively simple task based on national categories of levels of work, but the strongly-held opinion that both non-advanced and advanced work in nautical education should be integrated within one institution ensured a degree of collaboration between the Further and Higher Education Colleges. Thus, the IPC established an Academic Liaison Committee, consisting of seven from each institution, to promote close links between the two which was expected to lead to the 'optimal utilisation of physical and staff resources towards a comprehensive educational policy within the county and within the region.' In practical terms, this meant providing opportunities to comment on course development in each institution, the possibility of initiating courses of mutual interest and detailed consultation on the development of work with the Business and Technician Education Councils (IPC 11.11.1976, #11). However, the spirit of co-operation envisaged by the IPC proved elusive and a Working Party had to be established in 1978 to consider specific course and staff transfers, (GCP 16.10.1978, #6.2) The result of the Working Party's deliberations was the transfer of particular non-advanced courses and some staff from higher to further education, phased over several years, in Construction and Building, Electrical and Mechanical Engineering, Motor Vehicle related courses, and Science. The Working Party also urged both colleges to find ways of achieving closer and more effective links, though greater co-operation had to await the introduction of a Foundation Course in 1981 and the franchising of AFE work to the College of Further Education in the 1990s. (HBFE Sub., 5.7.1978, #2458; 15.11.1978, #2583).

To an extent, initial outline planning in the College in 1975/76 was driven by the urgency to establish the new institution rather than by a longer-term evaluation of the situation; the latter had to wait whilst the immediate issues arising from the merger were attended to. However, within a couple of years the College was able to undertake a more detailed and systematic appraisal of its position and its future. Planning took place within national, regional and local contexts which had to be balanced against each other with care. By 1978 the national context was characterised by uncertainty both politically and educationally. The Labour government was dependent on an understanding with the Liberals to preserve its parliamentary majority in the House of Commons and found its position totally undermined by the 1978/79 'winter of discontent' in which confrontations with public sector workers led ultimately to its defeat in the 1979 General Election. The implications for higher education arising from a change of government were unclear, but it seemed likely that the new government would continue its predecessor's intention to seek greater central control over higher education funding and greater management effectiveness in the public sector colleges and polytechnics. Furthermore, the new Conservative Government intended to reduce public expenditure on all fronts, and that could only mean less funding for public sector higher education.

Regional planning took place within the framework of national policy which had indicated a major growth in the public sector from 1972 to 1981 and which would continue into the 1990s (DES, 1978). The Yorkshire and Humberside Council for Further Education (YHCFE) encouraged individual colleges to plan on a rational and institutional basis rather than as ad hoc infill to cope with the decline of teacher education, and urged them to seek an appropriate balance between full-time and part-time courses, all of which ought to be of an acknowledged vocational nature. There is no doubt that the College's initial proposals fell within these broad parameters, and YHCFE acceptance of the College's attempt to set itself firmly in the context of the Yorkshire polytechnics, and its recognition of the county's need, as a development area, for a major higher education centre gave considerable heart to the College. However, the College was not committed exclusively to the region, having national and even international aspirations to balance its regional mission (*YHCFE Higher Education Committee Memorandum on Regional Planning*; A.Fieldsend to Principals, 21.3.1978 q.v. GCP&D .5.1978, # 3.1).

Planning also takes place with a local framework, and limited research showed that the College needed a greater understanding of the overall economic, industrial, commercial and educational trends on Humberside. Much of the material was available though it required considerable teasing out. Lines of communication with industry were less developed than they might have been, and a number of academic areas contained considerable economic potential for the College. In addition, the emergence of the city as a Gateway to Europe offered the opportunity to carve out a nationally important position in marine transport; fishing; management and engineering (Crampton 1981).

Against this background, the College set out its corporate philosophy in a 1978 Statement of Intent which identified its mission 'to develop .. a comprehensive educational community appropriate to a changing society,' a direct continuation of the overall objective established by the LEA in 1976. In terms of standard programmes, this meant the development of a balanced and broadly-based, flexible portfolio with internal transfer between courses, the encouragement of deferred entry, and the creation of variable modes of attendance and levels of study. Academic development would focus on courses rather than subjects and be guided by a number of principles. Courses must meet student need and be efficient; they should have central aims and objectives which would make a positive contribution to industrialised society; they should be college-based and have access to all expertise whatever the organisation of the college; and they should encourage students' independent learning. There was to be a commitment to local and regional industry, the professions and the trades unions, but also

Table 6.1   Student Numbers in Hull College of Higher Education

Year	Total Student Numbers	FTE Students
1976/77	6,286	4,814
1977/78	6,056	4,648
1978/79	4,811	4,490
1979/80	N/A	N/A
1980/81	N/A	N/A
1981/82	6,880	N/A

Source: Reports to Governing Council

a national and international dimension to its work. All of this would require considerable staff development, some of which would involve local industry, but the plan contained signs of convergence towards the polytechnics' argument that they were essentially national rather than local/regional institutions, and this trend was to be emphasised during the 1980s. Also, as the 1970s came to a close, it was becoming clear that central government funding of public sector higher education was likely to be controlled, and this would impose severe constraints on any development plans and require all colleges to plan realistically.

Accurate series covering student numbers for the early years of Hull College of Higher Education are problematic. However, as Table 6.1 indicates, overall student numbers declined during the early years of the College, partly due to the substantial reductions in teacher education and partly because of the transfer of courses to the College of Further Education. Nonetheless, it was anticipated that the built-in growth which would accrue from the introduction of new courses would stabilise overall student numbers, and the initial academic experience of the College could be viewed in a favourable light.

THE PROVISION OF HIGHER EDUCATION FOR THE REGION

One of the justifications for the creation of a major, unitary institution in the city had been to improve the provision of higher education opportunities in the region. Yet the College's initial experience in this respect was mixed. As the previous paragraphs indicate, it enjoyed considerable success in rapidly establishing a major centre of higher education in Humberside, thus providing new educational opportunities for local and regional students, but not all of its initiatives met with the same degree of success.

The first major opportunity to demonstrate its commitment to the region occurred during the formative period of the College in maritime and nautical education, an area traditionally at the heart of the region's economy and one in which it sought to develop a national reputation. Nautical education was the subject of an HMI report on *The Provision of Vocational Nautical Courses on Humberside* in 1975, though the lack of an agreed policy for the future development of nautical courses in the county led to limited advice on the development of advanced courses, the provision of equipment and the better utilisation of existing resources. However, in addition to serving the needs of local and regional industry, an opportunity existed to develop a centre of excellence in Marine Science & Technology and Fishing, a point made by the Minister of State for Higher Education, Gordon Oakes, at the official opening of the College on 19 March, 1978, but the Authority, in collaboration with its Colleges needed to take the initiative. At the heart of the problem was the relationship between North and South Bank development and, in particular, the traditional rivalry between Hull and Grimsby, and it is arguable that it was the failure to resolve this issue which led to the eventual loss of nautical and maritime courses in Humberside.

The crucial issue was the consolidation and location of non-advanced work between the two centres which would provide a springboard for the development of advanced courses but which would require substantial investment in at least one centre. Hull College proposed that a Fisheries Studies Centre, to operate on the Regional Management Centre model, should be set up within the College, operating within the Instrument and Articles of the College under a Policy Committee appointed by the Governing Council and representing the industry and educational/research institutions; initially, it would be supported by the College which would control its estimates and finance, but eventually it would become self-supporting (GP&F 21.11.1977). In contrast, the Local Authority produced a compromise proposal which would have retained a serious Grimsby involvement in this work. There would be a new and independent Humberside Centre for Fisheries Education to maintain present interest in fisheries and food studies, develop further courses locally, nationally and internationally, and promote related research and consultancy. The Centre would have its own Governing Council and Academic Board, and a full-time Director of Centre who would be assisted by two others, possibly seconded for up to years from the Hull and Grimsby Colleges, and its remit would include advising the Authority 'on the desirability of combining of rationalising courses in Humberside and on the suitable location for courses.' However, financially the new Centre would not be independent; it would receive no additional resources since its initial costs would be absorbed within the budgets of the existing Hull and Grimsby Colleges and it was expected to become self-financing eventually. (GCP 8.5.1977, #9).

The Authority's proposal was clearly an uneasy compromise, designed to take account of South Bank sensitivities, and the Centre's ability to fulfil its wide-ranging mission would have been undermined if, as seemed possible, it was also expected to act as a forum for settling local disputes between the Colleges. Sadly for the region, both Colleges continued to jockey for position. Neither was willing to yield to the other, and, sadly for the region, the opportunity to develop a national and perhaps international centre of excellence was missed. Three years later, the Local Authority agreed to be involved in the establishment of a National Fisheries Education Centre with Devon and Suffolk County Councils, and allocated £12,000 to the secretariat. (HBEC 17.9.1980, #3398). Also, a bid was being made to the EEC for £225,000 over five years to support the Centre (EC 11.3.1981, #3581), though it was not established.

Until the foundation of Hull College of Higher Education in 1976, the vast majority of the advanced further education in the city took the form of teacher training in the two former Colleges of Education. The reduction from 1,400 to 600 students in training associated with the reforms of 1974-76 were taken even further to 450 by 1979 caused Humberside Education Authority, in common with many others throughout the country, to make strenuous but unavailing protests to the DES, largely on the grounds that, since it recruited large numbers of its new staff from the two former Colleges of Education, primary and secondary education provision in the city and the county would be severely hit. However, the DES, strongly committed to a wholly numerical approach to higher education planning which involved a major reduction in teacher education, ignored all protests, and morale amongst the former College of Education staff in the new College was badly affected. Nonetheless, the new College was able to absorb many former teacher trainers into its wider academic structures, and radically reform its pattern of teacher education along the lines proposed by the 1972 James Report by introducing a consecutive model of training. The basis of the structure was the new two-year, general Diploma of Higher Education which allowed students to defer their choice of outlet until the second year of their course but which provided a satisfactory academic base for those who, from the outset, intended to train as teachers; those who did not were able to transfer, without loss of time, into degrees in Business Studies, Combined Studies and Applied Social Studies. Students who wished to train for teaching moved onto two years of specialist education training which required staff in that area to develop a totally new primary education degree to which an option in special needs was soon added. Throughout its existence in both Hull and later in Grimsby, the Diploma proved to be an attractive course for mature students seeking higher education, and offered a major opportunity to the region.

The College was also active in the area of wider professional training, thus seeking to fulfil one of its important regional objectives, by participating in a Local Collaborative Project (LCP) funded by DES and the Manpower Services Commission under the Professional Retraining Scheme (PICKUP) to investigate the ways in which all institutions of further and higher education could improve their response to regional adult training needs. The project recommended a Humberside Training Consortium to support the commercial and industrial development of the regional economy which was established by using Humberside County Council's PICKUP funding to support a director and seconded staff from the founder institutions to which the College provided two secondees equivalent to 0.4 FTE. (GCP 14.10.1985, #9). Specific management training in the region was handled through the Regional Management Centre based at Sheffield City Polytechnic, and there was a view that the sub-region of Humberside, which had minimal representation on the Centre committee, had been consistently neglected. Therefore, the College, with strong support from Grimsby and North Lindsey Colleges, set up the Humberside Management Centre from 1

January 1982 to enhance sub-regional education and training. (GCP 26.10.1981, #7.3)

The College was also mindful of its wider responsibility to the region, and, in 1978, created a School of Humanities and Community Education as part of an academic reorganisation with a remit to bring the College to the community. This was developed in 1981 by the establishment of a Unit, separate from but responsible to the School of Humanities and Community Education, to give a college-wide thrust to its work. Several initiatives were taken, including the introduction of an open lecture series; summer schools for American students; educational visits; and the continuation of work in community arts and broadcasting. However, with the progressive development of more advanced work in the College under the impact of government policies which contained disincentives for community education, much of this work eventually disappeared, although the Community Education Workshop did receive a new lease of life with Manpower Services Commission support for several years in the mid-eighties.

Two initiatives linking the College to its local community proved more resilient. In 1980, the School encouraged the establishment of a Foundation Course in the College of Further Education which was designed to provide opportunities for adult students with a second chance. Recognising that much potential existed amongst adults who had never had the opportunity to enter higher education at the traditional age, the Foundation Course provided them with the chance to sample study with a view to moving onto higher education, and particularly to the Diploma of Higher Education which had always held a particular appeal for mature students (GC 26.10.1981, #7.4). The venture was so successful that the Community Education Unit was able to encourage its adoption in all other Further Education Colleges in the county and one beyond, with the result that many mature students were able to confront the challenge of higher education with confidence and hope of success. Another successful venture was the establishment of a Local History Archive Unit which, with Manpower Services Commission support, was able to produce numerous documentary collections on the region's history were useful in schools, libraries and the College itself. In the mid-eighties, this work was transferred to the College of Further Education.

114

THE ACADEMIC CHALLENGE: VALIDATION AND THE CULTURE OF THE COLLEGE

One of the frustrations of course development was the long lead-time required for a course to move from germination to presentation to students. A major factor in development was the existence of academic control in public sector higher education through the requirement to obtain academic validation and, where necessary, professional recognition for the programmes which it wished to offer. Even before the creation of the College was agreed locally and approved nationally, the new LEA was compelled to confront a professional recognition problem in the School of Architecture in the Regional College of Art which, had it been unanswered, could have deprived the nascent College and the county of advanced level work in this important professional area. In the event, the crisis provided an opportunity for the LEA to demonstrate its strong support for the maintenance of AFE work in the county.

A visit by the Royal Institute of British Architects (RIBA) in 1973/74, which gave professional recognition to the work of the School, led to a report so devastating that the Authority felt obliged to announce its wholehearted support for the course, its determination to allocate whatever resources were necessary, and its willingness to take whatever emergency measures were necessary to guarantee the survival of the School. (HBFE Sub., 6.3 1974, #133; 11.4.1974, #183). The 1974/75 intake of students was deferred, the proposed move from Brunswick Avenue to Anlaby Road was postponed, and a full-time temporary consultant Head of School was appointed, charged with producing a report on the School's future; four administrators and technician were appointed and £150,000 committed to building works over the next two years, and DES approval was eventually given for £60,000 to be included in the 1975/76 building programme. The LEA's prompt action, reported to the RIBA in November, resulted in the grant of a two-year approval from the professional body and the re-introduction of student intakes in 1975/76 (HBEC 7.6.1974, #292; HBFE Sub., 17.10.1974, #441; HBEC 30.1.1975, #627; 3.1975, #711).

The Consultant Head, Michael Lloyd, produced a damning report, which was in complete agreement with recent RIBA criticisms, yet envisaged a rosy future for the School. Because of

115

long-term neglect, indicated by academic staffing being 30%
under establishment, administrative staffing almost non-existent,
a resultant absence of academic records in a school which examined
by coursework, inadequate buildings and impoverished facilities,
morale was very low and student numbers were inadequate for
a viable operation. Despite this, there was a strong possibility of
successful development with suitable investment, but the School
needed to 'discover its own identity, both for its own morale and
for its ability to make a national contribution to be a centre of
attraction to people of outstanding ability.' With its use of work
bases and some concentration on local problems, such as the
Selby coalfield and the Hull docks and town development, the
potential to develop a unique School existed (Report of M.Lloyd
to HBFE Sub, 17.10.1975). Obviously, the Authority's support
for the School was effective, and a subsequent visit by RIBA in
the Spring of 1976 led to approval for the standard five-year period
(HBFE Sub., 10.6.1976, #1438)

Following this rather bleak omen, the College addressed the issue
of academic validation. Prior to the merger, the separate colleges in
the city had been involved, principally in teacher education, with
courses validated at certificate and degree level by the local university, or in further education where qualifications were awarded by
a range of external and professional bodies as appropriate. In both
cases, a good deal of the responsibility for academic organisation
and administration rested with the validating or awarding bodies,
and in the former a close and detailed relationship existed at subject
level between college and university. Therefore, for many staff in
the new Hull College of Higher Education, accustomed to working
in monotechnic institutions, absorption into a polytechnic-style
college amounted to a culture shock. For some, it was dominated
by the transfer from local university control to the more brac-
ing environment of the Council for National Academic Awards
(CNAA); for others, it was the challenge of moving from lower to
higher level work, whether it was from non-advanced to advanced
or from diploma to undergraduate and postgraduate work, with its
demands for teaching, research and consultancy. For all, it was the
challenge of working and competing in a diversified College with its
requirement of a wider sense of collegiality than before.

Central to the College's initial foray into the broad higher
education arena was the support of a validating body, and it

was decided at the outset that its degree-level work would seek approval from the CNAA, though such a move was not without its critics nationally and in the institution where old loyalties to the University of Hull remained strong, especially amongst staff from the former Colleges of Education. Nationally, the Council suffered some criticism in the mid-1970s for an apparent severity towards new course proposals from ex-Colleges of Education in comparison to the validation offered by Universities, whose rate of approval of diversified courses was higher than that of the Council. Problems experienced by the Council included Colleges' lack of experience of both corporate and academic planning which led to complex and over-ambitious proposals; uncertainty that Colleges would be able to exercise appropriate supervision of courses and academic standards without the continuing local control exercised by previous university validation; the unsuitability of some staff for B.A. work and the small scale of some academic departments compared to the range of work proposed; and the complexities of combining integrated B.Ed degrees with B.A. schemes. The Council's own suggestions for dealing with these problems, unpalatable to staff in many former Colleges of Education, focused on the need to develop their own self-critical arrangements, including the improvement of internal course development and validation procedures to produce better matching of courses with staff, and a recommendation that colleges concentrate on Diploma of Higher Education and degree courses in the first instance, after which they might move to Honours degrees in the light of their experience (Diversification in the Former Colleges of Education CNAA q.v. GCP 23.5.1977, #7). Therefore, the College's plan to seek general CNAA validation for its degree courses presented staff with the major challenge of transforming it from a further education and/or teacher training emphasis to a broad, higher education context. Implicit in this was the creation of an internal organisation with considerable autonomy and wider responsibility for its own affairs without detailed external scrutiny once course approvals had been obtained; the acceptance of a greater responsibility for its own academic development within the local and national planning and funding frameworks; a realistic appraisal of its institutional strengths and weaknesses, the threats posed by its competitors and possibly its funding, and the opportunities available both regionally and nationally; the development of a range of central services, particularly in the area of institutional academic planning and administration; and the pursuit of a different balance of course provision in the face of initial teacher training reductions were all to be addressed (GCP 8.3.1977, #3).

CNAA approval was given at institutional and subsequently at individual course level. The former requirement was that a College be approved as a suitable centre to offer courses leading to the Council's awards, and this was achieved, for an initial period of two years, through the medium of an officers' visit on 19 October 1976, though it was clear from the report that much work needed to be done. The Council recognised the support given by the LEA, particularly in terms of library and staff development, which it hoped would continue, and noted the need for retrained and additional well-qualified staff, including a student counsellor, if the initial ambitious programme of course development was to be realised. It also urged that computing facilities across the College and student facilities at the Queen's Garden site be improved as quickly as possible. Given that the College was required to report to Council the progress made by December 1978 on academic structures, academic and estate development, the formation of policies for research and staff development, staff appointment procedures, and a development plan for library, learning resources and computer services, it is clear that the Council's initial approval represented a considerable act of faith in the ability of both the College and the LEA to provide the structures and resources necessary to fulfil its ambitious development plans. It is a measure of the combined efforts of staff and local authority officers and members that the required report resulted in an extension of institutional approval to 1981 (CNAA Officers Report 19 October 1976, GCP 8.3.1977, #8).

The first external commentary on the College' development came with a major institutional review by the CNAA on 25 November 1981. By that time, the College was able to argue that there had been a major achievement in Hull, exemplified by a period of rapid and widespread course development at advanced level, the development of a single institutional identity, and the creation of an institute of advanced learning, chiefly through a transformation of staff attitudes. Its academic development had three main characteristics. First, its courses were vocationally-oriented courses in business, science and social science on the one hand, the latter including opening up new areas such as Secretarial Studies, Fishery Studies and European Business Studies; second, a substantial programme of diversification had been undertaken in both arts and in-service education courses; and third, there had been only limited developments in science and engineering areas, areas which were notoriously unpopular with students nationally. Another important development was the move away from the aspiration of some initial campaigners for a comprehensive post-school provision of higher and further education college in the county, marked by the transfer of lower level work to the College of Further Education, a process which had been accelerated by some course closures in fisheries, nautical catering, music and secretarial courses consequent on local budgetary problems.

However, there were problems resulting principally from the pace of academic development. Whilst progress had been made in the library, in the development of its own computing facilities, and in the creation of suitable science and engineering laboratories through building adaptations, more needed to be done in all of these areas, particularly with respect to the better co-ordination of learning resources between the library and faculties. Furthermore, progress in research and more broadly-based staff development inevitably had suffered during the period of intensive course development necessary to establish the institution, and it was essential that the College made efforts to underpin the twenty-two undergraduate courses. The strong support of the Local Authority had been vital in this initial period, and it was vital for this to continue, particularly in area of capital expenditure, if its potential for becoming a regional rather than a local provider was to be fulfilled. (GCP 26.10.1981, #10.1)

The Council visit was successful with a five-year approval being given and support given for the College's intention to expand provison south of the Humber, though the Chief Officer noted that the Local Authority might be unable to continue to 'current generous support' in view of the changing national situation. (E.Kerr to J.M.Stoddart, 22.4.1982). The College's procedures for the maintenance of academic standards were commended though the Council reserved judgement on their long-term effectiveness, but research activity considered to be too limited (GCP 10.5.1982, #3.2).

STAFFING

The most important component of any development plan are the staff who have to implement it, and, in this respect, the new College had serious problems. Not only did it have to contend with the natural human inclination to avoid change, particularly when painful, and with an understandable loyalty to former institutions, but it also had to handle with sensitivity a staff from the disparate institutions whose recent experience had been discouraging. Kingston-upon-Hull College of Education had entered the merger unwillingly and both former Colleges of Education were demoralised by the massive cuts which had been imposed by central government on its teacher training quotas. The College of Technology had seen its limited advanced level work dribble away after 1966. The Regional College of Art was fearful for its recently-acquired CNAA degrees in Art and Design and the future of the School of Architecture seemed uncertain. The Nautical College required major staff development work if its pre-1976 ambitions for the development of advanced work were to be realised.

Central to the development of any institution, and particularly a new one, is the energy to confront challenges and a vision of the future. With that in mind, and conscious of the need to forge a sense of unity and loyalty to the new college, staff, students and courses were organised into five multi-disciplinary faculties, four of which - Administrative and Management Studies, Design Studies, Maritime and Engineering Studies, and Teacher Education and Applied Social Studies – absorbed the work of the individual colleges which composed the merger. A fifth – Combined Studies – consisting of science staff from advanced courses in Hull College of Technology plus some staff from the former Colleges of Education was to be the engine of new course development in the College. Each Faculty, with its component Schools and matrix of subject units to co-ordinate teaching and research activities, was located on a specific site all of which had been inherited from the previously separate colleges, though it was recognised that there would probably be considerable movement of staff and courses between sites as development occurred. However, in order to provide the necessary infrastructure for the plan to succeed, significant development was needed to enable the

College to support advanced level work. However, to underline the essential unity of the College, any physical development had to take place within a single comprehensive scheme. The principal developments were to be accommodated at Inglemire Avenue where major building works were required for specialist science, language and secretarial accommodation. In the medium term, a library and a teaching block were required at Queen's Gardens, and a significant student communal provision would have to be made within the six-year period. A decision was made immediately to maintain and improve the Brunswick Avenue site for Architecture and the development of civil engineering and building, and it was anticipated that there would be no attempt to relocate this work to Queen's Gardens during the first ten years of life.

The College compared favourably with other major institutions in terms of its staff-student ratio for academics (1:9.3 compared to 1:7 in polytechnics) and unfavourably in support staff, but set itself a target SSR of 10:1 for 1982/83, thereby intending to increase its efficiency. However, the principal need was for flexibility in both academic and support staffing, particularly in the areas of library, computing and languages, and it was decided that not less than 3% of the annual staffing budget should be set aside for staff development through secondment, short courses and conferences. The major needs in terms of additional academic staff, a sensitive matter in a context of job insecurity, were in Administrative and Management Studies which required £20,000 to support course developments, and in Maritime and Engineering Studies which had relied heavily on part-time staff and overtime by full-time staff. However, the most urgent element of the staffing problem in the new College was the diversification or reorientation of staff from the two former Colleges of Education consequent on the major reductions in teacher education. Thus, the IPC, supported by the local authority and in discussion with the professional associations, sought to adopt a speedy and sympathetic attitude to the problem. The basis of the College's approach was the opportunity for redeployment, with any necessary retraining, preferably in the College but also in the LEA where possible, and only in the last resort would staff be made redundant, In that event, the more generous compensation terms, known as the Crombie Code, were available.[2]

The overall impact of the development plan was for more rather than fewer staff, albeit in different subjects and with different emphases. Therefore, if involuntary redundancies were to be avoided, a major programme of staff development would be required from 1976-80, facilitated by a unit dedicated to that end. Some internal re-training was undertaken, and around ten staff for each of the next three years were seconded for postgraduate study or to obtain necessary experience in industry, commerce and the public service (IPC 11.11.1976, #12). Parallel to this retraining effort was the provision of opportunities to former teacher education staff to create their own futures in the College. Many redeployed staff were placed in a new Faculty of Combined Studies where specialists in the Humanities and the Sciences were encouraged to develop new diversified courses. Essentially a temporary device to provide diversification opportunities, the implicit threat of excision proved a great motivator, and the successful development of a free-standing Diploma of Higher Education, and subsequent related degrees, led to the Faculty's dismemberment into a number of Schools within two years. However, the opportunities for redeployment were not unlimited, though some staff whose subjects faced severe contraction were provided with opportunities to teach their subjects in other faculties. A number were located in Applied Social Science and a few were absorbed by the Faculty of Art and Design, though there were few opportunities there since that area of work was not expected to expand. The major impact of the cuts in teacher training fell on Education which required eight or nine fewer specialists in the new College. In addition, there were a number of staff whose subjects would be unlikely to be taught as major subjects in their own right in the new College, such as Archaeology and the Performing Arts. Others, such as Music, were unlikely to develop at AFE level outside of the reduced teacher education programmes. In all of these areas, redundancies were inevitable and, in the event, fourteen staff accepted compensation under the Crombie Code.[2] In 1978/79 the decline in teacher education numbers exceeded the build-up of new numbers, and the College put in place a process whereby staff could indicate their willingness and the College determine their ability to teach on other courses with or without retraining, and the declaration of redundancy for any who may be unable to be so absorbed (IPC 20.1.1977, #15).

Obviously, the College had to balance the needs of existing

courses and the expected academic development with the professional interests of staff, and the need to work within approved
revenue estimates. Staff were invited to indicate the faculties/de-
partments/areas of work in which they were interested, with a
so-called 'pencilling-in' process used by senior management where
appropriate, and interviews in other cases. There was a phased
publication of appointments by grade, and all work was completed by 19 March, 1976 (IPC 29.1976) to enable an interim
Academic Board to be established (IPC, 2.4.1976). Additionally,
IPC accepted that there would have to be a small number of
external appointments to introduce new blood and to supply staff
for new developments which could not be covered from existing
resources, and nine such appointments were made during the
first three months of 1976. The establishment of each faculty
was quickly agreed on the basis of existing SSRs in the Colleges
of Education, though it was recognised that the College would have
to move closer to national norms. (IPC 2.4.1976)

FINANCE: THE LOCAL AUTHORITY DIMENSION

Funding for higher education in the public sector was divided into
three major categories, all theoretically under the control of the
LEA. The normal running costs of the new College, its revenue
income, came from two principal sources. Advanced level work
was supported by central government via the AFE Pool, and NAFE
work was funded by the LEA from the rates. In addition, the Local
Authority, at its own discretion, could make additional revenue
grants to the College in order to support particular initiatives or
to increase the amount provided by central government; this latter
element, known as 'topping-up' became increasingly important,
particularly after the capping of the pool in 1980. The other
two major items within the College budget concerned buildings.
The first was known as minor works, for the maintenance and
adaptation of premises, and covered expenditure up to £2,500.
In common with most institutions, the amounts required by the
College were always greater than that which the Local Authority
could find, but the opportunity existed for the Authority to allow
the College to vire money within major budget heads, and this
device enabled the College to make many vital alterations to its

premises which would otherwise have hindered its development. The second item in the budget was capital for major building and developments on items over £10,000 which required central government approval and which had to come from the allocation made to the Local Authority for all its needs. Again, the College's requests regularly outstripped the ability of the Local Authority, providing a constant problem for the College. This was the only serious point of difference between it and the LEA, and the shortage of capital funding threw even greater strains on the adaptation of premises through minor works development which, in turn, were only able to be funded by virement from other budgetary heads, notably staffing.

Although it had to operate within the constraints of national expenditure patterns and despite the substantial financial implications of the initial plan, the LEA offered considerable and consistent support for the College's aim of becoming a major centre of AFE in Yorkshire and Humberside alongside the three polytechnics in South and West Yorkshire. The approximate revenue estimate for 1976/77, derived from the previous independent colleges, was £3.362 millions, with a further £257,000 in 1976/77 for academic developments, and an additional £70,000 in minor works for immediate building adaptations to facilitate the phased transfer of staff and students; by the end of the six-year planning period it was estimated that the annual revenue budget would reach £4.401 millions (IPC, 19.7.1976, #5). At the level of revenue, the County Council was very supportive, approving both the supplementary estimate of £75,000, and the cost of additional courses being included in the next estimates which meant £212,00 in a full year, though it was careful to stipulate the condition that the cost would be met by virement from the AFE Pool (IPC, 30.9.1976, #5). Within the financial plans, particular attention was given to the library budget which needed to be £120,000 p.a. for the subsequent three years in order to meet the demands of new degree programmes, particularly since the combined stock in 1976 was over 50% oriented towards teacher education due to decline from its initial 30% to 12% of the College's work, and the weakness of the bookstock in those areas in which the College wished to expand. In the area of equipment, needs were identified at £270,000 in 1976/77 and a further £200,000 p.a. for the next few years. In all of these areas, the Authority was as supportive as possible, though equipment estimates continued to race ahead of supply.

At the level of minor works for adaptation of premises, initially the Authority were very generous, recognising that there was a cost implied in its wish to develop a major centre for higher education. However, the College's requirement of £28,000 for minor works in 1977/78 and at least the same amount per annum for the foreseeable future, soon outstripped the Authority's ability to meet the need, and its provision of £8,000 meant that the balance had to be vired from College budgets. This set a pattern which was to be repeated throughout the Authority's stewardship of the College, though the Authority was very supportive of the College's wish to vire money from other budget heads into premises, so as to carry out vital alterations to its plant, even when it came from the staffing head resulting, on occasions, in the loss of courses and staff. Perhaps less acceptable to the College was the delay in other specialist conversions to its premises because of a shortage of design and development staff in the County Architect's department.

In the area of capital expenditure there was greater difficulty, and this created the most serious problems between the College and the LEA, though it was often the result of the latter's inability to obtain sufficient capital funds from central government to meet all its needs, with the subsequent prioritisation of projects across all sectors of the LEA's responsibilities. At the outset, the DES indicated that there was little likelihood of much capital money available in the next few years which meant that new buildings would not appear, major conversions (£50,000+) remained unlikely and the main burden would fall on minor adaptations and improvements. This made the situation particularly acute at Queen's Gardens, identified as a problem by the CNAA officers' visit, where a major building programme of c.£2.6 millions was needed, though conversions of the Cottingham Road Site library (£95,000) and Science (£200,000) had begun. In common with all local authorities, Humberside's allocation of capital continued to be paltry, and many important programmes had to be shelved. Thus in 1979, the proposed warehouse conversion for an FE/HE library in Queen's Gardens and the conversion of the Cumberbirch hall of residence at Cottingham Road into a conference centre could not proceed. (HBFE Sub, 28.6.1979, #2973).

However, the Local Authority found greater difficulty in responding to the second, technological phase of the College's academic development which was intended to counter its geographical isolation and respond to the needs of existing regional industry. The College's wish to continue its expansion was based on the low share which Humberside had of higher education provision in the region which, at 10%, compared unfavourably with Huddersfield (14%), Leeds (23%) and Sheffield (26%). The Authority's attention was drawn to the economic multiplier provided to Humberside by the College in the form of employment opportunities, including those through expenditure on buildings, the development of a skilled labour force, and total student spending estimated locally at £2.5m. per annum. From the outset, there had been concern over the provison of adequate computing facilities. Initially, the College had used the County Hall computer, but it quickly became apparent that this was inadequate, and after some enhancement at County Hall and much pressure from the College, it was agreed that the College should have a stand-alone computer, subject to any spare capacity being available for county council use; the cost was £120,000 plus annual revenue expenditure rising from £23,600 1978/79 to £138,350 in 1981/82. Other problems were experienced with crucial support staffing needs: thirteen new posts were required in the library costing £45,358 over three years and five in student services spread over three years costing £22,699 plus an additional £13,000. Additional academic requirements of thirty staff in Administrative and Management Studies to capitalise on potential, twelve for new growth in Technology, and twelve research assistants were needed to provide some pump-priming activity in an area which CNAA had found to be weak. Further adaptations to buildings were vital in order to develop Science and Engineering for the benefit of the region (HBEC 23.5.1979, #2886).

In 1979, the new Conservative Government announced its intention to cap the AFE Pool, thus precipitating a three-year period of financial stringency for colleges prior to the establishment of the National Advisory Body (NAB) for planning and funding higher education in England. As an emergency measure to begin to control the escalating funding of higher education at the national level, the incoming Conservative government fixed a £375m. ceiling on the size of the AFE Pool for 1980/81, representing a cut in real terms of c.9% nationally. In addition, its wider public expenditure cuts had a significant impact on Humberside County Council's education budget for 1979/80 which had to find immediate savings of £2.469m. from which the College could not be protected. As a result, the Education Committee required a 3% cut in staffing across the whole education service, and the College was required to implement those savings (HBEC 20.7.1979, #2981).The position became even more serious with the distribution of the capped Pool over the next two years which resulted in further real reductions in revenue and serious problems with capital and minor works allocations. For 1980/81, the Pool was distributed equally across the sector on the basis of 1978/79 student numbers which were the latest which the DES had available. Naturally, this approach failed to take any account of institutions, such as Hull, which had experienced growth since that date or had additional growth built into their development, and led to a reduction of the College's revenue estimates by 2.2% (HBEC 18.12.1980, #3496; 11.1.1981, #3579). In response to the severe criticism from institutions concerning the arbitrary distribution of the capped pool in 1980/81, the DES set up a committee to consider a more equitable way of carrying out the exercise for the subsequent year and to propose a longer term system for 1982/83 when the AFE Pool was capped at £539m. It represented a system-wide reduction of 6.5% differentially calculated at 9% for the polytechnics and 15% for the colleges of higher education.

Allocation in 1981/82 was based upon the concept of 'common funding' which allocated the majority of the Pool based on institutional staff/student ratios, and 'further funding' which provided additional finance for those institutions which had historically high costs which might result from operating on several sites, running centres of excellence, or even poor cost efficiency which, presumably the government was intent on driving out. It concentrated on the distribution of a pre-determined pool by a mechanistic application of a formula which required no educational judgement and took no account of educational considerations. Furthermore, it repeated its penalisation of those institutions which were still growing by its use of a previous year, 1980/81, as the base year for student numbers. However, even more serious for the College was the differential operation of the funding methodology between colleges and polytechnics. In its category, the College was perceived as a high-cost institution, arising from the fact that its work involved a wide range of activity not present in the vast majority of colleges which concentrated on courses in teacher training and the liberal arts. However, when compared with its natural allies, the College was no more expensive to run than the average polytechnic. Disaggregation of Polytechnic and Other Maintained Establishments (OME) funding showed that the College lost £674,000 by not being a polytechnic. A further difficulty was the derisory weighting of 0.15 FTE attached to part-time students which penalised those with substantial students in that category. Eventually, consideration was given to these points and the College received amelioration of £1.214m, and was relieved to learn that the broad category of OMEs would be examined to see if it needed refining. Still, but the significant impact of the allocation was that the College remained heavily reliant on the Local Authority for further support.

The allocation to the College represented a loss of £2.1 million (10.3%) against estimates for that year which was particularly severe on a new institution still experiencing considerable in-built and new course growth. That growth included the very recent approvals to develop degree courses in Engineering and Industrial Food Technology which would match the economic needs of North and South Humberside and create four hundred additional student places between 1980/81 and 1982/83. The actual result was that, for 1982/83, the Pool gave Humberside LEA £5.3 millions against a budget of £8.1 millions, which led to an adoption by the College of the SSRs used in the national allocation. The LEA advised the College to plan its future developments carefully in view of the likely reduction of a further 10% over the next two years, but encouragingly reaffirmed its commitment to the College's development plan (HBEC 7.4.1982, #4002; 24.9.1982, #4200).

Faced with cuts of this magnitude, the College and the Local Authority sought a measured view. The College realised that it was unlikely that the Local Authority, whatever its wishes, would be able to increase and may even have difficulty in maintaining its current level of contribution to the College, and it was inevitable that internal efforts to control costs would have to be made, even if that meant a reassessment of its portfolio and its development plans. In addition to establishing target revenue savings for the coming years, the College proposed to revise its SSR targets upwards to 12:1 by 1984/85, based on a 10-15 band across School, though this would cause problems in some Schools since the target implied an overall loss of 43.6 staff posts. The outlook was even more bleak when consideration was given to the requirement for essential continuing improvements to the library, learning resources, micro-technology and the need to protect the staff development budget if the College was to support and develop its range of undergraduate and postgraduate work (GCP 10.5.1982, #4.2). In the slightly longer-term, the College sought a wider planning framework than purely annual estimates and requested that it be involved at an early stage in the preparation of the Authority's AFE Pool claim, extracting from the Chief Education Officer the admission that 'if the Authority wished the College of Higher Education to sustain a major role in the region and nationally, there might be a need to increase the College's estimates' (EC 19.12.1979, #3121). Initially, however, the Authority failed to provide additional funds to supplement College estimates for 1979/80 and was dilatory in advising the College of the position, thus creating the only occasion when the two appeared at variance with each other.

However, the Authority's re-iteration of its support for the College's development plan led to a number of adjustments to policy and practice designed to assist the College. For 1980/81, revenue estimates were increased by £181,000, a sum which would be met from an increase in the College's short-course and full-cost activity (£85,000) and additional fee income (£95,000), though the Authority stipulated that no commitments were to be made before the money had been secured. Further flexibility was given to the College in the form of relaxation of the clauses in the Instrument and Articles whereby the ceiling on repairs and virement without county council approval was increased to £5,000 and £15,000 respectively; the sum of £24,000 was approved for capital equipment; sympathetic consideration was promised towards further equipment and building adaptation needs; and more generous virement facilities were made available whereby the College was able to transfer £20,000 for building works and £40,000 for equipment from the staffing budget. It further advised the Authority that the period 1980/81 to 1983/84 would require a further virement of £349,000 from the staffing budget which was likely to lead to the closure of some courses (HBFE Sub, 3.7.1980, #3336; HBEC 18.12.1980, #3496; 11.11981, #3579). In 1981/82, the revenue estimates were approved in their entirety, including the relocation of £106,000 from the academic to the non-academic staff heading, and the transfer from the Authority to the College of all responsibility and finance control of staff secondments and associated developments, and further flexibility was granted by the approval to spend any surplus income from net budget activities. A final gesture of support came with an expression of support for the validity of its capital bid for £550,000 over three years and an actual allocation of £170,000 for 1981/82 which compared with an allocation of £240,000 over the total of the previous five years. (GCP 10.5.1982, #3.1)

Chapter 7

Humberside College of Higher Education 1983–1989

INTRODUCTION

The early 1980s proved to be a critical period both for public sector higher education in general and for Hull College of Higher Education in particular. Following the immediate imposition of controls on public expenditure resulting in the capping of the AFE Pool, the search for a mechanism for the improved management of colleges and polytechnics came to fruition with the December 1981 announcement of the establishment of the National Advisory Body (NAB) which began work early in 1982. Although at that time neither its detailed impact nor its methodology could be clear, there was no doubt that increased central control meant retrenchment, consequently all colleges looked forward to a period in which the unit of resource would continue to fall, yet hoped that the squeeze would be enforced with a more logical rationale than had previously applied. For the College, this meant a tricky period in which it would have to continue its development against a much less encouraging funding regime. Locally, the period was marked by a number of developments. First, the conversion of Hull College to Humberside College of Higher Education in 1983 more accurately reflected the local and regional expansion of higher educational provision, but its impact was partly offset by the loss of both maritime and teacher education in the 'eighties. Second, the appointment of a new Director, Dr.J.C.Earls, previously Assistant Principal at Sheffield City Polytechnic, to replace J.M.Stoddart who had been appointed Principal of Sheffield City Polytechnic, coincided with a period which was to be characterised by consolidation rather than growth and by the gradual emergence of a national rather than a regional institution, though the College's polytechnic ambitions continued to be thwarted.

THE NATIONAL FRAMEWORK AND ITS IMPACT ON THE COLLEGE

During the 1970s, several factors combined to ensure greater control over higher education planning and funding. Apart from the apparent lack of control over funding by an open-ended Pool which responded to demand, the emergence in the DES during the 1970s of a purely numerical approach to the planning of higher education foreshadowed greater direction for the system. Furthermore, the belated realisation of the impact of declining birth-rates in the late sixties and the seventies on higher education implied possible decline in some areas and subjects, and experience suggested that this needed to be planned for more effectively than a decade earlier. Finally, the reforms of 1966-76 made the review of planning and funding systems inevitable, though local government reorganisation and the Layfield Committee on local government finance, which reported in 1976, delayed consideration until the late seventies.

By the end of the 1970s, future demand for higher education was predicated on the number of eighteen-year olds in the population through to the 1990s. The trends indicated that the figure would rise from 880,000 in 1976/77 to a peak of 941,000 in 1982/83, decline gently to 855,000 in 1986/87 and then precipitately to 630,000 in 1994/95. In its 1978 publication, *Higher Education into the 1990s. A Discussion Document*, the DES postulated a number of models to deal with the situation, all of which anticipated long-term decline in the demand for higher education even though all projections were based upon an increase in the age-participation rate (APR) from its existing 13.5% to 18.0%. However, the government's approach was based on an elitist view of higher education and its assumptions overlooked the fact that the APR was dominated by students from middle class and professional backgrounds, thereby ignoring the vast pool of students from working class homes which could be targeted for higher education.

Thus, the DES showed no real desire to develop a mass system of higher education which would meet the needs of a more diversified market with a wider variety of courses at various levels and in contrasting modes, primarily because of its fixation with reducing the size of the overall education budget, a concern which became an imperative with the return of a Conservative government in 1979 committed to major reductions in public expenditure.

The main problem was that the existing system was designed to deal with a period of development which had long passed. When the system of planning and funding was established under the RACs and the AFE Pooling Committee between 1946/7 and 1959, AFE provided only a minor part of higher education in Britain. The establishment of a tiered system of Further Education Colleges following the *1956 White Paper* and the creation of the polytechnics a decade later led to the emergence of a regional and proto- national system of AFE in the public sector which required more co-ordination than that which could be obtained through the existing system of local management. Moreover, the operation of the AFE Pooling System was open to criticism, partly because some Local Education Authorities were unhappy with the difference between their contribution and their allocation, but also because there was widespread dissatisfaction with a system which contained little incentive for financial accountability, a point reinforced by the *Layfield Report*. As a result, there was considerable interest in the problem which was addressed both by the Oakes Report, *The Management of Higher Education in the Maintained Sector* (1978), and by the House of Commons Select Committee *Report on the Funding and Organisation of Courses in Higher Education* (1980). Both argued for greater coherence and control in planning AFE, though Oakes assumed that local authorities would continue to have significant power whereas the Select Committee proposed the establishment of a national body which would seek trans-binary co-operation, thus encouraging diversity among institutions within a plural rather than a binary system, ideas which were fulfilled only in the 1990s. The Labour Government promoted a bill enshrining the Oakes proposals, but with its defeat in the 1979 General Election, the bill fell.

During the end of the seventies debate on the best way forward for planning and funding advanced further education, two views of the future emerged – a central solution favoured by the DES in its consultative paper, *Higher Education in England outside the Universities: Policy, Funding and Management A Consultative Paper* (1980) and a local solution proposed by the Council of Local Education Authorities (CLEA) in their hurriedly-prepared response *The Future of Higher Education in the Maintained Sector (1981)* , which sought to strengthen the existing role of local authorities. Although the two papers argued for greater managerial effectiveness, discussed new modes of funding and the scope for the new national body, and considered the value of the regional dimension and transbinary co-operation, they principally reflected the fundamental dilemma of central or local control of AFE. In fact, neither paper sought to provide co-ordinated planning between the two sectors of higher education nor made any provision for regional and sub-regional policy. Progress was slow until the government reshuffle of September 1981 brought Sir Keith Joseph to the Department of Education with William Waldegrave as his Parliamentary Under-Secretary with special responsibility for higher education. Their objectives were twofold. First, they sought some form of trans-binary rationalisation, for which a national body directing the public sector was a pre-requisite. Second, they wished to achieve the primary objective without worsening central/local relations, which meant avoiding any contentious legislation. The resulting compromise was the National Advisory Body for England (NAB). Its principal elements were a Committee and a Board. The former, the senior of the two, was chaired by the Parliamentary Under-Secretary of State for Education, consisted of six local authority representatives and the chair of the Board, and gave advice to the Secretary of State on the distribution of the AFE Pool. Below the Committee was the Board consisting of six members each from the LEAs, the DES and the institutions, together with three others from the TUC, the CNAA and the Business and Technical Education Councils. Aided by subject groups, the Board's main function was to develop detailed plans for the sector. However, although the NAB system appears to have emerged through typical British muddle and compromise, it did reflect a move away from the broad steer which sought to control, through manpower planning, effective and efficient management of the national system, and it did promise a system which was based upon planning rather than historical data.

A government decision in 1982 to reduce the AFE Pool by 10%

in real terms over the next two years ensured that the NAB's task of developing a national plan for the public sector of higher education would be carried out in a negative climate. To enable it to carry out its responsibilities, all institutions offering advanced level work were required to submit development plans with details of student numbers and forward planning to 1984/85 and, significantly, to identify their own areas of priority within their portfolios. This approach ensured that institutions were forced to take a rational view of their future and implied that, for the first time, public sector higher education planning would take place on the basis of future intention rather than previous student numbers, even though it appeared to involve cuts.

In the light of its recent origin and the under-provision of public sector higher education in its sub-region, the College rejected cuts in favour of growth and, in common with a number of other institutions, was unwilling to identify academic priorities because its portfolio was still developing. Regionally, there was an imbalance of provision in Yorkshire and Humberside in favour of the polytechnics in the west of the region which had limited the output of qualified manpower in Humberside which was 75% of the national average, with suitably qualified people going into engineering from Humberside only 50% of the national average. Its different employment structure, with 40% in a wide range of manufacturing and primary sectors and 55% in the service sector, required a balanced provision of higher education. In seeking to establish a major public sector college, with polytechnic characteristics and ambitions to meet regional need, initial development had been based on courses inherited from the colleges which had formed the merger in 1976, thus concentrating growth in Business and Technology and avoiding a major expansion in Humanities work. The most recent and regionally significant development, the enlargement of the College to become Humberside College of Higher Education, had substantially extended work in Technology matching the industrial needs of south Humberside, and the intention to grow to c.750 FTEs on the South Bank meant that planned growth in Hull would be reduced to enable Grimsby to be developed. However, whilst emphasising but seeking not to over-play its regional card, the College drew attention to its wider national and international ambitions, the former already evident in its novel degree courses in Secretarial Studies and

Fishery Studies and the latter by its European Business Studies programme with European partners which was one of the very few joint programmes of its type in the United Kingdom. This lack of clarity, if not contradiction between the regional and the national/international role of the public sector colleges, became more obvious as the 1980s progressed, and was illustrative of the arguments used eventually to justify the removal of local authorities from AFE provison in 1988.

Mindful of the NAB's need to consider some form of trans-binary planning and even rationalisation, the College pointed to its portfolio which was complementary to that of the University of Hull, even to the concentration on primary and middle school initial teacher education and the selection of Postgraduate Certificate of Education options not taught in the University. Indeed, the only overlap, which was small, was in the provision of part-time Humanities and Social Science which had been caused by recent developments in the University. In summary, during the previous six years the College had moved 'from a fragmentary and unbalanced provision of advanced courses to establish a broadly-based portfolio of courses firmly linked to the industrial, economic and social needs of Humberside' (NAB Response p.3). All of the developments had received the support of the CNAA in its recent quinquennial review of the College, and strong backing from Humberside County Council without whose support developments could not have occurred.

However, whatever the justification of its special regional case, the College recognised that it would not gain the full support of the NAB with a plan which emphasised growth only and which failed to respond to the national reduction in funds available for advanced further education work. Therefore, with an appropriate dash of realpolitik, the response noted that the College was 'essentially concerned with the balance between academic priorities and resources against the background of achieving defined and phased reductions in revenue expenditure,' thus choosing the efficiency option rather than a radical approach to strategic planning or portfolio analysis. In approaching this exercise, the College assumed the national 10% reduction in the AFE Pool and discounted any Local Authority top-up in the exercise, but did not propose to take a radical view and excise the work of a whole School or Faculty (GCP 29.11.1982, # 373). Recent cutbacks in targets would enable built-in growth in courses vital to the region's Economic structure, such as Engineering, Food Technology, Fishery Studies, European Business Studies and Higher DATEC, and there were planned reductions totalling £593,000 which would be achieved through the adoption of higher SSRs and through savings in non-staffing costs and increased efficiency (NAB Response p.6). Thus, the main features of the proposal were a small growth in overall numbers with an annual increase in AFE and Non-AFE work, the latter in Nautical, Marine Technology and Engineering; a substantial change in the balance of provision, involving a greater concentration on Engineering, Food Technology, Fisheries and European Business; the development of a 750-strong campus at Grimsby with the necessary transfer of resources and expenditure from Hull; the introduction and development of a College-wide part-time Scheme, and the continuation of all viable part-time courses; and a determination to be more cost-effective, resulting in an overall revenue reduction of £500,000 in 1984/85 and a further £250,000 in 1985/86 by applying internally-agreed SSRs targets and savings in non-staffing expenditure (GCP 14.2.1983, #3).

The first attempt to plan AFE in England on the basis of unit funding did move away from a dependence on historic to target student numbers, but, in the view of a member of the NAB Board, it failed to have any significant influence on the overall system. (Knight 1984). As far as the College was concerned, the initial NAB allocation was for 3338.1 FTE students giving a financial allocation of £6,066,000, representing strong support for the College's development plan and recognising the phase in which the College found itself. During the subsequent three years, various adjustments were made to actual NAB allocations, but, in line with national policy, they resulted in revenue reductions to the College of £600,000 in 1983/84 and £800,000 in 1984/85. In 1985/86, the college's bid for selective growth in programme areas with new courses all relevant to regional economic well-being in computer-aided engineering, applied science, and port and shipping management, was refused, but proposals for an HND in Plant Engineering (Refrigeration and Air Conditioning), an undergraduate degree in information Technology and a postgraduate diploma in food industry management were approved, though any numbers had to be found by internal redistribution of institutional target numbers. The resultant allocation of £6,684,000 represented a

10% increase in NAB funding and further demonstrated the Advisory Body's confidence in and the DES's support for the College's development (GPF 18.10.1984, #228; GCP 21.1995, #6). The overall result of the first NAB planning exercise was that College development was hindered, but its overall objectives remained intact. In the context of the national policy which the NAB was obliged to implement, the College was treated fairly, even sympathetically.

However, there were significant reductions compared to identified requirements and, if the position of the College was to be maintained, there appeared to be little alternative to further topping-up by the Local Authority, though the extent to which the one could continue to depend on the other was debatable. Thus, the College began to take internal steps to ensure that it at least made some contribution to the resolution of its problems. By 1984/85 it was apparent that a longer-term planning framework was required locally, despite the uncertainty of the external climate, and since the College needed to plan for development and change against the background of falling revenue. The major strategy adopted by the College in this climate was to seek continual improvements in student:staff ratios which freed revenue to be vired to other headings where there was a shortfall in allocation, thus availing itself of the flexibility first agreed by the Local Authority in 1981, and a series of planned reductions were put in place. Thus, planned reductions of a little over £1m were achieved and permission was received to vire £115,000 from staffing to other heads of expenditure between 1984/85 and 1986/87. However, such an approach had its limitations, and further reduction in supplies and services budgets and staffing could undermine the College's credibility with its validating and professional accreditation bodies; by 1987/88, the possibility for further estimate reductions on the staffing budget without compulsory redundancies had virtually disappeared. The reductions in the above areas provided revenue which was able to support some of the essential adaptation of premises to support the College's work, but the College was consistently seeking additional support from the Local Authority for these areas, and since expenditure on existing premises was fixed, the closure of annexes had to be considered.

Capital expenditure presented an even more serious problem. In 1984/85, there was a request for £220,000 for new equipment and for finance on an exceptional basis for special projects such as computer enhancement, together with a request that the LEA consider developing a policy for built-in obsolescence of equipment. A year later, it was estimated that capital finance requirements were likely to be £130,000, a reflection of Humberside County Council's loss of overall capital finance, and the potentially serious impact on the College's work was only mitigated by an agreement to transfer £50,000 from revenue (staffing) to capital. There was a view that the only satisfactory answer to the problem was to ask the LEA to introduce a rolling capital expenditure programme for the College with an increased annual allocation of £300,000, plus planned phasing of computer enhancement of £150,000 and a nuclear magnetic spectrometer £65,000. However, in the light of the national financial framework which allocated inadequate amounts of capital to all Authorities and the internal competition for that reduced sum within any one Authority, it was unlikely that Humberside could respond positively to such a request. The problem is best illustrated by the Authority's inability to increase capital funding for building works at the College for a four-year period which led to an estimate of annual need at £60,000 in real terms, and the same picture applied to minor works where £25,000 per annum was required. Given the impossibility of a positive response, the College had to seek permission from the LEA to introduce even more flexible arrangements for virement between minor capital building works, minor improvements, and equipment allocations, support which the Authority gave. However, the likelihood of there being no capital in 1987 had the serious impact of delaying the anticipated new building at Grimsby which impaired the development of that campus and ensured that work would have to continue in less than satisfactory premises (GCP 30.3.1987, #6).

The next major NAB planning exercise took place in 1987/88 and, like its predecessor, it took place within the context of continuing reductions in public expenditure, but more sophisticated attempts were made to plan future developments and to answer the serious concerns about the maintenance of academic standards in a period of consistently declining funding. The combined impact of the Secretary of State's reduction of the Pool and the NAB's wish to ease the concern about standards by protecting the unit of resource from further erosion was an overall cut of about 7% for the public sector. Therefore, in line with government vision of the role of the public sector, the overall reduction was to be disaggregated as 6% in the protected areas of engineering, science, construction, mathematics, business and management, and design studies, 11% in the medium protected areas of environmental science, other professional and vocational areas, and modern languages, and 17% in the non-protected areas of social science, humanities, and art. The result for the College was a loss of 107 FTE students from its intake (GCP 10.3.1986, #6). In response, the College reiterated its now familiar arguments concurring the comparative lateness of its origins which required it to develop within a more constrained resource climate than that in which the polytechnics initially flourished, and which meant that it required an expansion of its student intakes to provide a broad portfolio responsive to change and regional needs. The NAB was sympathetic to the College, recognising its special sub-regional case and the need to protect its critical mass, and reduced the proposed cut, prompting the College to ask for an additional 175 student places to allow for course development and to record its desire for a further 500-600 full-year FTEs over the next five years in anticipation of polytechnic designation (A Charlesworth to J.Bower, 4.4.1986; GCP 23.6.1986, #6). In the event, the loss of initial teacher education provided a means by which the NAB was able to largely meet the College's social case but remain within its overall policy imperative of reducing numbers. The College's immediate aspirations were met by transferring the ninety-three places lost through the closure of initial teacher training (+3) to other areas to provide for new developments in business studies and science, thus building back numbers against new course developments. Initially the NAB refused to take account of representations designed to allow growth in Humanities and mature students at Grimsby, but eventually conceded a further nineteen additional places, as against a bid of thirty, specifically to protect the Grimsby-based Diploma of Higher Education. In addition, the College was granted £137,000 for a range of special projects – to develop courses for under-qualified mathematics teachers in secondary schools; various research projects; participation in professional training under the PICKUP programme; additional technical support in Science, Food Technology and Engineering - all of which were valuable contributions to the College's ability to fulfil its regional role (GCP 2.10.1986, #6; GPR, 9.3.1987, #47).

Similar arguments were employed in response to the NAB's request for academic plans for 1987 and beyond which, it stipulated, should accommodate the overall pool cut of 2.3% by reductions in student numbers rather than in the unit of resource. Therefore, colleges were asked to respond for a 5% reduction and a 5% increase on total first year numbers 1984/85, with cuts falling selectively on Humanities, Social Science, Fine Art and Fisheries. The original development plan for 1987/88 was for 3520 students of whom 1565 were first-year, and the NAB request would have resulted in 3585 overall and 1630 first-year with a 5% increase and 3442 and 1487 with a 5% cut. The College was strongly opposed to any cut as it would impede balanced and efficient provision, and sought at least 5% overall growth with additional selective growth to sustain its student and employer responsiveness, efficient and effective operation, its commitment to open and continuing education, and its new collaboration with the University of Hull in initial teacher education, a proposal which emerged from the DES. Opposition to a cut was based on the serious diminution of local opportunities, particularly for mature and non-standard entrants, many of whom were to be found in the non-preferred areas such as Business and Social Sciences; the damage which would be done to related part-time work and interlocking courses such as the part-time scheme which crossed disciplinary boundaries, thus promoting efficiency; and the threat to professional links in the non-preferred areas, including the police, probation and health services, and to the new Humberside Training Consortium under the PICKUP initiative. Other areas of development which would be undermined by any reduction in numbers and income included postgraduate work and the continuing development of the Faculty of Business as a European centre, and important new ventures, such as the combination of Business and Technology, and Art and Graphic Design degrees, would be jeopardised (GCP 14.10.1985, #11).

For 1988/89, NAB proposed to reduce targets to monitored elements but not increase them where there was over-achievement. In the event, there was a net loss of eighty-two FTEs on all year numbers, which left the College with sixty-five more places than the original NAB proposals, which was felt to be a fair settlement, though there was regret that there was inadequate compensation for over-recruitment in those areas which had succeeded. Further

Table 6.2 Full-Time Equivalent Student Numbers in Humberside College of
Higher Education 1983/84 to 1988/89

Year	FTEs	Year	FTEs
1983/84	3,747.6	1986/87	3,299
1984/85	3,359	1987/88	3,396
1985/86	3,303	1988/89	3,479.6

support came from the NAB in the form of £50,000 as part of its
special research initiative. (GPR, 10.3.1988, #78). The overall
impact of NAB controls on student numbers can be seen in Table
6.2. Given the severe reductions in public expenditure over that
period, it is clear that the College's drive for efficiency mitigated
against the worst impact of NAB cuts.

The position of the College was also complicated by the uncertainty attaching to additional revenue which the Local Authority
agreed could be used in addition to estimates, but which was
often affected by circumstances outside the immediate control of
the College. Thus it was anticipated that the closure of maritime
education courses after 1984 would be the principal contributor
to a shortfall in tuition fee income of £66,700, (GCP16.7.1984,
#11), whilst a shortfall of £76,270 in the following year was the
result of a delay in new course approvals at regional level and
a reduction in overseas student numbers, some of which had
attended maritime courses (GCP14.10.1985, #14). In 1987, the
budget included a cut of £199,000 resulting from the loss of initial
teacher training, and this was increased to £301,500, largely as a
result of the new arrangements for staff development in the light of
DES *Circular 6/86* (GCP 18.5.1987, #57).

Perhaps a cameo of the financial problems faced by both the
College and the Local Authority can be seen in the financial
situation in the final year prior to incorporation. The College's
estimates were presented in the knowledge that a substantial
financial reduction would be required by the Authority. Savings
of £750,000 had been agreed previously, to which was added a
further £208,000 for costs related to supernumerary posts being
temporarily carried, and £400,000 for the transfer of NAFE work
to further education. In response to its capital bid of £207,000,
the College anticipated £70,000 which was disappointing given
that DES had indicated £127k was available for higher education
work in Humberside (GCP 10.3.1988, #114). The final revenue
shortfall was £1,282,000 which was met by savings from staffing

(mainly Crombie) £791,530; premises £60,760 ; supplies and services £285,710; £119k by removing the subsidy for catering; and £25,000 income from the Conference Centre. (GCP 4.7.1988, #92)

THE SEARCH FOR ACADEMIC AUTONOMY AND POLYTECHNIC STATUS

From the mid-seventies, the CNAA had begun to consider ways of modifying its rather formalised method of validating courses, though its concern was in the context of the larger and more experienced institutions rather than relatively new ones such as Humberside College. By the end of the 1970s, as a result of two CNAA papers, *Partnership in Validation* (1975) and *Developments in Partnership in Validation* (1979), proposals had evolved which suggested that the responsibility for academic standards might eventually be shared between the CNAA and the institutions. These ideas led to two experiments being set up, at Newcastle-upon-Tyne and Sheffield City Polytechnics, the success of which led to a further CNAA proposal for new forms of relationship with its colleges in its *Consultative paper on the Development of Council's Relationships with Institutions* (1984). The Council's position was undoubtedly influenced by the impending Lindop Report, *Academic Validation in Public Sector Higher Education* (1985) which stressed that the responsibility for academic standards should rest with a college.

The CNAA quinquennial review visit to the College in 1981 was successful with a five-year approval being given and support offered for the intention to expand south of the Humber, though the Chief Officer noted prophetically that the LEA may be unable to continue its 'current generous support' for all the college's plans (E.Kerr to J.M.Stoddart, 22.4.1982). The College's academic standards procedures were commended though it would take time to establish that they were actually effective. Attention was drawn to the relative paucity of research activity given that the College offered twenty-two undergraduate courses, and to the need for greater co-ordination of learning resources between the library and the various faculties (GCP 10.5.1982, #3.2).

In view of the fact that most polytechnics had been operating under the CNAA's formal system for almost twenty years, the College's bid in 1984 to be one of the six institutions which would be invited to establish partnership arrangements with CNAA following the success of the Council's experiment with Newcastle Polytechnic since 1981 might be thought to have been a little premature (GCP 16.7.1984, #459). However, whilst the move represented a significant move for the College and an indication of its developing self-confidence, the proposals were relatively conservative compared to the Lindop suggestion that colleges could be licensed for validation and review by the validating body subject only to periodic institutional reviews. In establishing a partnership, the College did seek responsibility for organising the validation and review of all courses, and delegated authority to monitor and review progress on those courses with indefinite approval and to approve certain specified changes, but it also proposed to involve CNAA members in validation and review visits and make formal reports to CNAA with whom final approval would rest. Furthermore, the proposed scheme would be reviewed after one year, and, if successful, quinquennially thereafter. A vital element of the proposal was that the CNAA should make an 'appropriate financial contribution for the additional work covered by the College.' (GCP 14.10.1985, #12)

In the first instance, CNAA cautiously decided to allow nominated College staff to participate in validation and review events as full members of visiting parties, but the 1987 quinquennial review resulted in a recommendation that CNAA enter into a standard institutional agreement with the College. This was followed by a pilot delegated authority agreement in December 1987, and the final stage in the development of its academic autonomy under the CNAA umbrella came in 1988 when its bid for accreditation, based on the success of the partnership agreement granted after the 1987 Review, was approved. The College set up an academic control system with Academic Board carrying the ultimate responsibility for academic standards, and the actual responsibility for monitoring placed with course teams. Other objectives included the replacement of confrontation by involvement, and the development of less bureaucratic systems, though the adequacy of the administrative underpinning for the system gave cause for some concern. The achievement of accreditation was seen as a vital development which would enhance the college's status in the eyes of the new funding body to be established by the 1988 Education Reform Act, and thereby strengthen its bid for polytechnic status. (GCP 4.7.1988, #122)

The LEA and the College never lost sight of the original 1974/76 intention to create a polytechnic in Hull, and both waged a consistent campaign to achieve that status which was an important element of the College's search to increase its academic autonomy, particularly when well-informed opinion seemed to suggest that the CNAA may well produce differential schemes for polytechnics and colleges of higher education. At the time, it appeared that the rules were constantly changing and the goalposts moving, and the creation of Humberside College of Higher Education in 1983 pro-vided an opportunity to raise the issue with the DES; the case was based on the college's regional position and its course and student profile. In the various campaigns, the regional card was played very strongly, although it was perhaps a little ironic that the group of institutions which the College aspired to join seemed more con-cerned to establish their national and international credentials, with some even wishing to sever the formal link with their authorities. With Polytechnic provision in the region concentrated in south and west Yorkshire, Humberside was presented as a sub-region with its own specialist industrial and training needs, and with only 8% of its students on full-time and sandwich courses when it had 17% of the region's population, a factor which was strengthened by its increasing population with an above-average percentage in the 0-29 age group. The sub-region's economic development had lagged behind the rest of the country, and its manpower training needs could not be met by existing regional institutions. The output of graduates per head of population was only 75% of the national average.

In its rationale, the College's polytechnic character was clear from its emphasis on vocational commitment to the needs of Humberside industry, with a course profile similar to a small polytechnic spread across both degree and higher technical level, with twenty-two CNAA courses and a further ten receiving plan-ning approval, and with a higher proportion of part-time students on advanced courses than in most polytechnics. Compared to the Other Maintained Establishments with whom it was grouped for funding purposes, it had more undergraduate courses and a much greater range of work than any other College of Higher

Education and was the only one with courses in all three categories of work as defined by the NAB. It was, at 3359 students, larger than any OME that had over 50% of its work at advanced level. It was also larger than some polytechnics, and, with 80% FTEs on AFE pool courses and rising, its proportion of advanced level work would have been even higher if the proposed 1982 closure of maritime work went ahead (GPF 13.7.1982, #4.3). Behind this impressive, though not immediately persuasive, set of statistics was the belief that polytechnic status would encourage regional Economic growth. Evidence suggested that manufacturers sent students out of the region for advanced training in accountancy, engineering, management and public administration, and the absence of a polytechnic led to loss of talent to the region since many did not return after their studies elsewhere, and a loss of opportunity to the less mobile in the region. Although it is difficult if not impossible to establish direct causation, there was a view that the achievement of polytechnic status meant far more than additional resources to the institution. Crucially, it would convey government's confidence in the region, thought to be an important factor in determining industrial location.

When this request was ignored by the DES, another approach was made in 1984 after some encouragement from preliminary consideration by the NAB Chairman's Study Group which had advised the NAB Board and Committee that a case existed for new designations, and it was hoped to have an answer by Spring 1986 (GCP 16.7.1984). However, despite a very strong recommendation for designation from the NAB, publication of the 1987 *White Paper* produced a further delay in resolving the issue. Despite this disappointment, the College continued to press for designation, a position which the White Paper seemed to support, and sought to reflect the polytechnic character of the institution in all its promotional literature (GCP 18.5.1987, #54). It is indicative of the good relationships which existed between the College and the Local Authority that, despite its opposition to the proposals to grant corporate status to institutions, the Local Authority continued to support the College's bid (GPR 9.3.1987, #48), and it is rather sad that the delay in designation until 1990 prevented the LEA from fulfilling an ambition for which it had worked so hard.

THE COLLEGE'S REGIONAL ROLE IN THE 1980S

Since its inception in 1976, the regional role of the College had been perhaps the single most important reason for its creation and for the generous support which it had obtained from the LEA. In this context, the experience of the 1980s was decidedly mixed. The concept of Humberside as a sub-region with its own different character and needs within the national planning region of Yorkshire and Humberside received a considerable boost with the formation of Humberside College of Higher Education in 1983 from the merger of Hull College and the advanced level work in Food and Fishery Studies at Grimsby College of Technology. On the other hand, two proposals, apparently made on the basis of national planning with little or no regard to regional requirements, severely affected the College's ability to meet its responsibilities. The closure of advanced nautical work in 1983, which led to the demise of non-advanced work in that area, and the loss of initial teacher training in 1986 were both the subjects of strong but unsuccessful College and Local Authority protest, and the College's role as a national rather than a regional institution was inadvertently strengthened.

MARITIME AND NAUTICAL EDUCATION
Surprisingly in a city which depended so much on the sea for its economic well-being, little progress had been made in establishing an important centre for advanced work in the maritime and nautical areas, due at least in part to the inability of local interest groups to determine a co-ordinated approach. In the area of maritime education, a Maritime Advisory Committee (MAC) was established in the College in 1981, rather later than competitor institutions, to advise the Governing Council on the development of maritime education and its direct relationship to and service of the maritime industry. Three major areas needed attention, all of which required strategic direction. First, the College needed to place any developments in the context of the probable rationalisation of training nationally, given the reduction in the size of the British fleet. Second, any development needed to focus on the crucial question of specialisation. Traditionally, maritime education in Hull had been comprehensive, but had concentrated strongly on non-advanced work, and if the College

were to make an impact nationally, consideration would have to be given to the development of a range of specialisms which would sustain advanced level activity. Finally, the College needed to improve its relations with the industry, by marketing itself more intensively and effectively to local shipping companies preferably by direct personal contact by staff (GCP 26.10.1981, #11).

In an attempt to take advantage of the buoyancy of overseas demand for courses and consultancy, the Faculty of Science, Engineering and Maritime Studies was restructured into five schools, three in the Maritime area – Electronics & Communications; Technology; Nautical Studies – one in Science and Engineering, and one in Architecture, plus a Centre for Fisheries Studies. A major problem facing the College in seeking to sustain developments and enhance its position in this area was the need for substantial and expensive equipment, including a (preferably) new navigation simulator, additional staff with an academic bias, and appropriate building developments and adaptations, all at a time of public expenditure retrenchment nationally (GCP 10.5.1982, #9). However, in the midst of these deliberations, the College received the NAB Board's proposal to close advanced nautical education in Hull, a decision which seems to have been taken on the basis of a national manpower planning exercise for this academic area rather than on the specific economic needs of the region.

The NAB Committee, which made this proposal, recommended that there should be four rather than five centres for nautical education, although the rationale for this decision was obscure and the concept of a minimum intake of 80-100 students to provide a viable unit was not proven. Given that the Humber ports together ranked fourth nationally in terms of cargo value and tonnage, that there was a significant seafaring community in the area, and that some 80% of the College's AFE nautical students came from Humberside, the case for continuing support for this work was clear. Central to the College's case was that it was the only centre providing integrated NAFE and AFE training in all three disciplines – radio, nautical and engineering - and the closure of AFE clearly implied a threat to the continuation of the non-advanced work which was equally vital to the region.

However, although the protest mounted by the College and the LEA was accepted by the NAB Board, it was overturned by the NAB Committee, with consequent voluntary early retirement being made available to staff. (EC 14.11.983, #5189; 15.2.1984, #5386). The Governing Council established an Advisory Group to consider the future, but although the College transferred some courses to the School of Engineering, they declined rapidly in the absence of academic progression to higher level work and in the face of the rapid decline of the British merchant fleet (GPF 30.1.1984, #208). The human consequences were fifteen redundant posts out of a total of twenty-seven, with nine transferring to a new Centre for Maritime Transport, and three internal redeployments. Positive developments from the closure were the retention of the Centre for Fisheries Studies and the introduction of the Centre for Maritime Transport which maintained existing full-cost, short-courses and which developed the first full-time postgraduate degree courses in the College. Eventually, during the planning for incorporation in 1988/89, the two centres were located in the new School of Food, Fisheries and Maritime Studies, based at Grimsby, though the Centre for Fisheries Studies was transferred to the University of Hull within a year. Overall, the closure indicated the extent to which national decisions affected institutional strategy overall, in that the resulting compulsory redundancies required twelve months notice, thus giving the College an uneconomic staff profile for that year (GCP 16.7.1984, #462).

FROM HULL COLLEGE TO HUMBERSIDE COLLEGE
In the light of national moves to reform the management and control of the funding of higher education in the public sector, foreshadowed in the government's Green Paper *Higher Education in England outside the Universities: Policy, Funding and Management,* national speculation suggested that course rationalisation, particularly the concentration of advanced courses in predominantly higher education institutions and their removal from or even closure in colleges of further education, might well feature prominently in many central initiatives. Mindful of Hull's dominance of the county's advanced provison (75%) compared to the small amounts in Grimsby (<20%) and North Lindsey College at Scunthorpe (<6%), the LEA re-opened the 1974/76 issue of the county-wide provision of higher education and sought a unified higher education plan for Humberside (HBFE Sub 7.10.1981, #3792/93)

In the view of the Governing Council, the issue was not if but where and how the College should expand its regional role. It was believed that Hull College of Higher Education had largely fulfilled its initial role of creating a broadly-based institution of higher education in Humberside firmly linked to the industrial, economic and social needs of the region, and the College felt that the time was ripe, with the opening of the Humber Bridge, to consider the establishment of a South Bank presence. The concentration of advanced work in one location was neither practical nor desirable, and it was anticipated that a combination of the low take-up of higher education in Humberside, the College's existing but limited links in South Humberside, and a national policy of concentrating advanced work in larger institutions offered an opportunity for overall expansion of the College on the South Bank of the Humber by 600-1000 FTE students. Recognising that an associate college and an outcentre model would limit provision, support was widespread for the more ambitious concept of a dispersed Humberside College, with a centre located in Grimsby. This would create a large, diversified, polytechnic-type institution which would allow for the rationalisation of provision within the county, provide opportunities for course development beneficial to the existing food science and technology base in Grimsby, allow some modest undergraduate developments in non-science areas on the South Bank, and find favour in the national planning and funding context.

Local political opinion was not entirely unanimous. Humberside Education Committee proposed the creation of Humberside College of Higher Education, selecting a name which reflected the new College's county-wide role, and determined to use the expansion as an opportunity to petition the DES for designation as a polytechnic. On the other hand, Great Grimsby Borough Council, perhaps suspicious of the potential in the proposal for asset-stripping of Grimsby College of Technology, objected to what it saw as the undue haste of the development and sought a delay in the new College's designation to enable capital expenditure to be allocated to the Grimsby site. When the County Council rejected the request on the grounds that it was protecting advanced work at Grimsby, the Borough Council sought to protect the local position by obtaining a seat on the new Governing Council, a request which was equally unsuccessful (EC 23.6.1982, #4105; HBFE Sub 6.10.1982, #4228).

The emergence of Humberside College of Higher Education,

with the need for rapid promotion of courses relevant to the requirements of South Bank industry and commerce, meant a major reconsideration of the 1981 Development Plan, though its broad aims remained largely intact, with its regional role enhanced through the development in South Humberside. In order to encompass an initial 400 FTEs at Grimsby, rising to 1,000 within five years, there was marginal growth of existing numbers for 1982/83 with Grimsby encompassed in that total, and internally it was necessary to excise c.180 places in non-laboratory subjects and to seek an increase in Technology places of c.19; the overall impact, represented a major shift towards poolable work in the College as a whole. Central to the development was not only the preservation but also the enhancement of work in Fisheries and Food Studies which were augmented by a specialist Refrigeration Engineering group detached from Hull and located at Grimsby. Equally important, given the Authority's commitment to the South Bank, was the build-up of courses in Business, Humanities and Social Sciences, achieved by transferring the Diploma of Higher Education course from the North Bank and expanding existing Higher National Diploma in Business Studies with options different from those available in Hull.

Inevitably, the revenue implications of these developments were severe, given the necessity of meeting the reductions already agreed with the LEA over the next few years, and the transfer required to support Grimsby. All were dependent on the provision of adequate accommodation which included temporary additional and remodelled premises and enhanced library facilities (GCP 14.2.1983, #2). The Local Authority made a major effort to ensure that adequate provison was made for advanced work in Grimsby in order to reassure both the validating bodies and the local community. A temporary library was created; major remodelling work undertaken in the Nun's Corner site gave a whole floor of the Grimsby College of Technology to the College of Higher Education to provide suitable facilities for higher education; and the old wing of the residential Humber Lodge was converted for non-specialist teaching accommodation. Eventually, DES approval was given for a £650,000 major building programme at Grimsby to provide new teaching and library space which was included in the major building programme for 1987/88, but a combination of severe reductions in capital expenditure and the advent of incorporation ensured that the proposed building never got off the ground (GPF 2.7.1985, #40; GPR 23.2.1987, #42). In the initial stage, the Local Authority's freeze on filling vacant posts, a response to the wider economic climate of the day, caused some problems, but by the end of 1983, the Governing Council felt able to record that 'the development at Grimsby had been achieved remarkably smoothly . . . and the initial anxieties of staff had to a large extent been allayed.' (GCP 5.12.1983, #425.2)

REGIONAL ROLE: TEACHER EDUCATION

Following the White Paper *Teaching Quality* (Cmnd. 8836, March 1983), the Government's *Circular 3/84* established a national advisory council for the accreditation of teacher training courses and required local professional committees to be set up representing the training institutions, Local Education Authorities in the area, local practising school teachers, and individuals from outside the teaching service, with a particular interest in establishing and promoting links between the training institution, schools and the community. Every initial training course had to be sent to the National Council for the Accreditation of Teacher Education (CATE) for approval with the backing of the local CATE committee which the College was required to establish in October 1984. The latter's brief was to advise the college on all aspects of initial and in-service training, professional staff development and research.

Teacher training was the only element of higher educational planning which was completely in the hands of the DES, a crucial factor in determining the nature of reductions and reorganisations in 1974-76. Although there was little confidence in the system in the Department's planning ability, the statistical approach to the development of teacher education continued into the 1980s with steady reductions in national numbers which had a differential impact locally. The result was that by the mid-eighties Humberside had an unsatisfactory balance of approximately 50:50 between initial and in-service training numbers against a more normal pattern of 66:33. Furthermore, its initial training allocation of sixty-five was one of the smallest in the country and the future of ten of those was uncertain given the proposals to disband specialist courses for mental handicap training (HCHE to NAB, 13.12.1984 in NAB File). The Advisory Committee on the Supply and Education of Teachers (ACSET) was the body on which the DES relied for advice on the projected demand for newly-trained teachers, and it identified a shortfall in the area of primary education, the area of the College's main training course. Therefore, when the NAB was asked to advise the DES on the total size, distribution and balance of teacher training places for 1986 and beyond, the College made a bid for a substantial increase in initial teacher training places in order to redress the imbalance and to provide a stronger staff and resource base to sustain and develop the relatively large in-service provision made (GCP 21.1.1985, #6). Consequently, the DES proposal in 1986 to cease initial teacher training at Humberside College came as a major surprise, particularly since it was made against a background of a 20% increase in teacher training nationally.

The LEA deeply regretted the Secretary of State's 'catastrophic and scandalous' (Earls to GC, GCP 23 June 1986, #5) proposal and was actively involved in the major campaign mounted to seek a reversal of the decision, a campaign which was supported by both the NAB and the CNAA. The regional implications were alarming, and the Authority drew attention to the educational and economic disadvantages which would accrue to the region if the proposal were confirmed. In reality, the tenth largest city in Britain, together with two industrial towns on the South Bank, were largely dependent on the College for beginner teachers. In 1985, 60% of the entrants to the profession were local and 50% took up local posts. For its part, the College contested the decision on the grounds that it was based largely on outdated information and an alleged weakness derived from the Department's own early policies. The College was also mindful that the closure would mean income shortfalls of £273,000 and £444,000 in each of the next two years which suggested a loss of six to eight staff in each year (GPR 9.3.1987, #45 & GC 30.3.1987, #75). The Secretary of State's letter drew attention to the small size of the unit, ironically a direct result of previous reductions by central government, the pattern of past recruitment which had tended to emphasise a strong mature student component emerging from the Diploma of Higher Education, the lack of distinctive provision in mathematics and science, and the lack of provision for early years. Much of this information was culled from a major Inspection of teacher education in the College carried out in 1984, suggesting that the information base at the DES was out-of-date as a number of developments had occurred, some of which responded to HMI criticisms. Since the Inspection, a new concurrent B.Ed.(Hons.) had been validated and introduced; early years training existed in both the B.Ed. and Postgraduate Certificate in Education despite the Department's apparent ignorance of the fact; there was science and mathematics provison at degree level in the College and a flourishing Mathematics Centre for Teachers which was integrated into initial training. Equally perplexing were the inconsistencies in the proposal which scheduled not only the B.Ed courses but also the Postgraduate Certificate for closure, despite no criticism being levelled at it, yet expected that the College would be able to make a continuing in-service provision. The College pointed to favourable external judgements on its teacher education work. Only one year earlier, the NAB had noted that Humberside's teacher education numbers should be increased for the remainder of the decade, and reports from the CNAA, external examiners, and HMI were very supportive (HBEC 18.1.1986, #6412; GCP 23.6.1986, #5).

Despite the vociferous and high-profile campaign mounted against the proposal, the Secretary of State confirmed his decision towards the end of the year, and drew attention to the size of the unit as being inadequate 'to provide robust and effective provision,' an argument whose speciousness was perhaps recognised by the DES willingness to compensate any redundant staff according to the Crombie Regulations which had been available nationally at the time of the 1976-79 reductions. Given the reliance on an argument which was entirely the product of previous government policy, the failure to respond to the specific arguments with which the College countered the Department's reasons for closure, and the attitude of DES officials, it is difficult to avoid the conclusion that there was never any likelihood of the original proposal being overturned. However, perhaps mindful of the damage which his proposal may have on teacher supply in Humberside, the Secretary of State suggested that the College and the University of Hull might wish to prepare detailed proposals for a joint unit for primary training drawing on the strengths of both institutions (Baker to Earls, 30.10.1986 in GCP 2.10.1986, #5). Despite the surprise with which this proposal was received, it was welcomed by both institutions and intensive discussions led to a proposal for a joint unit of two hundred students on a BA/BSc degree with a further sixty on a postgraduate certificate course, the awards to be made by the University but with both partners operating on an equal basis in terms of allocation of students, and subject and professional contribution. Agreement was reached and proposals presented to the College's Governing Council and the University Senate by May 1987 (GPR 18.5.1987, #56). The submission met the characteristically tight deadline imposed by the DES, but there was considerable cynicism in the College when the University Grants Committee approved a 50-place primary postgraduate certificate of education at the University without any reference to the joint proposal, and the College was left with the task of phasing out initial teacher education for its remaining students (HBEC 18.6.1986, #6412 and 8.3.1989, #8188).

Chapter 8

The Emergence of Humberside University 1989–95

INTRODUCTION

The short period since the late 1980s has witnessed a revolution in British higher education in general and in Humberside in particular. The College, which had begun life as Hull College of Higher Education in 1976 and was enlarged to Humberside College seven years later , moved rapidly to Polytechnic status in 1990 and achieved University status a mere two years later. However, the transformation has been much more than nominal. Along with all other polytechnics and colleges in the former public sector, it was incorporated in 1989, thus accruing to itself a wide range of responsibilities previously in the hands of its LEA, and this has brought major change, particularly in the sphere of governance and management. However, in the midst of constitutional change was a high degree of institutional continuity as Humberside has remained faithful to its 1976 origins, seeking to continue to offer a predominantly vocational curriculum to a wide range of students, local, regional, national and international.

CORPORATE STATUS: THE WHITE PAPER 1987

The DES White Paper, *Higher Education. Meeting the Challenge* published in April 1987 and the subsequent 1988 Education Reform Act (ERA) heralded a revolution in the control and administration of public sector higher education in England and Wales. However, the reforms represented the denouement of a drama which had been being played out since the 1970s, and the DES now felt that it could adopt formal control of higher education. In common with many other official publications of the previous decade, the *White Paper* appeared to be directed more at those universities which the government believed to be making an insufficient contribution to the social and economic issues facing the country, and it clearly believed that institutions in both sectors could be encouraged to become more aware of their responsibilities if they were under more direct government control. The social and economic responsiveness of polytechnics and colleges such as Humberside was acknowledged in the *White Paper*, and perhaps the most significant change for them was the offer of autonomy within a context of national control.

Central to the DES position was the creation of a strong public sector, independent of local authorities, and led by national planning rather than uncoordinated regional initiatives, though it also argued, somewhat contradictorily, that local and regional links should remain strong and distinctive. Further, good management in the institutions was suffocated by local authority control, particularly with respect to finance and staffing. Therefore, a Polytechnics and Colleges Funding Council (PCFC) would plan educational provision in the sector by making funds available for capital expenditure and by contracting with institutions to encourage less dependence on public funds, thus sharpening institutional accountability and strengthening their ability to deliver courses with a strong industrial and commercial element. A particularly important function of PCFC as far as Humberside College was concerned was its remit to advise the Secretary of State on the possible designation of new polytechnic designations 'in a positive spirit, paying attention not only to candidates' attributes but also to their capacity to expand to meet national and regional needs.'

The College greeted the *White Paper* with mixed feelings. Whilst it had enjoyed good relations with and received consistent support from the Education Authority and its officers, and although it had never sought corporate status, there was no doubt that separation from the LEA would enable the College to plan over a longer cycle than one year, a factor which had caused severe difficulties during the 1980s. On the other hand, the College remained committed to that element of the *White Paper* which expected that public sector institutions would continue to fulfil their social and economic responsibilities within their regions (GCP 30.3.1987, #11). For its part, the LEA was strongly opposed to the granting of corporate status, feeling that the objectives of the White Paper could be achieved within the existing framework. However, local authority protests counted for nothing and incorporation was to take place on 1 April 1989. This left the existing Governing Council in charge until that date, thus requiring continuation of the good working relationship between the College and the County Council which had generally characterised the previous twelve years. Despite its unhappiness with government policy, the Humberside Education Authority adopted a mature approach to the issue, and a measure of its commitment to the College was that it reiterated its support for polytechnic designation even if it were to be removed from local control.

PREPARING FOR INCORPORATION

In the interim period between the approval of the Education Reform Act and the advent of Vesting Day on 1 April 1989, the College continued to be governed under the 1983 Instrument and Articles by the Governing Council responsible to the County Council, but was required to establish a Formation Committee to oversee the preparations for incorporation. Although having no formal powers, it was the Formation Committee, rather than the existing Board of Governors, which prepared for incorporation, though co-operation between the two was essential since the latter remained responsible for day-to-day management until 1 April 1989. Perhaps to ensure the necessary co-operation, the Formation Committee, which required and received DES approval, consisted of six members of the existing Governing Council; four independent members who would become members of the new corporation (Messrs. Hooper, Dunn, Edwards, Milner), an LEA representative who was the Education Committee chair (Councillor Bird), and a staff representative (L.Cross). The Director and his two deputies also attended meetings of the Formation Committee whose major task was to advise the Secretary of State on the proposed membership of the new corporation, and to make whatever arrangements were necessary to prepare for vesting day on 1 April 1989.

Within the constraints of the legislation, the Formation Committee adopted an open approach to the issue of corporation membership. It was decided immediately that the new Board of Governors should consist of twenty-five members which was the maximum allowed under the Act, a position adopted by 24% of the institutions in the sector (Bastin 1990). The Board would consist of thirteen independent members, eight nominees, three additional nominees, and the Director of the College, thus maintaining many of the categories, though not the balance of membership of the unreformed Board of Governors. Although the Secretary of State sought nominations for the additional nine independent governors from other regional and national organisations and passed them to the chair of the Formation Committee, the Committee's own nominees were proposed and eventually approved by the minister. Thus the initial independent membership of the Board was broadly representative of the criteria proposed by the Director, namely geographical considerations within and beyond the region, the world of the creative arts, communications, and the public service as well as the more traditional professions, and the need to achieve some gender balance. (FCP 23 May & 21 June 1988). The nominated members, in addition to the Director, were to consist of three LEA representatives all of whom would be drawn from and nominated by Humberside County Council, despite a desire by Hull City Council to be represented, two Academic Board representatives, one elected academic and one elected non-academic staff representative, one student representative, and three additional nominees; elections for the internal members were supervised by the Committee. The LEA nominees were chosen to reflect the Authority's political composition and earlier strong interest in and support for the College, one being nominated from each of the three main political parties including the Chair and Shadow Chair of the County Education Committee. The three additional nominees included the former Chief Executive and the then Chief Education Officer of Humberside County Council, further reflecting the desire to maintain good relations between the two bodies, despite the Authority's disappointment at its loss of direct control of the College; the final nominee was a representative from the local trades unions. Within the initial Corporation, independent members were to serve for three years, LEA and staff nominees for two years and student nominees for one year from the date of incorporation; additional nominees were to serve for three years from their dates of appointment (FCP 30 August, 30 October 1989).

Consonant with government intentions of reducing significantly

the role of local authorities and staff members in college governance, the responsibilities of independent members was enhanced.
It is true that the appointment of new members to the Board
lay with the Corporation, but an appointment had to be made
within three months of a vacancy occurring; otherwise the independent members would become the appointing authority. Equally
important was the provison that appointments to the group of
independent members could only be made with the agreement of
that constituency.

Other issues vital to the formation of a corporation which the
Formation Committee addressed included commenting on the
model Instrument and Articles provided by the DES; welcoming
the initiatives to establish national bargaining machinery through
the Shadow Employers' Forum, provided that it was not totally
restrictive or locally inhibiting; noting the broad agreement with
County Council regarding property which would ease the work
of the Education Assets Board; overseeing the establishment of
financial management systems in the College, and of basic services
such as banking, payroll, legal services, insurance and external
auditing, though guidance was awaited from DES on a number of
issues (FCP 23 May, 21 June ,25 July, 31 August, 3 & 31 October
1988; Shadow BGP 21 November 1988; Board of Governors 19
December 1988).

Equally vital in the approach to incorporation was the severe
impact on the College of the loss of its financial support from the
LEA, and the Formation Committee was actively concerned in the
development of plans to enable the newly-incorporated College not
only to remove the deficit created but also to develop plans which
would ensure a sound financial base for the new institution. The
impressive support which the LEA had given to Humberside over
the years suddenly became a liability for an institution which was
to be incorporated. Initial estimates suggested that the 'topping-up'
of the College's budget by the LEA amounted to some £2.3m,
and this did not include the £1.6m. cost of NAFE work which,
under the terms of incorporation, authorities could contract to their
former colleges. The initial strategy adopted, in order to mitigate
the extent of the financial difficulties and to enable the College to
maintain its bid for polytechnic status, was to seek expansion from
3,500 to 4,000 students as soon as possible, with a further target of
4,500. Nonetheless, it was clear that the brunt of any retrenchment

would fall on staff, since this item accounted for some 66% of the College's total expenditure, and it was estimated that, using 1987/88 as a base and adopting an SSR target of 13:1, there would be a minimal loss of sixty-eight FTE academic and sixty-six FTE non-academic posts. From the College's point of view, the situation was also aggravated by the no-redundancy policy of the County Council, and the Formation Committee regretted that financial constraints appeared to be driving academic development As immediate measures, the Governing Council agreed that a higher target SSR should be adopted, and an embargo was placed on permanent external appointments except in special cases agreed by its chair. Further, the Policy & Resources Committee was given delegated authority to act on behalf of the full Governing Council on staffing and other issues arising from the *White Paper* (BGP 22.6.1987).

By February 1989, thirty-two academic and ten non-academic members of staff had accepted voluntary redundancy or premature retirement to take effect on dates up to and including 31 March 1988 and a further eleven had made enquiries; in addition twenty-one teacher education staff agreed to leave prematurely by the same date under the Crombie compensation regulations. Alongside these developments was an administrative restructuring exercise which saved 30.7 FTE posts. A review of technical establishment saved a further 2.5 FTE posts. More positively, the College introduced a new and leaner academic structure, reducing to eight Schools, from 1 April 1989, though it was only through cultural change rather than structural change that the overall objectives would be achieved. Other opportunities for retrenchment were available through the rationalisation of sites, particularly by vacating annexes as quickly as possible, and considerable progress was made towards an amicable agreement on the property transferred from the LEA to the College. Indeed, senior management was sufficiently confident with the progress made by March 1989 that the temporary embargo on new appointments was lifted, though due caution was exercised whenever a proposal was made (FCP 10 March 1988).

GOVERNMENT AND MANAGEMENT[1]

Prior to incorporation, the College was governed, under an Instrument and Articles, within a regulatory framework which enabled the Local Authority to control all aspects of its work, including the crucial areas of finance, employment and estates, though the strong civic pride which the Humberside County Council had in the College led to very supportive relationships and to the eventual *de facto* delegation of a range of responsibilities to the College. Both governance and management took place within a culture of participation and shared responsibility between the Governing Council, dominated by local authority and College members, and senior management and representatives of the staff operating through Academic Board and its committees. With incorporation, the reforms of 1988 and 1992 stimulated a more professional and business-like approach to the government and management of colleges by replacing a regulatory bureaucracy with a corporate body, and by introducing a culture of power relationships into the polytechnics and colleges, investing in both the Board of Governors and the Director powers which had hitherto rested with Local Authorities. In the new context, the Board, on which independent members were to be in an absolute majority, was directly and solely responsible for the educational character and mission of the College, for the effective and efficient use of its resources and its solvency, and for the employment and conditions of service of all staff. Central government anticipated that the dominance of independent members would introduce a culture of efficiency to institutions.

Equally crucial was the strengthening of the role of the executive at the expense of elected academic representatives in determining the strategic direction as well as in establishing more effective and efficient means of managing institutions. The Director, later Vice-Chancellor, strengthened considerably in his role as Chief Executive responsible for implementing the decisions of the Board, carried full responsibility for making proposals concerning the educational character and mission to the Board of Governors, thus reducing the role of Academic Board to that of advisor; furthermore, he held executive responsibility for the organisation, direction, and financial management of the College, and the management of staff, with direct control over senior postholders and student discipline. Two major devices, common to most corporations, developed to assist the Director in the management of the institution. The widespread concept of a Senior Management Team in pre-incorporation institutions, often carrying out considerable iteration with Academic Board, evolved into a more formal

Executive Committee structure which became not merely the dominant unit but the major locus of power and authority within the institution, developing policy and practice independent of the traditional academic channels. At the centre has been an inner cabinet, consisting of the Director/Vice Chancellor and his immediate colleagues, each of whom exercised portfolio responsibilities under the supervision of the Chief Executive. The Executive also made considerable use of specially appointed sub-committees or working parties, usually led by a member of the Executive Board and with a limited life, to drive forward the work of the institution; thus the major task of converting the University's academic portfolio to a modular structure in 1993/94, and the establishment of a new international strategy in 1993 were carried out by such groups. The position of management was also strengthened on the new Academic Board which was reduced to twenty-nine members, of whom sixteen were ex-officio and two co-opted, and its powers, which were exercised in an advisory capacity to the Director, were confined to the quality and academic standards of the work in the College.

The 1992 Further and Higher Education Reform Act, which brought academic autonomy and offered University status to the Polytechnic, provided an opportunity for government to continue the trend of its earlier reforms whereby the governance of institutions was dominated by independent members and the position of both staff and LEA members was diluted. Staff and LEA representatives were removed from the initial Board of the revised corporation, and the independent members were given power to co-opt up to two teachers nominated by Academic Board, up to two students nominated by the Students' Union, and between one and nine other members, one of whom must have experience in the provision of education (1992 ERA, Schedule 7A). The independent members sought to continue the principles which had informed the composition of the previous Governing Council, both by retaining its number, twenty-five, and by co-opting two teachers, two students, three local councillors and the Principal of the local College of Agriculture. In accordance with the opportunity contained in the Act, the University seized the opportunity to increase the size of the Academic Board of forty members, the increase of ten reflecting the need to provide greater representation of the new academic structure of the institution which had recently been disaggregated from four to thirteen Schools; its responsibilities were unchanged.

It has been suggested that the corporate model of governance and management, where power is located and exercised only at the centre, thus running the risk of alienation, develops a management style which is political and tactical, operates within a short-to-medium term time frame, and is best suited to crisis situation (McNay, 1995). Certainly, the marginalisation of the Academic Board from the decision-making process produced a feeling of disenfranchisement amongst staff, and recognition of the longer term difficulties which can ensue from this issue led the University to seize the opportunity offered by the 1992 Act to increase the size, though not the responsibilities of the Academic Board. More recently, in response to the University's Audit Report from the Higher Education Quality Council (HEQC), further steps have been put in hand to encourage greater iteration between the Executive and Academic Boards without surrendering the Vice-Chancellor's legal responsibility for the academic development of the University. Accusations of short-termism can, in Humberside's case, be refuted by the energy which has been devoted to the production of five-year strategic plans, but such is the context of permanent change, largely though not exclusively produced by central government policy, that medium and longer-term planning can appear to be undermined. Whilst the word crisis is inappropriate, the incorporation of the College did present new and significant challenges, though the move to more efficient management and strategic planning had been foreshadowed by the NAB the forerunner of the PCFCP. Nonetheless, the scale of reform required urgent and dramatic change, and it is arguable that centralisation of power was the only means by which energy necessary to achieve the objectives could be harnessed.

THE DEVELOPMENT OF CORPORATE SERVICES

The crucial means by which the Secretary of State would control the development of higher education in the Polytechnics and Colleges of Higher Education was through the distribution of financial support. This was done on the recommendation of the PCFCP whose major initial concern was to develop a funding methodology which met the government's proposal for contract funding in place of the grant system, and through it to obtain lower unit costs in individual institutions, better value for money via greater accountability, and increased competition. In this work, PCFC dealt directly with individual institutions thus requiring them to accept a wider financial responsibility than previously, and also to develop a range of services, such as estates and personnel management which had previously been carried out by the local authority, to underpin the academic plan deriving from the College's mission.

The financial impact of incorporation was two-fold. First, in addition to the loss of its annual 'topping-up' facility, a number of new elements, from which the College had been protected, such as the requirement to pay value added tax, the impact of inflationary pay awards and wages drift through incremental progression, and other general inflationary pressures gave the newly-incorporated institution an immediate and substantial problem. (1989/90 Financial Estimates: Initial Revenue Appraisal. BGP/89/19 30.1.1989). Second, it became necessary to establish a corporate financial services on a scale and with a range of expertise not previously required. Although the College possessed a Finance Department prior to incorporation, much of the work relating to government funding and all the implications of becoming an employer of staff introduced a wide range of new responsibilities which had to be handled immediately from 1 April 1989.

Premature retirement and/or voluntary redundancy, and leaner academic and administrative structures, made a substantial contribution towards eliminating the 'topping-up' deficit, though this was little more than urgent corrective surgery to control the problem. More essential was the establishment of a financial strategy to place the College on a healthy, even robust footing from which it could take advantage of the opportunities afforded by incorporation. From the outset, the College determined to adopt a balanced budget, even though initial estimates suggested that further savings amounting to £1,429,000, would be necessary in order to produce a small balance of £159,000 at the end of the first year. The objective of financing the academic plan within the confines of a balanced budget and with an intention to make a contribution towards the establishment of reserves and to minor works remained the central plank of the College's financial strategy after 1989. In order that this strategy could succeed, it was essential to exercise close control of costs, and senior managers introduced thorough internal estimates and budgetary procedures which enabled the College to prepare realistic proposals for approval by the Board of Governors. Oversight of the College's financial position was exercised by the new Employment and Finance Committee of the Board of Governors which undertook regular and detailed scrutiny of the College's financial performance.

The major element of the College's income came by an annually agreed contract with the Funding Council and tuition fee income through local authorities which, together, did not fall below 80% of total income in any one year since incorporation, thus emphasising the need for accurate student projections during the bidding process introduced by PCFC, particularly in view of its practice of clawing back grant where contracted numbers were not achieved. Thus, the need to make realistic proposals to the Funding Council exercised an important discipline on the College, though its guarantee of 90/95% of the previous year's grant as core funding for the subsequent year, and the opportunities offered for growth through the bidding process for the balance, did give some stability to the year-on-year operation. However, the coincidence of the government's intention to cap growth in student numbers from 1993/94, achieved by manipulation of the tuition fee for library-based courses, and the advent of the Higher Education Funding Council for England (HEFCE) in 1993 indicated the problems of pursuing independence within a controlled environment. The crucial decision was the change to the tuition fee structure with the reduction in Band 1 fees by £550 making the concept of marginal students no longer tenable, thus ensuring that self-generated growth was no longer an option for the University. An indication of the planning problems which this external decision caused can be seen from the fact that the University had 63.8% of its full-time and sandwich students and 50.9% of its part-time students in Business & Management and Humanities & Social Science, all of which were in Fee Band 1. As a result, the University was constrained to keep 1993/94 numbers in these areas to their 1992/93 levels, thus implying severe restraints on recruitment that September. Since incorporation, the scale of expansion in these areas had been a significant factor in the expansion which had led to the achievement of polytechnic status, and the reassertion of greater central control over student numbers presented the University with serious problems.

Table 8.1   Institutional Income and Expenditure Accounts (£000s)[2]

Year Ending	Annual Income	Annual Expenditure	Annual Net Surplus
31 March 1990	17,443	16,424	983
31 March 1991	21,589	19,717	1,895
31 March 1992	27,301	25,928	1,252
31 July 1993	47,434	42,013	5,418
31 July 1994	46,587	42,013	5,802
31 July 1995	43,916	38,662	5,231
Total Surplus 1989–95			20,581

Source: University Annual Financial Reports 1989/90 to 1994/95

Amongst the financial advantages of incorporation has been the ability of the university to carry forward money from one year to the next, to earn interest on its balances, and to create a reserve out of revenue income if it wished. The result of these opportunities, together with strict financial management during the first six years of incorporation, has been the creation of a healthy, even robust financial platform from which to support its academic plan, as indicated in Table 8.1.

The most obvious measure of its success in this area is the fact that, not only has the academic plan been fully underpinned, whilst major improvements have been made to the estate and judicious investments made to strengthen corporate support services such as estates, finance, personnel and administrative computing, but a surplus has been achieved every year and reserves of some £20 millions created. However, it was clear that such achievements could only be realised at some cost. There was a significant increase in the staff:student ratio (SSR), and the revisions to the strategic plan in 1990 set targets for Art & Design of 15:1 and Business Studies and Social Science of 25:1. Where possible, new academic posts have looked for new blood, and therefore relatively low cost appointments, focusing primarily on support for the European strategy, and it was intended that by 1992/93 10% of all academic posts would be funded from full-cost activities.

ACADEMIC DEVELOPMENTS

During the second half of the twentieth century, central government has taken a progressively greater interest in higher education, stimulated by the latter's ever-increasing demands on the public purse, and the reforms of the late 'eighties and early 'nineties have seen the culmination of that process with the subordination of universities, the take-over of advanced institutions from their original providers, both municipal and religious, and the creation of a unified system. As a LEA college until incorporation in 1989, Humberside belonged to the advanced further education sector which had been developed since the 'sixties as one of the strategies for modernising higher education and, in particular, making it more responsive to the needs of the economy. Prior to incorporation, the institutions in the public sector had been characterised by their close connections with the economy of their regions which was reflected in an accessibility to students of a wide range of ability, and by their municipal origins and links which had encouraged a sense of accountability rather than autonomy, though this accountability was widened to a national context with the advent of the NAB in 1981.

The dominant theme of government reform was the offer of academic autonomy to institutions which was to be exercised by strong local management within a framework of government centralisation through its control of finance. The body established to control the development and finance of public sector institutions, the PCFCP, was an instrument through which government objectives could be achieved and policies implemented, though a precedent had been set by the NAB which had operated a system of central government control of public sector institutions' finances with its distribution in the hands of local authority members who dominated the NAB. Its operational framework was established in the 1987 *White Paper* and the 1988 ERA, but more significant was the continual stream of advice and instruction emanating from the Secretary of State for Education and Science who saw the sector making a major contribution to the social and economic needs of the country. In practical terms, this meant the need to expand access for mature students, the desirability of a shift towards more numbers in science, engineering and vocational subjects, increased links between industry and education alongside a more constrained view of research funding, and an emphasis on delivery in return for public funds which may include rationalisation to create stronger institutions and departments. (BGP/89/13, 30 Jan 1989).The twin controls by which PCFC sought to fulfil government policy were a requirement for detailed strategic planning which, once agreed, would form the basis for financial allocations to each institution.

An incidental by-product of the binary system had been the emergence of two rather monolithic sectors which encouraged convergence between institutions both within and between the two. On the one hand, Polytechnics formed an increasingly cohesive group and a model which aspirants such as Humberside found it necessary to emulate; on the other hand, the quest for equal status with the universities, on the grounds that the public sector institutions were providing courses and making awards at the same level as universities, encouraged academic drift. One of the principal objectives of the ERA was to attempt to rectify this situation by providing an environment in which a degree of diversity between the sectors might ensue, though it was to take the reforms of 1992, in particular the elevation of polytechnics and some colleges to university status, before that became a real possibility and even then other factors, such as the research assessment exercise, continued to encourage convergence. Nonetheless, the PCFC sought to present polytechnics and colleges with the challenge of determining their own future by requiring the rapid production of strategic plans. Humberside College of Higher Education's mission for the first three years of its existence, 'to become an enterprising, accessible and highly regarded polytechnic with a strong European and regional orientation and 8,000 (5,000 FTE) satisfied students' (Strategic Plan, BGP 12 June 1989), continued its traditions of offering accessible, vocational higher education to its region whilst seeking to capitalise on its well-established European experience. Central to this mission was the bid for polytechnic status which had been the fundamental aim of the college since the early 1980s and which had been strongly recommended to the Secretary of State in 1987 by the then NAB, but which had been shelved pending enactment of government reforms. The College's case, by now familiar, was based upon its character and achievements on the one hand, and its potential for development on the other. Its academic case was based on the size, spread, and balance of its academic portfolio, in which it compared favourably with a number of the smaller polytechnics, its recent accreditation by CNAA, and its recognition externally for innovative programmes, particularly in the area of European

169

programmes. Its potential for growth was strong in an area of almost one million people, traditionally under-provided with vocational higher education, based principally on its favourable geographical location as a major seaport on the east coast of England in the light of the emergence of a unified European market in the early 1990s (BGP 89/89 30.10.1989).

During the 1970s and 1980s, public sector institutions had been at the forefront of the provision of professionally- and vocationally-oriented courses to a wider group of students than before at a significantly lower cost than the education provided by the universities. In placing itself firmly in this tradition, the College was a willing participant in the gradual development taking place in Britain over a twenty-year period from an elitist to a mass system of higher education, though it has been argued that these developments occurred within a continuing elitist system which failed to produce the mass higher education system required by a post-industrial society (Trow, 1989). Central to the College's mission was a strategy of growth in student numbers from an existing 6,500 to 8,000 students, most of whom would be in the vocational areas of Information Technology, Computing and Mathematics; Business and Management; Humanities and Social Science; Art, Design and the Performing Arts; and Teacher Education, provided that the DES supported the bid for a joint primary education unit with the University of Hull. This target for planned growth of some 23% over three years was ambitious, though some of it was in-built, but, in the light of PCFC advice to the Secretary of State that new polytechnic designations should be made only where institutions had at least 300 full-time higher education students in a majority of the Council's nine programme areas, a higher education enrolment of at least 4,000 full-time and a substantial number of part-time (c.1,500), and have over two-thirds of its full-time higher education students on degree level courses, there was a degree of inevitability about the College's dash for growth (R.Dearing to J.MacGregor 28 8.1989, in BGP 30.10.1989).

During the period of the initial strategic plan, revisions were made to the targets, normally in an upward direction with increased growth being achieved by further development of the College's European programmes, by an increased emphasis on access and on franchising elements of courses to Further Education Colleges in the region, and by course developments in new vocational areas

170

such as Tourism, professionally-related areas such as psychology and social work, and Environmental Studies. In 1991, it was envisaged that there would be growth in all areas, but particularly in Information Technology, in Health and Social Sciences, and in Business Studies, and in Engineering through the introduction of an undergraduate Technology and Business Programme.

By the time that PCFC required a new strategic plan to cover the period 1992-97, the educational environment had changed substantially. The impending disappearance of the binary system and the creation of a sector containing over eighty universities and a number of other major colleges challenged the institution to position itself more clearly in a system which was meant to have the potential for greater diversity than had previously existed. The government's planned increase in the participation rate, both numerically and socially, provided new opportunities for growth, though it was clear that the achievement of those targets against the background of a declining unit of resource would pose its own challenges in terms of curriculum content, delivery, student support, modes of attendance and flexibility and pace of study. Finally, there appeared to be possible pressure for institutional alliances including joint-ventures and mergers.

Government, therefore, sought to provide a context within which greater institutional diversity might develop by offering universities the opportunity to define the character of an institution within the framework of a market managed by government control of overall finance. Against this background, Humberside elected to become an institution providing mass higher education as exemplified by its 1992 mission, 'to be the region's accessible and enterprising European university, developing skills and capabilities through a commitment to quality education.' Conversion to university status would not deflect it from its primary commitment to providing vocational higher education to the region and to Europe, and it expected to grow from 10,700 to 14,000. Whilst such ambitions implied increases in student numbers in all academic areas except in-service teacher education, much of it would be achieved by widening access off-campus by the provison of study centres throughout the region, and by the expansion of formal agreements with local and European colleges, some of which would be able to obtain associated status.

However, there were new emphases, particularly in the detailed implications of the broad mission. First, the commitment to vocational education led to a stress on knowledge, skills and capabilities, the latter two often implicit rather than explicit in traditional university education in the U.K. With the stimulus provided by the Enterprise Project, the European Competencies Project and the British Petroleum Endowment to be used for learning development work, the university intended to introduce broader approaches to curricular content and structure and to student learning in order to achieve this aim. The new plan proposed the introduction of common cores of Foundation Studies for all undergraduate courses, thereby enabling students to defer choice of academic or professional specialism, and placed an emphasis on the development of generic skills and capabilities allied to academic knowledge but relevant to employment in the twenty-first century. It was also assumed that a mass higher education university committed to teaching and learning and to the provision of vocationally relevant programmes, would have to produce courses which would be more flexible and student-centred than had been the case hitherto. Thus, a major transformation was proposed in terms of the development of more flexible, unitised structures, the support for Credit Accumulation and Transfer Schemes (CATS), increased flexibility in modes of study, including semesterisation, the introduction of learning outcomes as key organising principles of units and courses, and an increased emphasis on student-centred learning. Second, there was a new emphasis on the provision of quality education which, in reality, meant a search for continuous quality improvement in all aspects of the university's work.

However, although the revised mission statement was intended to apply to a five-year period from 1992, externally-imposed changes in the system compelled the university to reconsider its position in the summer of 1994. First, government decisions to cap growth in higher education, the decline of 18 year olds in the population, and the emergence of the new further education corporations as providers of certain types of higher education all increased competition, and placed a premium on the need to develop a distinctive reputation for high quality performance. Second, the introduction of league tables, based largely on traditional university criteria placed Humberside in a relatively unfavourable light, and it had to be recognised that it had limited areas of recognised academic excellence, reflected at least in part by its low research base and the correspondingly few staff with national reputations. Thus, it was necessary for the university to improve its image in the market place. In addition to the impact of changes in the external environment, the announcement, in May 1995, of the University's involvement in the Lincoln project which was to lead to the creation of the University of Lincolnshire and Humberside with campuses in Lincoln, Hull and, until 1999, in Grimsby transformed the planning environment.

Thus, a combination of external pressures and internal opportunism required an early revision of the university's mission for the remainder of the decade. The new mission, 'to provide our students world-wide with the best employment prospects and to equip them to become life-long learners', sought to invest for quality whilst maintaining its accessibility and business-like character, to maintain and expand the key elements of previous statements, by emphasising the vocational nature of the education provided, to recognise the need to produce students with specific characteristics, and to claim a regional, national and international market. Behind this vision are a number of key ideas which will be tested during the next few years. The concept of a regional university involves more than simply operating within a region; rather it reflects a commitment to the region and, in particular, to raising the base-line of higher-level skills and to applied research knowledge in support of the region's economic development. Similarly, an international university is seen as something more than recruiting international students and participating in international student exchanges. Rather it seeks to prepare increasing numbers of its students to operate in transnational economies and societies, through strategic alliances and joint-ventures abroad, and delivery of courses overseas, all of which will also assist the reputation of the university at home. Quality vocational learning implies a concern with the whole process of student learning which will be flexible, responsive and innovative and which will be underlined by applied research which will sustain the concept of a 'teaching-first' rather than 'teaching-only' university (BGP 94/52 13.6.1994).

Clearly, the newly emergent plans to develop a University of Lincolnshire and Humberside represent a high profile partnership within the region, but other, related developments, based on the new technologies, will further underline that commitment. Despite government intentions to consolidate student numbers, this development will inevitably lead to some growth, associated primarily with Lincoln, but the plan envisages a far greater diversity of student need which will require correspondingly greater flexibility in the provision of vocational higher education. Central to this vision is the new learning environment whereby students will become more responsible for their own learning and progress, and flexible academic structures which include a rationalisation of subject offerings in Hull and Lincoln though it may be significant that, for the first time, the university's strategic plan contains a marketing section, recognising the fact that the developments envisaged in the next few years may well run ahead of the natural conservatism of both students and employers, amongst whom considerable promotion work may have to be carried out.

In a number of crucial respects, Humberside has sought to create for itself a distinctive role within the national system and, through its emphasis on access to vocational higher education, has sought to avoid convergence with the old universities. However, in a number of ways, largely in response to the pressures of the market place, developments have occurred which have pointed in the opposite direction. Government attachment to the 'gold-standard' of GCE Advanced Level for entry to higher education and to the concept of a national standard for degrees; the apparent desire of most universities to maintain the three traditional elements of research, professional training and collegiate ethos; and the relative conservatism of the student applications and graduate recruitment market have all militated against differentiation within the system. In Humberside, as elsewhere, this has led to a subtle shift from a teaching-only to a teaching-first University in order to facilitate research, and therefore prestige and income, in particular niche areas; the encouragement of professional education, particularly through the Enterprise Project; and the search for devices to maintain the sense of intimacy which characterised the former elite system. Similar developments have occurred in what might be termed the paraphernalia of higher education. In common with other CNAA validated institutions, the College had held traditional Awards Ceremonies prior to incorporation and continued to do so after 1989. However, perhaps mindful of the perceptions of its wider public, including both students and parents, a number of developments occurred with the advent of university status which suggested that, at least at the image level, attempts were being

174

made to imitate the traditional universities. The power to award its own degrees obliged the university to create its own academic dress for graduands, but the opportunity was also taken to create ceremonial robes for the Vice-Chancellor, though not for other senior colleagues, The imitation was completed in May 1995 with the installation of a mace and of the University's first Chancellor, Dr. J.H. Hooper who has chaired the Board of Governors since the formation of Hull College of Higher Education in 1976. In a similar vein, the College decided prior to incorporation to introduce professorships, though this did not occur until after 1989. However, in establishing criteria for the award of the title, the College set itself against the traditional approach of coupling the award with a particular post, and introduced criteria based on achievement in educational innovation and leadership, in research, consultancy and scholarship, in professional activity, or in major contribution to regional or European development. Accordingly, the award was open to all staff who could apply to a panel which included two external assessors, and the result has been a very sparing award of the title (BGP/89/85, 12.6.1989).

PERFORMANCE

ACCESS AND THE GROWTH OF STUDENT NUMBERS

Access is concerned essentially with opening higher education to previously disadvantaged or under-represented sections of the population, such as members of the working class and ethnic minority groups. Humberside had a traditional commitment to access through its promotion of courses in the local Colleges of Further Education from 1980, mixing a radical approach of empowering the disenfranchised and disadvantaged with a strong and pragmatic vocational emphasis, but it is clear that access was downgraded in the dash for growth to achieve polytechnic status.

In achieving the growth elements of its Strategic Plan, the Polytechnic was extremely successful, outstripping its targets in all years, a rate of growth which placed it second of the thirty-three polytechnics during those years. In the period from incorporation until 1994/95, overall student numbers increased by 106%, though the growth was confined largely to full-time (208%) and, to a lesser extent, sandwich students (89.9%). During this early period,

Table 8.2   Number of Students Enrolled 1989/90 to 1995/96

	Full-Time	Sandwich	Part-Time	Total
1989/90	2,775	1,250	2,817	6,842
1990/91	3,880	1,506	2,583	7,969
1991/92	5,252	2,186	2,903	10,341
1992/93	6,602	2,387	2,570	11,559
1993/94	7,779	2,654	2,147	12,580
1994/95	8,553	2,374	3,155	14,102

Source: Annual Reports 1989-1995

government policy encouraged rapid growth towards its improved participation-rate targets provided that institutions could absorb additional students to those agreed with PCFCP at the tuition fee only, thus lowering overall unit costs and creating greater efficiency. This was an important incentive for those institutions which wished to and were able to grow in this manner, and Humberside made a particularly strong showing with 2,834 fees-only students in 1990/91 and 2,718 in 1991/92.

However, the Polytechnic's success in achieving polytechnic status resulted from its emergence as more of a national than a regional institution, and resulted in greater convergence within the sector. Thus, it might be argued that this success was achieved at the expense of its access policies, though the evidence is not fully convincing. Table 8.2 shows that the number of part-time students remained stubbornly stable with a growth of only 12%, and Table 8.3 reveals a steady decline in the number of students enrolling from the county of Humberside, but Table 8.4 suggests that the proportion of both mature and female students have been maintained during the last seven years.

However, there have been signs, with the 1995/96 intake, that the period of spectacular growth may be coming to an end, though the

Table 8.3   % All Students by Region of Origin

	1989/90	1990/91	1991/92	1992/93	1993/94	1994/5	1995/96
Humberside	54	46.7	41.1	36.4	36.3	34.8	
Yorkshire & the North	14.9	)	24.7	28.3	28.6	28.9	
Midlands	10.8	46.7)	10.9	14.4	15.0	7.9	
South	6.6	)	9.6	10.3	10.0	17.9	
Remainder of U.K.	2.9	)	3.3	3.2	2.9	2.9	
Europe	7.8	4.4	6.7	5.5	5.5	5.3	
Rest of the World	2.7	2.2	1.7	1.9	1.7	2.4	

Source: Annual Reports 1989-1995

176

Table 8.4   Access as Indicated by the Proportion of Mature Students and Female
Students

	Total Mature Students	Female Students
1989/90	50.6	47.6
1990/91	44.8	48.5
1991/92	N/A	49.6
1992/93	53.5	49.4
1993/94	51.3	47.8
1994/95	57.0	49.3

Source: Annual Reports 1989 to 1995

plan envisages a further 42.8% growth by the end of the decade, principally in off-campus, full-cost students. Much will depend upon developments at Lincoln and overseas if that ambitious target is to be realised, and it seems likely that future strategic aims are likely to focus on quality, innovative and cost-effective learning development, long-term development of global relevance, reputation and recruitment and franchising. Other important measures during this period relate to the structure of the student population. During the five years under consideration, the proportion of women on university courses has reached almost a half in each year, and the proportion of mature students has been in the high forties, thus indicating a measure of success in reaching its access objectives.

How satisfied these increasing numbers of students were is more problematic to assess since the polytechnic does not appear to have undertaken any systematic monitoring of student opinion, a reflection of the fact that the 1989 five-page strategic statement gave no guidance on how this item was to be either assessed or achieved. However, many school-based annual surveys, together with comments made in HMI Inspection reports suggest a reasonable level of student satisfaction.

REGIONAL IDENTITY

In demonstrating its commitment to the region, the University has enjoyed a marked degree of success. An obvious measure in this respect has been the continued healthy if decreasing recruitment from the region to its courses, and Humberside has never failed to produce at least 35% of the total student body and 25% of full-time and sandwich students. Similarly, figures show that the institution has, and continues to serve the north of England, with over 64% of its students originating there in each year for which reliable records exist. The health of part-time recruitment, an obvious measure of regional success, has been maintained, though numbers have remained rather more stable than was anticipated. However, recruitment to courses is but one indication of the university's commitment to its region. The expansion of access to learning has been a major plank in its strategy, and this was achieved first through the establishment of the Humberside Polytechnic and Partners Authorised Validating Agency in 1990/91 (AVA), which formalised the long-standing local initiatives under national co-ordination; through this scheme, all students who successfully completed an access course at a validated centre were guaranteed a place on a higher education course in the Polytechnic and in the period 1990/95, of the 622 students who completed access courses, 547 obtained places in higher education. A major enhancement of the University's commitment to access came with the decision to franchise a number of courses, primarily at first-year level, initially in part-time and later in full-time mode, to local Further Education Colleges; by the end of 1992, all five Further Education Colleges in the county, and one from outside, together with the local College of Agriculture, had obtained associate college status, and 3,876 students had enrolled for franchised courses in them in the period 1992 to 1995 (AVA Annual Reports 1990/91-1994/95, and University's Annual Operating Statements 1992/95). The latest stage in these developments came when the College of Agriculture became a full partner college of the university in 1993, allowing joint strategic and financial planning by the two institutions and enabling a distinctive range of courses to be run at the College, validated by the University.

The County of Humberside has one of the lowest higher education participation rates in the country, and initiatives within the University sought to address this problem. In 1992/93 the University's Enterprise in Higher Education Project launched a student tutoring scheme, by which students spent time in local schools as part of their degree courses, encouraging pupils in their studies and trying to motivate them to continue onto higher education. Another initiative in this area was the establishment of a scheme whereby young people from Hull and Grimsby inner-city schools, not traditionally associated with progression onto higher education, should be encouraged to do so by following a College Studies programme alongside 'A' levels, which produced a record of achievement to be taken into account in offering a university place at Humberside. Finally, the University introduced an associate student scheme, designed to encourage local people to sample postgraduate study without committing themselves to a full programme.

Other important contributions to regional development saw the University active in seeking to improve the skills-base of the region. The University developed a linked Engineering degree with British Aerospace in 1989, at nearby Brough, specially tailored to the company's needs and enabling students to be employed in a part-time capacity by the company after a full-time year in the university, thus combining professional practice and academic study over the final three years of their course. The Professional Updating for Women returning to Work course, supported by the Training Agency and LEA, and by the European Social Fund in 1991/92, gave professional women the skills and confidence they need to return to work after a career break, whilst the growth of the Diploma in Management Studies, eventually developed into an integrated postgraduate management programme, provided a part-time support to the region's smaller and medium-sized businesses. A major step forward in the University's interface with regional industry, which involved national recognition of the University's reputation in this field, came in 1993/94 with the launch of the Food Innovation Centre in Grimsby, funded jointly by the University and the Ministry of Agriculture, Food and Fisheries as part of the latter's initiative to stimulate innovation and the transfer of Technology within the food industry. Finally, enhancement of the region's cultural opportunities have been afforded by the first part-time masters' degree in Fine Art in collaboration with other regional providers, and by the sponsorship of one of the annual concerts given in the city by the Hull Philharmonic Society.

The response of the region to the University's contribution can be seen through the increasing sponsorship which has taken place since incorporation. Local companies have supported students on the modular Food Studies degree; other food firms have made substantial donations to the specialist food Technology library in Grimsby; two chairs have been sponsored by local companies; and there have been an increasing number of prizes donated to outstanding students in a range of areas for presentation at the annual Awards Ceremony.

TOWARDS A NEW CURRICULUM FOR THE TWENTY-FIRST CENTURY

The development of mass higher education, with its emphasis on education for capability, implies reform of both curricula and teaching and learning strategies. The enrolment of increasing numbers of students wishing to study at their own pace in a variety of modes, perhaps using widely dispersed centres, requires a revolution in approaches to teaching and learning in which Technology will be only a part, albeit an important one. Core capabilities have been put at the heart of the University's search for a vocationally-oriented curriculum, and it seeks to distinguish between generic, occupational and professional competence. The latter two imply an ability to perform specific, recognised occupational activities to particular standards, and are redolent of a narrow vocationalism which the University has sought to avoid, whereas generic competence is more conducive to higher education in that it encourages a convergence between knowledge and intellectual development on the one hand and particular skills on the other (Gaskell 1989). It is perhaps better described by the term capability which implies an integration of knowledge and skills within one person. The University's search for the most appropriate form of education to fit its students to thrive in the twenty-first century was given an initial fillip by its participation in the national Enterprise in Higher Education Project (EHEP) from 1989 to 1994, and it has been able to maximise the benefits of that experience by moving towards a new learning environment under the auspices of the British Petroleum Endowment made to the University in 1992.

ENTERPRISE IN HIGHER EDUCATION

In its Green Paper *The Development of Higher Education into the 1990s, (DES 1985),* the Government was uncompromising in its criticism of higher education's failure to make a significant contribution to the economic needs of the nation. It expressed particular concern at the inability to produce sufficient graduates with the skills and competencies required by an enterprise society, though it did recognise that institutions in the public sector had made a significant contribution in this respect. The same point was made, though somewhat less stridently, in the 1987 White Paper *Higher Education. Meeting the Challenge*, which promised 'to encourage and reward approaches by HEIs which brought them closer to the world of business' (DES 1987), and it was no coincidence that the Department of Employment's Manpower Services Commission, later renamed the Training Agency and finally the Training, Enterprise and Education Directorate (TEED), established the Enterprise in Higher Education initiative in the same year. Its advent alongside incorporation for public sector institutions was represented by the Department of Employment as 'a happy coincidence', affording an opportunity to institutions to move more quickly in a direction in which they were beginning to wish to move in 1987, and to explore models of management in the face of social, Economic and academic change (EHE 1989, p.4).

The attempt to transform higher education, and universities in particular, into suppliers of suitably-trained students did not meet with universal acclaim, especially as critics saw it as a means by which the Government sought to control the values and the content of higher education through the application of a market model which some rejected as incompatible with higher education. (Prickett, 1994; Tasker & Packham, 1994). Even the supporters of the scheme were inclined to agree that 'enterprise' was not a particularly happy choice of title, and some staff in Humberside College were out of sympathy with the ideological implications of the title, though they were receptive to its specific application by the College (Humberside EHEP Annual Report, 1991, p.11). In fact, the enterprise initiative was one of the means by which government sought to challenge the traditional view that there was 'a happy convergence between what higher education provides and what the labour market needs' (Kogan 1993 p.53), and tried, through specially dedicated funds, to exercise greater influence over the direction and content of higher education.

Behind this broad aim were three specific objectives. First, higher education was to become more responsive to the demands of the labour market and its rapidly changing needs. Thus, rather than needing detailed knowledge which may become redundant quite quickly, students would require more broadly-based skills such as resourcefulness, flexibility, innovation, teamwork, risk-taking, effective communication, and computer literacy, all of which would produce more effective workers for a changing world and offer personal fulfilment. Second, its courses were to become more accessible to an increasingly varied clientele. The anticipated decline in the number of young people entering higher education by the traditional route and the advent of increasing numbers of mature students with more varied backgrounds and entry qualifications would require a greater commitment to access and a greater willingness to give educational credit for previous learning. Finally, courses needed to become more concerned with students' learning outcomes and their assessment rather than centred on tutor-designed aims and objectives. These objectives would be achieved by a partnership between employers and institutions, with the direct involvement of the former in curriculum design, delivery and assessment, the provision of placement and real work experience, designing projects and case studies, and the support of staff secondments and exchanges. Critics of the EHEP feared the development of a narrow vocationalism which was felt to be inappropriate for higher education, a point emphasised by employers and by the recent history of polytechnics and colleges, where degree-level studies in some academic areas had seen a careful blend of knowledge and capability (Kogan 1993, p.54). The central conception was not the promotion of a narrow vocationalism which might be thought capable of achievement by adding modules in business studies to all programmes; nor did it displace the need for high level expertise in specialist areas. Rather it was concerned with individual empowerment and intended to integrate the new objectives with existing educational provision (EHE 1989). One of the great benefits of the EHEP was its lack of specificity and the opportunity it provided for institutional interpretation and development according to local needs, (Wright 1992) though any tendency towards fragmentation was countered by the requirement to negotiate local objectives with the Training Agency, and later TEED, on an annual basis.

A year after the launch of the initiative, the College was successful in seeking development funding of £50,000 to prepare a bid which was approved for £1 million over five years, and detailed work began in January 1990. Since only eleven institutions had been funded in the initial round and a further seven in the development stage, recognition of the bid conferred considerable prestige on the College. However, it is clear that Humberside's EHEP did not signal a major transformation of its educational rationale and philosophy, nor herald major changes in its work

8. The Queen and The Duke of Edinburgh at the opening of the
new Lincoln Campus, October 1996

9. The new Lincoln Campus, 1996

10. City Campus, 1990s

and course portfolio. In embracing EHEP, the College was con-
firming its commitment to the principles and practices which had
informed its work since its inception in 1976. The aim of the
national enterprise initiative was to re-direct the education process
towards the development of personal qualities, effectiveness and
key skills so that students might become more enterprising, better
communicators, life-long learners, and experienced in the world of
work. Through its EHEP, the College's emphasis on the need to
develop students' potential by a transformation from tutor-centred
to teaching to student-centred learning involving independence,
team work, and partnerships with employers, closely matched the
overall intention 'to become an enterprising, accessible and highly
regarded Polytechnic', thus underlining the congruence between
the national EHEP and the College's mission.

Central to the achievement of this mission were a number of
objectives. First, it was essential to establish a management and
organisational framework which ensured that EHEP was at the
centre of college developments, appropriately resourced, effectively managed, properly subject to monitoring and evaluation,
and with its achievements eventually embedded within the fabric
of the College. Second, a coherent programme of curriculum
development had to be devised so as to promote change across
the whole College, reaching all students. Third, strategies had to
be determined to involve employers more closely in the planning
and implementation of the students' experience, with particular
emphasis upon work experience and projects undertaken in a real
setting. Finally, as an initial priority, a major staff development
programme was required to enable them to meet the demands
made by the EHEP.

The EHEP was overseen by an Enterprise Management Committee which included both Chair and Vice-Chair of the Board
of Governors, thus ensuring support for the project at the highest
level, as well as a range of business and academic interests in the
region, and the active support of the committee was instrumental in
maintaining the high profile of the project in the College. However,
since EHEP's launch came at a time when collegiate rather than
managerial leadership still prevailed, there was less central direction
than might have been the case had it been introduced a few years
later, and it is arguable that a more centrally-driven project may
have had a wider impact on the College. Nonetheless, EHEP

organisation in the College did recognise the need for some central direction as well as local ownership. The central Enterprise Office, headed by a senior member of staff as Project Director, gave an institutional direction to the project, and his ex-officio membership of Academic Board, Academic Affairs Committee, the later Quality Management Committee, and the Senior Management Group, ensured that EHEP had a high profile with the senior Executive and academic management in the College. However, since EHEP was a hearts-and-minds initiative, the commitment of a wide range of academic staff was crucial in delivering what the College had contracted with the Training Agency, and, in order to promote the project throughout the College, the Enterprise Team consisted of staff drawn from every School, appointed by open competition and promoted to Principal Lecturer grade for the duration of their association with EHEP. Once identified, those staff were responsible for identifying School objectives and contributions within the framework of the overall project, and for forming links with a number of employers to facilitate other aspects of the project. There is little doubt that this 'bottom-up' approach to the organisation and management of the project was instrumental in gaining the commitment of staff throughout the College, and the enthusiasm with which Enterprise Managers undertook their work localised ownership of EHEP work and encouraged staff to innovate. However, such a grass-roots approach contained within it the seeds of fragmentation, and towards the end of the project the need for more central criteria became apparent, particularly in the need to establish central criteria by which the adoption of EHEP principles could be tested across the range of the University's work (EHEP Final Report, 14.5 p.32).

In order to begin the task of promoting curriculum change, the Enterprise Office undertook an audit of all courses. This was designed to establish a curriculum model with which to examine each course from the point of view of the opportunities available to introduce business awareness; to identify key transferable skills and personal qualities; to realise the concept of student-centred learning and associated appropriate assessment; to increase employer involvement, not merely through the provision of work placement but also by contribution to course design, delivery and assessment; and to identify those staff development activities to support the changes envisaged by the project. Since the success of the project depended largely on staff conversion and enthusiasm, the last objective was the first priority, and early responses to an initial two-day staff awareness programme were extremely positive. By September 1990, 88% of the Polytechnic's academic and some of its academically-related staff had been through the initial, events-driven programme, leading to staff demands for further development activities such as information technology for non-specialists and workshops on student profiling, both of which were funded by a donation of £15,000 from Digital Plc. However, the structure and organisation of EHEP located the primary initiative for follow-up work with staff in the Schools, thus providing an opportunity for the enthusiastic to dominate the project and the sceptical to ignore it, but the extent of EHEP penetration throughout the institution will only become apparent with the passage of time. Follow-up topic workshops continued until the end of the project, and the University's commitment to EHEP and its embedding in future work can be seen in the establishment of a Staff Development Unit (SDU) whose programme of over one hundred events for 1995/96 contained some 60% which could be considered to be derived directly from the EHEP. The challenge facing the SDU is to become fully integrated into a focused rather than a formalised organisational strategy for staff development (Brown & Sommerlad 1992).

During the life of the EHEP, which came to an end in 1995, many initiatives were taken at both School and institution level, involving students and staff, sometimes separately but also in partnership. The University's mission and portfolio has always pointed to its involvement with business and commerce, industry and the professions, particularly in its region, and the Enterprise Project gave a fillip to that work, but it also encouraged the less-obviously vocational aspects of the University's work to engage more fully with the world outside of education. The directly-vocational aspects of the University's work gained considerable benefit from involvement in the Enterprise Project. The School of Food, Fisheries and Environmental Studies was awarded a company Teaching Company Scheme, the first ever by the Ministry of Agriculture, Food and Fisheries, and a research project into European competencies in the UK and Humberside was funded by the Department of Employment and the Humberside Training and Enterprise Council. Existing links with industry were promoted vigorously with over 50% of student projects originating in industry, final-year students being required to confront the problems of relating theory to practice by spending one day managing a factory production line at Northern Foods, and staff developing an introductory open learning programme in food technology aimed at food industry Executives. Similarly, in the Humberside Business School, where professional links were the norm, courses were redesigned to provide an even more realistic approach to content, and Business students carried out marketing projects for fledgling entrepreneurs in receipt of enterprise allowances from the Training Agency. In other vocational areas, engineering students designed pieces of equipment for CMB Packaging, and science staff worked with BP Chemicals, Reckitt and Coleman and Northern Foods to develop learning packages on total quality for use in the polytechnic and in the companies.

It is clear that the Government's desired growth in science, engineering and technology students carried an implied threat to the continuing expansion of the liberal and creative arts, but the College sought to confound that rather simplistic view by embedding the principles of enterprise in that unlikely soil. An excellent example of this type of development was the formation of an Arts Business Centre which co-ordinated the development of a professional studies input into undergraduate courses in art and design so that students could engage with the commercial issues facing practising artists and designers. The Centre also provided a link between the School of Art and Design and economically active art and design practitioners, partly through a short course programme to develop the managerial and business expertise of arts providers in the region. Wider contributions to the interface between the University and the region's industry and life included collaboration between architects and Humberside Police resulting in a publication linking the design of the built environment and issues of health and safety; the design and supervision by students of the construction of the Kay Kendall museum in nearby Withernsea, supported by a £35,000 grant from relatives of the late film star; the establishment of formative links with Britain's largest Housing Action Trust; and the detailed involvement of one student in the production of an exhibition entitled 'Hull in the '40s Exhibition'. Progress was also made in the School of Social and Professional Studies, another area less-popularly associated with the world of work and including Humanities and the Social Sciences. Here a central development was the introduction of Personal Programme Management, a compulsory unit which required students to negotiate the content and the means of assessing their own learning experiences with staff. Live projects carried out by students included contracted survey work for Humberside County Council, the Training Agency, and the Housemartin Housing Association; participation in a BP Chemicals project concerned with the impact of their work on the local environment at Saltend; the direction of a play, performed in Grimsby, as part of an independent study unit of work; and a staff survey of dwelling stock and housing need for East Lindsey District Council. Other research projects enabling enterprise aims to be fulfilled included a survey of employment training relating to child care for the Training Agency, and a county-wide survey of under 5s provision, one of the largest research exercises into this area undertaken anywhere in the United Kingdom.

Under the direction of the Enterprise Project, innovative moves were made at the institutional level where the work of the Unit was recognised by Digital Plc. which committed £20,000 to support the programme for two years. This enabled the Project to create a post which sought to develop students' personal and transferable skills by involving the Students' Union in programmes of extra-curricular activities such as recruitment, induction of new students, career planning and links with alumni. Also, during 1992/93, the Enterprise Project launched a student tutoring scheme, supported by Humberside TEC, BP Chemicals and Community Service Volunteers, by which volunteer students committed themselves to a school for at least a term, during which time they would assist pupils with their learning and encourage them in their education. In addition to providing much needed assistance in schools and providing additional stimulus for pupils, students were able to develop important transferable skills to assist them in their future search for employment. The take-up on these voluntary schemes has been modest, but there is little doubt that those who have participated have benefited.

The national EHEP has been described as 'a major programme of curricular development' whose flexibility encouraged institutions to move away from course development by disciplinary incrementalism towards strategic course development (Wright 1992). How did

Humberside responded to that challenge ? To what extent have the principles of Enterprise been embedded into the institution's work ? It has been suggested that the main areas of the University's EHEP mission have been achieved. Students undertake courses which include enterprise skills such as collecting, analysing and organising ideas and information; expressing ideas and information; planning and organising activities; working with others in teams; using mathematical ideas and techniques; solving problems; using technology; and are encouraged to be more responsible for their own learning. Furthermore, these skills and competencies are handled in the context of particular knowledge pertinent to the academic areas which individual students study, thus emphasising the importance of fusing the high-level, general competencies with specific knowledge and so avoiding the trap of narrow vocationalism (King 1994).

Other developments also took place within the University which reinforced the work of the EHEP in this respect. The University Planning and Development Committee produced a Course Planning Manual in 1992/93 which requires courses to be designed from the basis of student learning outcomes rather than teaching aims and objectives, and includes vocational and transferable skills as categories to be addressed in course design. However, although all courses and units are now required to present their material in this way, the response has been variable, and the lack of explicit identification of skills required by some courses suggests the need for centrally-derived and imposed criteria by which the actual achievement of EHEP learning outcomes can be assessed fully at validation. At the moment, the enterprise competencies seem to be fairly well embedded in Humberside curricula, but less significant progress has been made in the assessment of those competencies. Never easy to assess, there is a danger that, where such units form compulsory parts of courses but are not assessed or are assessed by traditional methods, students may gain the impression that they are dealing with issues of secondary importance, thus undermining the whole thrust of EHEP which was intended to place competence at the heart rather than on the periphery of the curriculum. Another crucial legacy of EHEP is seeing the introduction of the quaintly-named 'fifth column' in all University courses from 1996 whereby all those programmes which do not have a clear and obvious vocational focus will include a strand throughout a three-year degree which requires students to confront a first-year unit 'Learning to Learn' in which they accept responsibility for their own learning; a second-year unit 'Learning to Work'; and a third year unit of independent study.

In other EHEP areas, the University has built upon existing experience. Employers, including those on the Board of Governors, have long been involved in all aspects of the University's work, through provision of and support for student placements and the provision of live projects, to course design and review; staff involvement in the new approaches to teaching and learning has ensured their willing co-operation in the developments, and this continues to be the case. In seeking to enhance links with employers, the college sought to transfer existing best practice across the college and to expand the network of employers which already included British Aerospace, BP Chemicals, Humberside County Council and Humberside Health Authority. The involvement of employers, defined as any organisation outside higher education, was an essential part of the scheme, and a target of £3.3 million was set for the five-year period, mainly costed in terms of staff time; the Polytechnic was delighted with the initial progress when £72,000 was 'raised' in the first three months against a target of £20,000. By the end of the five-year project, employers contributed £4.45 millions to the project, demonstrating both their commitment to the University and, in particular, its EHEP-related activities, and EHEP's success in involving local and regional employers in the project. However, a number of elements of University-employer relationships require further development. The input by employers to course design and review is more variable than might be desired, and their role in the assessment of students' work, particularly placement and live projects, is limited, at least in part by the time which companies can afford to devote to collaborative work.

The EHEP project was designed to be a change agent, particularly with respect to curriculum, but also with respect to the relationships between universities and the world of work. An interim assessment suggested that it represented a series of lost opportunities (Brown & Sommerlad 1992). However, it is likely that the former public-sector institutions, including Humberside, would claim to have accepted the opportunity through which previously-determined goals could be given greater internal and external visibility, and be achieved more quickly and easily. The same review was also implicitly critical of the rather peripheral role of senior management in the project and it may be that, at Humberside, the initial dependence on grassroots initiative limited the impact which might have resulted from a more centrally-driven approach. But, in terms of managing change at institutional level, EHEP assisted the University's transformation into a more efficient organisation by highlighting and supporting its vision, by requiring it to foster critical but supportive external advice, and by requiring it to engage in the process of annual contracting (Crothall D. 1994).

THE NEW LEARNING ENVIRONMENT

The creation of a high quality new learning environment is central to the University's strategic mission of increasing access, internationally, to its courses and enhancing the employability of students, particularly through the development of greater independence in learning, enhancing transferable skills. Internally, this development has become known as the 'New Learning Environment,' though it would be wrong to see it as the creation of an appropriate climate in which students learn. Rather it is a search for curricular convergence, even a core curriculum, through which students are encouraged to develop a wide range of transferable skills such as communication, problem-solving, teamwork, managing others, planning and organisation; interpersonal skills; innovation and flexibility; analytical ability, self-motivation, competence with information technology, and with research methods, numeracy, and leadership.

One of the implicit aims of the national Enterprise in Higher Education project was the transformation of teaching and learning strategies within higher education, and the University's commitment to that objective received a tremendous boost in November 1991 when a £1 million endowment from British Petroleum, initially for seven years, facilitated the establishment of a strategic development fund to support research into new methods of teaching and learning. The establishment of the British Petroleum Strategic Development Fund was announced at the Polytechnic's Awards Ceremony by the then chairman of BP, Mr. Robert Horton, who noted that Humberside was the first polytechnic to be supported by BP in that way. The endowment of £1 million would provide income of £50,000 in 1991 which would be uprated for inflation during the subsequent six years of the initial period, and it was agreed that the Polytechnic would match that sum annually; in fact, the Polytechnic's initial contribution was £75,000, subsequently increased to £170,000. The two parties were to agree on the major objectives of the scheme which would be 'in general relevant to the wider interests of industry,' and at the outset, it was determined that the fund should be used to support major programmes of activity which would last for periods of three to five years. In keeping with its mission and strategy and to develop and focus the work of the Enterprise Project, the first commitment was to a five-year investment programme 'to harness modern media and technological developments to further the growth of mass and vocational higher education by the Polytechnic' (A.A.Dunn to R.P.King 2 January, 1992 in BPSC Papers, 25 February, 1992).

In contrast to the management of the Enterprise Project, the new initiative was directed by a small but influential Steering Group (BPSC) consisting of the Director and a Deputy Director of the Polytechnic, the Works Manager of BP and the former Works Manager who was also Vice-Chairman of the Polytechnic's Board of Governors. They were to be joined by the new Professor of Learning Development on appointment. The Steering Group's function was to give focus and direction to the project, thus ensuring that its work was consonant with the aims and central to the development of the Polytechnic, a crucial function which has been and continues to be carried out through control of the strategy and finance of the project. With the appointment of a Professor of Learning Development and the establishment of an Open Learning Resources Centre (OLRC), the BP Project began to address the issue of providing a student-centred, competence-oriented, quality educational experience for a growing number of diverse students, of whom increasing numbers were likely to be off-campus. In practical terms, this meant the provision of flexible, interactive learning and resource systems which were equally appropriate for standard classroom delivery, and for open and distance learning. The achievement of these ambitious objectives was heavily dependent on staff enthusiasm, and the experience of the EHEP was useful in this respect. Following its pattern, four academic staff were seconded part-time to the OLRC from each School to give the project a high profile throughout the Polytechnic, but, unlike EHEP, staff development activity was confined initially to those who were centrally involved with specific projects approved by the Steering Group. Within two years, the original initiative had burgeoned into a Learning Development Unit, funded by the annual £50,000 yield from the BP endowment and more than matched by the University, with the aim of planning and evolving a 'New Learning Environment' (NLE), which, amongst other things, sought to build on the work of the original Enterprise Project whose funding was shortly to expire.

The main ingredients of the NLE are the development of flexible academic structures based upon a learning outcomes model; the production of high quality learning materials which would enable students to study independently, both on and off campus, at a pace which suits them; the wider and more varied use of information technology; and the production of capable students committed to life-long learning. The achievement of these aims would demand substantial changes in the traditional approach to higher education, not least amongst staff, and an extensive programme of development has been put in place, including a strategy to obtain the award of 'Investors in People.'

During its first three years, the BP Project has passed through three distinct, though overlapping stages, and has now embarked on a fourth. The first stage, centrally-conceived, saw the conversion of existing postgraduate management modules into a form which would enable them to be delivered in partner institutions overseas. The scale of this operation provided an early opportunity to promote the BP Project across the Polytechnic with the production of thirty-two modules in open learning format by thirty authors covering three of the Polytechnic's then University's four Schools, and it also enabled the OLRC to develop standards and procedures for the production of open learning materials. During the second stage, Schools were involved more fully in the development of new learning methods, and individual staff were invited to bid to the Strategic Development Fund (SLF) for support of initiatives which were assessed for their congruence with University and OLRC objectives, their transferability across the institution, and the extent of financial support offered by the School concerned. By the end of 1994, fifteen projects were in operation some of which were School and/or subject specific, others being University-wide such as staff development for administrative staff through the support of NVQ awards. In the third stage, the University made its first foray into the development of distance-learning materials which led to the commencement of a final level course being offered through specially-approved Centres throughout the country and in a limited number of places overseas. It is likely that this will form a major thrust in future development.

However, the development of School-originated projects, whilst showing what could be achieved, was liable to be piecemeal even though they were required to conform to the criteria established by BPSC. In this situation, the University was unlikely to achieve its strategic objective of transforming the learning environment and process without the development of teaching and learning strategies at departmental level under the guidance of the LDU. Essentially, the projects in the early stages of the BP project were experimental, providing valuable insights into new teaching, learning and assessment methods, but it soon became apparent that there was a need for consolidation and extension to the wider University community. Accordingly, during stage two, the LDU initiated a process of consultation throughout the University to consider the character and components of a new learning environment which would be required to achieve the University's objectives of increasing the degree of independent learning amongst growing numbers of students located in a range of partner institutions in the U.K., overseas, at home and in the workplace. As might be expected, the exercise revealed a range of responses from the enthusiastic to the sceptical, though it was clear that there was a general sympathy with the overall intention to support and improve student learning. Scepticism was confined largely to the methodology being employed

The consultation exercise concentrated on the five major components of the NLE – the creation of more flexible academic structures designed to maximise student curricular choice; the provision of learning materials in a form to encourage independent learning; the development of staff to ensure that they can support students within the NLE; the encouragement of student capability to utilise the NLE; and the systematic application of new technology to the learning process – and detailed reactions indicate some of the areas which will require attention if the overall objectives are to be achieved. The development of more flexible academic structures has two elements. In the first place, the actual units and courses available to students have been undergoing change under the influence of the EHEP, but there is some evidence to suggest that the learning outcomes focus of EHEP has been more cosmetic than real. There is a pressing need to design content and particularly assessment strategies to be compatible with learning outcomes in order to offer all students a core of vocational and independent learning regardless of specific curriculum selection. Second, the development of learning materials will need to be sufficiently flexible to enable them to be delivered by a variety of methods, dependent on student demand, and this in itself will raise issues of quality conformance and quality standards, though the experience of IM3P will be valuable to new products in this respect.

The creation of a new learning environment makes new demands on staff and is based upon assumptions about the market place. As far as staff are concerned, the development will not merely have to overcome the sceptical view that the NLE is motivated by the search for efficiency gains through the introduction of new technology into the learning process leading to de-skilling of staff, and is nothing more than the current fad; it will also have to address the fundamental re-professionalisation of the roles of some staff which represents nothing less than a cultural change. The NLE, and the EHEP before it, are predicated on the necessity for universities to respond to and satisfy the needs of the market place, though the latter concept is not easy to define. Certainly, the demands on employers for students with capability is being addressed widely throughout the system and not only at Humberside, but the needs of students and their reaction to the diet on offer is less certain. It is true that the advent of many schemes to introduce more independent and work-related learning in schools will help students adjust to the University's approach, but as long as government continues to adhere to the 'gold-standard' of Advanced level for the majority of entrants, student reaction to the NLE is uncertain. It is clear that new students will require intensive introduction to the approach to learning which they will confront, particularly if they have come from cultures where a didactic approach is favoured, though the advent of increasing numbers of non-traditional entrants who are likely to have undergone more varied experiences of learning should reduce the severity of this problem. (Report: The BP Strategic Development Fund , in BPSC 26.4.1995, # 3.1)

Many of these issues require a central initiative, and further corporate direction to the development of the NLE was given in 1995 by the formation of an NLE Committee under the chairmanship of the Vice-Chancellor; then this became a sub-committee, under the leadership of the BP Professor, of the new Academic Development Committee and the chairmanship of the Pro-Vice Chancellor (Academic Developments). An initial proposal issuing from this body, is that all University degrees should have a competence strand worth 12 CATS points per level with students undertaking activities which will be assessed through a portfolio to demonstrate specific competencies – communication; problem-solving and decision-making skills; working with and managing others; planning and organising; innovation and flexibility; analytical ability, and including the integration of career planning - excluding numeracy and IT which are central to learning-to-learn. This could also form part of the Certificate of Personal and Professional Development (CPPD) – now a generic award, arising out of Food and Fisheries placement work - which requires 10 core and three additional competencies to be demonstrated, thus keeping the concept of the degree-plus which is attractive to employers.

At the time of writing, the development of the NLE is at an early stage, but it is clear that, like all revolutions, it will be embraced by the enthusiastic and resisted by the sceptical.

EUROPEANISATION AND INTERNATIONALISATION

Traditionally, international higher education was based upon the twin foundations of academic excellence and assistance with social and Economic development. The pursuit of academic excellence internationally found expression in networks of scholars pushing back the frontiers of knowledge through joint research programmes, often aided by visiting fellowships and occasional international conferences. Furthermore, universities in the first world accepted an obligation to advise on the development of new institutions overseas, and to assist those societies by training students from developing countries who were able to study in the U.K. on subsidised fees. During the last twenty-five years, a number of developments have occurred which have had a dramatic impact on British universities' approach to higher education. In a broad context, the emergence of different international economic groupings, such as the European Economic Community and the European Free Trade Association, have created an awareness of both opportunities and the need to widen the concept of international education to embrace greater student and staff mobility and exchange, and to design courses which are more appropriate to what has become known as the global economy. More narrowly, the economic policies of British governments since 1979 have changed the context in which universities recruit and teach international students from outside Europe. The imposition of 'full-cost' fees for international students from 1980 led to a drop in the number of overseas students in universities, polytechnics and colleges from a peak of 60,700 in 1979 to a trough of 47,600 four years later. In response, institutions embarked on intensive marketing and promotional activities in the major supplier countries with the result that the decline was initially arrested, the 1979 peak recovered by 1987 and finally overtaken by 1990.

Although active in both the European and the wider international arena for many years, in the 1980s the College concentrated on developing its European expertise, and enjoyed a leading position amongst British institutions. The University's commitment to the Europeanisation of its work dates back to 1981 with the foundation of the first joint degree with the Fachhochschule Munster in Germany, and that programme quickly expanded to include partners in France and Spain. The initial development extended the College's vocational objectives by recognising the long-term implications of Britain's membership of the then European Economic Community for higher education in general and Hull in particular, given its position as a premier east coast port. From the beginning of the 1980s the College provided a European context for some of its Business Studies students and an international flavour on its campus by the presence of exchange students from the continent. Therefore, at the time of incorporation, the College had a wealth of European experience on which to build its strategy for Europe, having over two hundred and fifty European students on courses in Humberside, partnership agreements with ten European universities and polytechnics, and student mobility programmes supported by ERASMUS to the extent of £108,000 per annum. The University was starting from a position of strength in attempting to develop a strategy which focused particularly on the education and training needs which would be generated by the enlarged single market to be introduced at the beginning of 1993 (BGP/89/92 30.10.1989)

Initial analysis suggested that, if the College was to gain an outstanding reputation as a 'Polytechnic for Europe,' courses would have to be developed and additional partnerships established to enhance student capabilities in respect of Community policies, processes and legislation, and provide opportunities for greater student mobility, as well as promote language facility and cultural awareness. These aims could only be achieved by the Europeanisation of the curriculum, the development of joint courses with European partners, participation in European academic and scholarly gatherings, and increased promotion of student mobility. In addition, the College set out to attract Community students to its full-time courses, particularly through programmes in business which enabled Europeans to convert diploma awards to British degrees. To co-ordinate the whole initiative, a European Development Centre was set up to assist Schools in their development of European curricula, to co-ordinate learning resources for languages, and to organise the College's participation in student mobility schemes; crucial to its success was the direct involvement of every School which nominated staff to act as change-agents in their own fields. Rapid progress was made in some areas, and by the summer of 1990, the College was able to announce the establishment of four new European courses, additional ERASMUS support for student and staff mobility, and the establishment of initial connections with universities in Eastern Europe which led to the eventual award of a contract from the 'Know-How Fund' for the development of business education in Hungary through the College of Foreign Trade in Budapest (BGP/90/35, 25.6.1990 & 91/44 19.6.1991).

By 1992, the university had sixty-four formal partnerships with higher education institutes in Europe, of which forty-five involved student exchange programmes normally funded by the ERASMUS programme, and all Schools had achieved or were in the process of planning joint degrees with European partners which enabled students to spend periods of their course abroad, either studying or on placement. Since incorporation, the number of named European courses had grown from one to fifteen and covered all Schools. In terms of student numbers, the University has had between six and seven hundred European students studying in

Table 8.5   Number of European Students in the University

1989/90	304	1992/93	636
1990/91	347	1993/94	688
1991/92	696	1994/95	745

Source: Annual Reports

Humberside each year from 1991 to 1994, a figure in excess of its national competitors in this area, and there was, at that time an expectation that it would grow considerably, though this has not been realised to the extent that was planned.

Perhaps more important in assessing the success of the strategy was the growing external recognition of the University's strengths in this field. In 1990 the Polytechnic was awarded the Cable and Wireless Prize, one of the coveted Partnership Awards, an industry-backed scheme which seeks to recognise innovation in higher education teaching and learning; in awarding the prize to the European Business Studies degree, the judges commended the course for its ability to provide a thorough preparation for business in Europe. In 1991, the Council for National Academic Awards agreed to host a major conference in the Polytechnic on the future of higher education in Europe; the Polytechnic was appointed a regional centre for Yorkshire and Humberside for PICKUP Europe, and was selected by the Department of Employment to undertake a major European competencies curriculum project. In 1992, a Hungarian 'Know-How Fund' contract was awarded, a link which later led to recognition of the College of Foreign Trade as a Centre for the delivery of its International Modular Masters Programme (IM3P); the University was invited to organise, on behalf of the European Commission, the inaugural London conference on the EC Memorandum for the Future of Higher Education in the European Community, held in the Queen Elizabeth Conference Centre in September; in 1994, under the auspices of the Trans-European Co-operation Scheme for Higher Education (TEMPUS), the University was invited to develop an inter-university post-graduate management centre in Sofia with three Bulgarian universities, based on the Bulgarian system but using IM3P materials; and in 1994, the University was awarded the third Joint Industrial and Commercial Programme (JICAP) involving participation in the education of eastern European business people who were seeking understanding of western approaches to a business Economy. Another 'Know-How' contract was awarded to the School of Food, Fisheries and Environmental Studies to assist in solving the problems of food distribution in Estonia which led to the establishment of a Food Quality Centre in the University of Tallinn (BGP/92/69 16.11.1992).

In recent years, the European Union has begun to address issues other than economic ones which are central to the concept of European integration. In the field of higher education, it has concentrated on the recognition of degrees and the financial support for students as well as the long-established schemes for student mobility, but it is arguable that it is the pioneering work of individual universities which has led the way towards greater integration in the sphere of higher education, and this may be the model which should be adopted for all areas of cultural integration (Gellert, p.19). During the 1980s, Humberside was one of the leading British institutions in this respect, but changing priorities in Europe began to impact upon the University's position by the end of 1993, including external developments such as the enlargement of the EU to embrace a number of former EFTA countries and the opening-up of Eastern Europe, and internal matters like the restructuring of the Education and Training Programmes and the Fourth Framework for Research and Technological Developments. Parallel with these developments was the emerging view that student demand for European Business Programmes may have peaked, though there appeared to be opportunities for European courses in areas such as Tourism, Social Sciences, and Art, Architecture and Design, whilst the combination of Technology and Business, pioneered by the University, was gaining more support. However, other initiatives in Europe continued to bear fruit. The attraction of the International Modular Masters programme in Management (IM3P) was growing and provided opportunities for expansion, particularly in countries where English is the accepted business medium and which have non-university sectors anxious to develop postgraduate programmes, and in those countries where the private sector was seeking to develop a perceived gap in state provision (VCIC 4.1 (c), 22.4.1994).

In the light of changing circumstances, the University sought to address the increasingly important issue of its relationship to the extra-European world as it reformulated its mission in 1992 and again in 1995/96. The University, and its earlier component colleges, had solid experience of international education, both through the recruitment of students from many parts of the world, particularly in its niche markets of Architecture and Food and Fisheries, and in the development and management of student exchange programmes in the United States, and this work had been organised within a small International Office. It was becoming clear that, just as the 1980s had seen the University concentrating on preparing students with the capabilities to work in Europe, so in the 1990s it was necessary to equip them with the knowledge and competencies to operate effectively in the global Economy. Modern graduates will work in an economy without national boundaries, and success in this competitive environment will come to those who have both the necessary business knowledge and skills and an understanding of other societies and cultures. Furthermore, companies will need to adopt more flexible and sensitive approaches to the problems of expatriate entry to foreign assignments and their eventual repatriation if they are not to lose financially from playing in this global market (Adler, 1985). Recognising that international education is now a major export industry (Altbach & DeWit, 1995), the University sought to build on its European experience, particularly in the Pacific Rim and Australia, and, in so doing, helped to broaden the concept of an international university. Hitherto, internationally-recognised universities were those with reputations for academic excellence, often based on staff exchange and consequent joint research. Humberside's strategy suggests another definition of the international university, based upon high-level, often postgraduate, professional training, with both staff and students developing the capability for operating in international and global markets and societies. These objectives were to be achieved through a variety of strategies, some traditional and others more progressive. Amongst the former were continuing direct recruitment of overseas students to courses in the University which had been designed principally for the home market but which met their needs. Amongst the more progressive approaches are the franchising of University courses, and parts of courses, for delivery by selected partners abroad, building on the European experience; the validation of partners abroad to deliver courses leading to University awards; and the development of institutional partnerships or joint-ventures which allow the flexibility of delivery required by some training markets (Limberd, 1995); and collaboration with partners in research and consultancy. In order to co-ordinate this enhanced function, the International Centre was founded in 1993, subsuming the former European Development Centre and the International Office, to manage and monitor the delivery of Humberside programmes overseas, to co-ordinate international recruitment, and to develop links with international institutions.

The University targeted two main markets in this development. At the undergraduate level, arrangements to be sought included an expansion of existing advanced entry schemes which recognised the value of courses in overseas institutions as equivalent to the earlier years of Humberside degrees, thereby affording increased credibility to those institutions through direct association with and recognition by a British university, and direct franchising to institutions which were deemed capable of offering parts of Humberside programmes. At the postgraduate level, the focus was on training existing practitioners, whose demands for flexible delivery were met by the development of the International Modular Masters Programme (IM3P). This modular postgraduate management training programme, based on a common core curriculum, leads to specialist named awards through option modules, and permits various patterns of delivery according to local need. Its highly-structured teaching and learning materials, together with prescribed assessment strategies, helped to minimise the problem of variability between centres (BGP/93/24 15.3.1993).

In order to enhance international recruitment to its home programmes, the University gained increased visibility abroad through its membership of the British Council's Educational Counselling Service, active in the ten principal student donor countries, and has made judicious use of locally-based recruitment agents in some countries. The response in terms of student recruitment has been mildly encouraging. In the five years immediately preceding incorporation, the number of international students in the college averaged one hundred and eighty-seven per annum, whereas in the first five years of incorporation, they have averaged 157, though this disguises a major fall to 131 in 1991/92 which has since seen a growth to over 200 in each of the last two years and 255 in 1995/96. (AR 1989 to 1995). Bilateral links with overseas institutions have increased substantially, particularly in south-east Asia and Australia. In Malaysia and Singapore, agreements exist with seven institutions which enable students who

Table 8.6   Number of Full-Cost International Students Attending the University

	Targets	*Annual Numbers*
1989/90	120	176
1990/91	126	175
1991/92	106	174
1992/93	125	223
1993/94	140	213
1994/95	204	266

Source: Annual Reports 1989 to 1995

have completed locally-delivered awards to proceed to the later years of undergraduate and to postgraduate programmes. Student exchange programmes continue with colleges and universities in the United States, and in 1994/95, the University received its first exchange students from Finland, Hungary and Singapore, as well as a group from the University of Technology, Sydney who were the trailblazers on a new joint degree in international business. In international tourism, a similar initiative with Southern Cross University, New South Wales, has been launched and is now in the second year of reciprocal exchange.

The flexibility and level of the IM3P named awards have proved to be increasingly attractive to partner institutions in both Europe and the wider world. Initially offered at centres in the Netherlands from 1993, this programme is now delivered to students at the College of Foreign Trade in Budapest, Herning Business School in Denmark, the Escuela Superieur di Gestion in Madrid, and the European College of Arts and Sciences in Thessaloniki; furthermore, the University has developed a joint-venture partnership with a Singapore management training company, and IBMEC Ltd. offers elements of the IM3P scheme, together with post-A level courses which will eventually enable successful students to attend the University on a range of undergraduate business programmes. In keeping with the design of the course, students in these different centres follow their programme in a variety of modes of attendance, and in all cases, are taught by a mix of locally-appointed and Humberside University staff whose global experience and competence is developed as they teach in different parts of the world. The colleges in Budapest and Thessaloniki, and the University of New World Economics, Sofia in Bulgaria, are also partners in undergraduate programmes in European business courses. Even more recently, the University has begun to develop partnerships in the Middle East, and the final year of undergraduate courses in international tourism and business information systems are taught in Skyline College, Sharjah, one of the United Arab Emirates. In 1995/96, some 1,400 were enrolled on programmes overseas leading to University awards.

The University has been less obviously successful in developing international research and consultancy, but good progress has been made in the School of Food and Fisheries which has obtained external contracts for work in Bangladesh, Indonesia, and Thailand, and has been the joint promoter of two international conferences with the University of Karachi in Pakistan.

QUALITY IN HIGHER EDUCATION

Quality in education has become a major industry in the 1990s and no university can afford to take a relaxed stance on this subject. The reasons for increased interest in quality are both educational and financial. When higher education was confined to a minority of the population, the traditional notions of quality were almost taken for granted, but the movement towards mass higher education has been encouraged by a government which, at the same time, wished to see academic standards at least maintained and preferably enhanced. Not only has higher education become available on a far greater scale to a student population which includes more adults and part-timers; the range of educational qualifications at entry and the diversity of content offered, especially through modular courses, was undermining the traditional concepts of quality which had drawn strength from the single subject honours course and the more recent CNAA-inspired approach to course quality. Furthermore, the market climate which government was seeking to create encouraged students to define themselves as customers and adopt a consumer mentality; it was no longer adequate for institutions to decide what was good for students. The financial stimulus was premised on the need for accountability in institutions which were in receipt of considerable sums of public money.

Coincidental with the advent of incorporation, Humberside College was accredited by its main validating body, the CNAA, and it was anticipated that the major institutions would develop a relationship with the validating body which would result in virtual self-validation. This arrangement, together with a strengthening of the external examiner system and the continuation of Inspection of teaching by Her Majesty's Inspectorate would meet the need for the assurance of quality. However, the reforms introduced in 1992, giving polytechnics and some colleges the power to award their own degrees meant the abolition of the CNAA and an imperative need to develop systems of quality control and assurance which were both externally credible and internally effective. The decision to require universities to be responsible for quality control systems, the efficacy of which would be audited by a Higher Education Quality Council (HEQC), but to place quality assessment in the hands of HEFCE, produced an inefficient and hybrid system which is currently under review. Perhaps more problematic is the issue of quality for a mass higher education system with its increasingly flexible structures and delivery methods, and its hitherto unadmitted agenda about the maintenance of academic standards which were established for a different and more elitist system.

Whilst participating in quality audits and quality assessment visits with generally satisfactory outcomes, Humberside is seeking to amend its internal quality control structures and systems, which were derived from its CNAA experience and quite suitable for an approach in which the course was the central element to be evaluated, to ones which are more appropriate to an institution offering mass higher education on a global scale. Issues which require attention in the future include the relationship between the Executive's responsibility for academic development and the Academic Board's responsibility for the quality assurance of the resulting programmes; the better integration of the new learning environment initiative into the University's formal mechanisms for the assurance of quality of teaching and learning; the maintenance and development of effective mechanism for ensuring the quality of its awards which are taught overseas; and the issue of student response. In common with most institutions, satisfied students appear amongst the objectives of the University, but the University does not appear to have undertaken any systematic monitoring of student opinion, though many school-based annual surveys, together with comments made in HMI Inspection reports suggest a reasonable level of student satisfaction. Nonetheless, the changes involved in the work of the University will require serious strategic thought in this area. Is the creation of a new learning environment, with a major emphasis on independent learning, precisely what the students require ? Are the provision of learning resources adequate? How can the quality of work and experience in a varied range of centres, national and international, be controlled and its standards guaranteed ?

THE FUTURE

Although the revised mission statement was intended to apply to a five-year period from 1992, externally-imposed changes in the system compelled the university to reconsider its position in the summer of 1994. First, government decisions to cap growth in higher education, the decline of 18 year olds in the population, and the emergence of the new further education corporations as providers of certain types of higher education all increased competition, and placed a premium on the need to develop a distinctive reputation for high quality performance. Second, the introduction of league tables, based largely on traditional university criteria, placed universities like Humberside in an unfavourable light, and it had to be recognised that it had limited areas of recognised academic excellence, reflected at least in part by its low research base and the correspondingly few staff with national reputations. Thus, it was necessary for the university to improve its image in the market place. In addition to the impact of changes in the external environment, the announcement, in May 1995, of the University's involvement in the Lincoln project which was to lead to the creation of the University of Lincolnshire and Humberside with campuses in Lincoln, Hull and, until 1999, in Grimsby, transformed the planning environment.

Thus, a combination of external pressures and internal opportunism required an early revision of the University's mission for the remainder of the decade. The new mission, 'to provide our students world-wide with the best employment prospects and to equip them to become life-long learners', seeks to invest for quality whilst maintaining its accessibility and business-like character, to maintain and expand the vocational nature of its provision, to recognise the need to produce students with specific characteristics, and to claim a regional, national and international market. Behind this vision are a number of key ideas which will be tested during the next few years. The concept of a regional university involves a commitment to supporting the region's economic development by meeting its needs for highly-skilled personnel. An international university is one which prepares increasing numbers of its students to operate in transnational economies and societies, and which develops strategic alliances and joint-ventures abroad, and which delivers courses overseas, all of which will also assist the reputation of the University at home. Quality vocational learning implies a concern with the whole process of student learning which will be flexible, responsive and innovative and which will be underlined by applied research to sustain the concept of a 'teaching-first' rather than 'teaching-only' university.

Clearly, the plan to develop a University of Lincolnshire and Humberside represents a high profile partnership within the region, but other, related developments, based on the new technologies, will further underline that commitment. Despite government intentions to consolidate student numbers, this development will inevitably lead to some growth, associated primarily with Lincoln, but the plan envisages a far greater diversity of student need which will require correspondingly greater flexibility in the provision of vocational higher education. Central to this vision is the new learning environment whereby students will become more responsible for their own learning and progress, and flexible academic structures which include a rationalisation of subject offerings in Hull and Lincoln. This last issue may be the most interesting of all as the University moves towards a position which might involve internal differentiation between its main sites, with the move to Lincoln establishing a more traditional, elitist approach and the campuses in Hull offering mass higher education.

References

CHAPTER 1

1. This brief economic survey is based on the relevant sections of Allison K.J. (1969), *A History of the County of York. East Riding I.* The various boundary changes which affected the city make it difficult to produce precise comparative figures for the population, and the changes can be followed on pp. 2-10, 190 and 215. The figure for 1992 is to be found in *Humberside Facts and Figures 1992* (Beverley).

2. Two useful comparative studies are Leonard (1975) on *Constantine College, Middlesborough* (Middlesborough) which became the University of Teeside, and Burgess, Locke, Pratt and Richards (1995), *Degrees East. The Making of the University of East London 1892-1992* (London). A valuable introduction to the general background is Argles M. (1964), *South Kensington to Robbins. An Account of English Technical and Scientific Education since 1851* (London).

3. A valuable introduction to this topic can be found in Stansky P. ed. (1973), *The Victorian Revolution. Government and Society in Victoria's Britain,* whilst Fraser D. (1973), *The Evolution of the British Welfare State* covers both nineteenth and twentieth centuries.

CHAPTER 2

1. The following paragraphs on voluntary provision in Hull, unless otherwise indicated, are based on Allison K.J. (1969), *The Victoria History of the County of York. East Riding I London.*

2. The material on the origins and early provision of municipal Technical education and teacher training is based on

a range of sources in the Hull City Record Office. The principal documents are the printed minutes of the Technical Instruction Committee (TIC) and the printed minutes of the Higher Education Sub-Committee of the Education Committee (HESC). During this period, the printed minutes contain the annual reports of the Heads/Principals of the various institutions (PAR). Occasional reference is also made to the minutes of the Education Committee (EC) and to the Finance and General Purposes Committee (FGP).

3. The discussion of Endsleigh College is based on McClelland M.G. (1993), Early Educational Endeavour: A Study of the Work of the Hull Mercy Nuns 1855-1930. Hull M.Phil.

4. For a fuller discussion of the economic development of Hull in the period 1870-1914, the reader is referred to Allison, *East Riding I*, pp.245-60.

CHAPTER 3

1. The discussion of the impact of the formation of the University College, Hull on the provision of advanced further education in the city is based on Bamford T.W., (1978), *The University of Hull. The First Fifty Years* Oxford, unless otherwise indicated.

2. The Rt. Hon. T.H. Ferens, chairman of Reckitt & Sons one of the city's major employers; Liberal M.P., for Hull 1906-19; leading Wesleyan Methodist; benefactor of the Ferens Art Gallery towards which he provided £55,000 between 1905 and 1922.

3. As in the previous chapter, the discussion of developments in further education is based on the Higher Education Schools and Colleges Sub-Committee Minutes (HESC) which, until 1930, contain the annual reports of the Principals of the Colleges.

CHAPTER 5

1. Unless otherwise indicated, the detailed discussion of Hulls' response to *Circular 7/73* is based upon the private papers of Dr. C.Bibby, Principal of the Kingston-upon-Hull College

of Education and the most vociferous opponent of a unitary college for the city. Bibby kept copious notes, formal and informal, of the numerous meetings which took place between the College Principals and the two Local Education Authorities concerned, and they are to be found in the archives of the University. The accuracy of the narrative and the interpretation given here have been checked with other participants in the reforms, notably Mr.T.Berry, former Principal of the College of Commerce.

2. The remainder of the chapter is based on Humberside LEA's Response to *Circular 7/73*, a copy of which is in the Bibby Papers.

CHAPTER 6

1. The principal sources used for Chapters 6 and 7 are the minutes and papers of the Humberside LEA and the Hull, later Humberside College of Higher Education Governing Council Papers; where appropriate, specific references are made in the text. Further comment on the organisation, content and location of these papers can be found in the bibliography.

2. The Crombie Code was the shorthand name given to the Compensation Regulations which were used to deal with staff from Colleges of Education who were made redundant because of a decision made by the Secretary of State for Education and Science.

CHAPTER 8

1. The main source for this chapter is the University archive which is discussed in more detail in the bibliography.

2. The figures are derived from the University's Annual Financial Statements, with adjustments to allow direct comparability. The 'Income' column includes interests received from investments, and the 'Surplus for the Year' column takes account of depreciation of assets, taxation, and any exceptional items.

Bibliography

PRIMARY SOURCES

LOCAL AUTHORITY COLLECTIONS

Hull Corporation Technical Instruction Committee Minutes 1891-1902 (TIC) are published in the Corporation's series of official documents and copies are in the Hull City Record Office.

Hull Corporation Education Committee Minutes 1902-1974 are published in the same series and available in the same archive. In addition to the main Education Committee minutes (HEC), which are of a very formal nature, reference should be made to relevant sub-committees which undertook most of the work. The principal sub-committees are the Higher Education and Secondary Committee 1902-1945 (HESC) and the Colleges and Schools Sub-Committee 1945-74 (CSSC). The HESC minutes also contain the printed Annual Reports of the Principals of the various Colleges, Known as Headteachers' reports in the early years but listed here as PAR, up to 1930 when they cease. The CSSC minutes contain the minutes of the Governing Body of the various colleges for which it was responsible. In addition, occasional reference is made to the Education Committee's Finance and General Purposes Committee (FGP). All of the committees referred to in this paragraph have separate Report Files accompanying their minutes. These Report Files consist of papers which were presented to the committees, but they are rather disappointing and appear to have been thinned out before being deposited in the archive; for example, there is nothing concerning the bid for and rejection of polytechnic status in 1966/67. All copies are in the Hull City Record Office.

Additional material on the individual colleges prior to 1974 is sparse. Hull City Local History Library has various prospectuses, though the runs are far from complete. College of Art 1950-1976;

College of Commerce 1931-1976; College of Technology 1929-1976; The Nautical College 1956-76. As Dr. Bibby's jubilee history of the Municipal Training College (1963) makes clear, there are no records pertaining to that College prior to 1958, though subsequently, there is a wide range of material dealing with the minutiae of its work in the 1960s found in the University Archives. It has proved impossible to find any material on Endsleigh College of Education.

Humberside County Education Committee Minutes 1974-89 (HBEC), with its Further Education Sub-Committee Minutes 1974-83 (?) (HBFE Sub) and its Higher and Further Education Sub-Committee (HBESC) 19183-89 are printed and available in both the East Riding of Yorkshire Record Office, Beverley and in Beverley Reference Library. The minutes are also accompanied by separate Report Files deposited in the East Riding of Yorkshire Record Office; these Report Files are accessed through reference numbers contained in the printed minutes.

UNIVERSITY PAPERS
The major institutional sources used for this study have been the various papers of the successive Governing Bodies of the institution as it has been transformed from College to Polytechnic and finally to University. Hull College of Higher Education Governing Council Papers 1977-1982 (GCP) and its various sub-committees such as Policy and Resources 1977-83 (GPR). Humberside College of Higher Education Board of Governors Papers 1983-1989 (GCP) and its sub-committees such as Policy and Finance (GPF) 1983-1989). Humberside College Formation Committee Papers 1988-89 (FCP). Humberside College of Higher Education/ Humberside Polytechnic/ University of Humberside Board of Governors Papers 1989-95 (BGP) and relevant sub-committees such as Employment and Finance (GEF). All papers to 1989 in this group are located in the University, and those since 1989 are with the Clerk to the Board of Governors. All consist of Minutes and related agenda papers.

The Bibby Papers consist of private notes and official documents relating to the reorganisation of higher education in Hull 1972-76, and form part of the Univeristy archive.

Other papers in the University archive which have been used in this study include the NAB File 1982-89, University's *Annual*

Reports (AR), the Enterprise in Higher Education Archive, the BP Steering Committee Papers, the International Committee Papers, and the New Learning Environment Archive. The massive amount of material relating to Faculties and Schools, and to student admissions since 1976 are also available, but were not used in this study.

GOVERNMENT PUBLICATIONS

Circulars
1946.48
1956/305   Organisation of Technical colleges
7/59   Governing Bodies for major establishments of further education
1/60   The future development of management education and of business studies: revision of joint examination schemes.
3/61
15/61   Organisation of Business Studies in Colleges of Further Education
7/63   Management Education
8/66
11/66   Technical College Resources. Size of Classes and Approval of Further Education Courses
2/67   The Government of Colleges of Education
7/70   Government and Conduct of Establishments of Further Education
7/73   Development of Higher Education in the Non-University Sector
6/74   Development of Higher Education in the Non-University Sector: Interim Arrangements for the Control of Advanced Courses
10/76   Approval of Advanced Further Education Courses: Modified Arrangements
1/82   Approval of Advanced Further Education Courses in England
5/82   Approval of Advanced Further Education Courses in England; Revised
4/83   Arraignments for the Approval of Advanced Further Education Courses in England

5/84	Arrangements for the Approval of Advanced Further Education Courses in England 1985/86
2/85	Arrangements for the Approval of Advanced Further Education Courses in England 1986/87
3/86	Arrangements for the Approval of Advanced Further Education Courses in England 1986/87 and 1987/88
4/87	Arrangements for the Approval of Advanced Further Education Courses in England 1987/88 and 1988/89

White Papers and Green Papers (WP or GP)
DES (1956), *Technical Education* London
DES (1978), *Higher Education into the 1990s. A Discussion Document* London
DES (1985), *The Development of Higher Education into the 1990s* London
DES (1987), *Higher Education. Meeting the Challenge* Cm 114 London
DES (1991), *Higher Education: A New Framework* Cmnd 1541 London
DES (1989 & 1991), *Statistical Bulletins 11/89 and 20/91* London

SECONDARY SOURCES

Adler N.J.(1985), *International Dimensions of Organisational Behaviour*
Allison K.J. (1969), *The Victorian County History of York. East Riding I*
Altbach P.G. & DeWit H, (1995) 'U.S. Risks Losing Competitive Edge' in *NAFSA: Association of International Educators*, vol.47, no.2, November
Annual Reports of the University of Humberside (AR)
Argles M. (1964), *South Kensington to Robbins. An Account of English Technical and Scientific Education since 1851* London
Bamford T.W. (1978), *The University of Hull. The First Fifty Years* Oxford
Becher T. (1987), *British Higher Education* London
Bibby C (1963), *The First Fifty Years. A Brief History of Kingston-upon-Hull Training College 1913-1963*

Bibby 1975, In Defence of Colleges of Education in *British Journal of Teacher Education*, 1, pp.19-29

Booth C. (1987), 'Central government and higher education planning' in *Higher Education Quarterly*, 41, 1.

Brosan G., Carter C., Layard R., Venables P. & Williams G (1971), *Patterns and Policies in Higher Education* Harmondsworth, U.K.

Brown H & Sommerlad E. (1992), 'Staff Development in Higher Education - Towards the Learning Organisation' in *Higher Education Quarterly*, vol.46, no.2, pp.174-90

Cantor L. & Roberts I.F. (1986), *Further Education Today. A Critical Review* 3rd edition London

CNAA (1975), *Partnership in Validation* London

CNAA (1979), *Developments in Partnership in Validation* London

CNAA (1984), *Consultation Paper on the Development of Council's Relations with Institutions* London

Coldstream P. (1988), 'Industry Finds its Voice – and Higher Education an Unexpected Ally' in *Higher Education Quarterly*, vol.42, no.4, pp.370-77

Crampton P. (1981), 'Spatial Planning of Higher Education Facilities and Economic Policy – the Case for a Humberside Polytechnic' in *Journal of Local Studies*, 1,2, Spring 1981, pp25-32 Hull

Crossley A ed. (1979), *A History of the County of Oxford IV* London

Crothall D. (1994). 'The University's Vision Post-Enterprise' in Noble M (ed.), *Achieving a new Learning Environment. Building on Enterprise* UH Conference Proceedings

Davis M. (1990), 'Technology, institutions and status: Technological education, debate and policy 1944-56' in *Summerfield & Evans*, pp.120-44

EHE (1989), *Key Features of the EHE Proposals 1988-89* pp.2-6, Dept. of Employment

Gaskell S. M. (1989), 'Education and Culture: A Perspective from Higher Education' in *Higher Education Quarterly*, vol.43, no.4, pp.318-332

Green V.H.H. (1969), *British Universities*

Greenslade M.W. & Johnson D.A. (1979), *A History of the County of Stafford History of the County of Stafford*, VI London

Gribbin T.K. (1950), 'The Population and Employment of Kingston-upon-Hull 1921-1948' in *Yorkshire Bulletin of Economic and Social research*, 2,1 p.129-154

Gellert C. (1993), 'Introduction: Changing Patterns in European Higher Education' p.19, in Gellert C. (ed.), *Higher Education in Europe*

Harding, 'Circular 7/73 and the Development of Higher Education in the Public Sector up to 1981' in *Colleges of Education and Reorganisation* Coombe Lodge 1974).

Harris E.R. (1980), *A History of the County of Chester* III London

Hawson H.K. (19), *Sheffield, The Growth of a City 1893-1926* Sheffield

Hencke D. (1978), *Colleges in Crisis* Harmondsworth

Henry E (1981), *Oxford Polytechnic. From Genesis to Maturity 1985-1980* Oxford Polytechnic

HEQC (1996), Quality Audit Report on the University of Humberside

HMSO (1963), *The Robbins Report* London

HMSO (1972), *Education. A Framework for Expansion*

Hoskins W.G. & McKinley R.A. (1955), *A History of the County of Leicester* III London

Jones D.R. (1988), *The Origins of Civic Universities* London

Jones S. (1984), 'Reflections on a capped Pool' in *Higher Education Review*, 17, 1.

Kelly T. (1970), *A History of Adult Education in Britain* London

King R.P. (1994), 'The Achievement of Enterprise' in Noble M (ed.), *Achieving a New Learning Environment. Building on Enterprise* UH Conference Proceedings

Knight P. (1981), 'Diverse difficulties in surfacing from the Pool' in *Times Higher Education Supplement*, 13 January, 1981

Knight P. (1984), 'The 1984/85 NAB planning exercise: how great a failure?' in *Higher Education Review*, 17, 1.

Kogan M. (1971), *The Politics of Education* Harmondsworth

Kogan M. (1993), 'The end of the dual system?' in Gellert C. (ed.), *Higher Education In Europe*, p.53.

Leonard J (1981), *Constantine College* Stockton

Limbird M. (1995), 'International Advancement: It's Your Job', in *NAFSA: Association of International Educators*, vol.46, no.7, June/July

Lindop N. (1985), *Academic Validation in Public Sector Higher Education* London

Locke M., Pratt J. & Burgess T. (1985), *The Colleges of Education 1972-1982: The Central Management of Organic Change* Croydon

Lukes J.R. (1975), 'Government policy over teacher training' in *Aspects of Education*, 18

McClelland M.G. (1993), Early Educational Endeavour: A Study of the Work of the Hull Mercy Nuns 1855-1930. Hull M.Phil.

McNay I (1995), 'From the Collegial Academy to Corporate Enterprise: The Changing Cultures of Universities' in Schuller T. (ed.), *The Changing University ?* Buckingham

Ministry of Education (1957), *HMI Report on Endsleigh College* FETC 58/57

Mitchell R.H. (1975), The Development of Hull College of Technology (formerly Hull Municipal Technical College) from 1943 to 1973. Hull University B.Phil.

Mitchell B.R. & Deane P. (1962), *British Historical Statistics*

Phillipson P. ed. (1983), *Universities, Society and the Future* Edinburgh

Pratt J. (1970), *Policy and Practice: The College of Advanced Technology* London

Pratt J. (1976), 'Pooling: some revised conclusions' in *Higher Education Review*, 8,2.

Pratt J. & Burgess T. (1974), *Polytechnics. A Report* London

Prickett S (1994), 'Enterprise in Higher Education: Nice Work of Ivory Tower versus Exchange and Mart' in *Higher Education Quarterly*, vol.48, no.3, pp.169-181

Richardson G.B. & Tomlinson W.W. (1916), *The Official Handbook of Newcastle- on-Tyne* Newcastle

Scott P. (1995), *The Meanings of Mass Higher Education* Buckingham

Sheahan J.J. (1866), *History of the Town and Port of Kingston-upon-Hull* Beverley

Simmons J. (1974), *Leicester Past and Present. II the Modern City 1860-1974* London

Sister Imelda (1993), Middlesborough Diocesan Year Book

Stephens W.B. (1969), *A History of the County of Warwick VIII* London

Summerfield P. & Evans E. eds. (1990), *Technical Education and the State since 1850: Historical and Contemporary Perspectives* London

Tasker M & Packham D (1994), 'Training Minds for Tomorrow: A Shared Responsibility' in *Higher Education Quarterly*, vol.48, no.3, pp.182-193

Technical Education and Training, 9,7, July 1967

Thompson E (1976), National Policy in relation to the Training and Supply of Teachers in England and Wales 1960-1970. Hull University M.Ed.

Times Higher Education Supplement, 7.5.1967; 12.7.1984.

Timmins G., Foster D. and Law H. (1979), *Preston Polytechnic. The Emergence of an Institution* Preston

Trow M (1989), 'The Robbins Trap: British Attitudes and the Limits of Expansion' in *Higher Education Quarterly*, vol.43, no.1, pp.55-75

Vice-Chancellor's International Committee Papers (VCIC)

Wright P (1992) 'Learning through Enterprise: The Enterprise in Higher Education Initiative' in Barnett R., *Learning to Effect*, pp.204-213 OUP

Index